Personality and Persuasibility

EDITED BY CARL I. HOVLAND AND IRVING L. JANIS

Personality and Persuasibility

BY

Irving L. Janis

Carl I. Hovland

Peter B. Field

Harriet Linton

Elaine Graham

Arthur R. Cohen

Donald Rife

Robert P. Abelson

Gerald S. Lesser

Bert T. King

New Haven and London, Yale University Press

© 1959 by Yale University Press, Inc.
Third printing, January 1966.
Set in Baskerville type.
Printed in the United States of America by
The Carl Purington Rollins Printing-Office
of the Yale University Press, New Haven, Connecticut.

Library of Congress catalog card number: 59-7284

Originally published
in Yale Studies in Attitude
and Communication.

PREFACE

Two years ago the Yale Communication and Attitude Change Program inaugurated the present series of monographs after consideration of the advantages of having studies closely related in theoretical implications within the covers of a single volume. The success of our first volume, *The Order of Presentation in Persuasion,* has encouraged us to bring out a second monograph of similar type.

The present volume deals with "general persuasibility." This term refers to a person's readiness to accept social influence from others irrespective of what he knows about the communicator or what it is that the communicator is advocating. Two lines of inquiry as to the nature of individual differences in susceptibility to influence converge in this volume. The first began with the series of studies conducted by Janis on the personality correlates of persuasibility. The second line of attack, involving a series of studies of developmental aspects of persuasibility in children, was initiated by Abelson and Lesser under the auspices of the Yale program and later supported by a United States Public Health grant and by Adelphi College.

A number of other psychologists associated with the Yale research program have also made significant contributions on individual differences in persuasibility. All the pertinent studies are brought together in this volume.

Four of the authors, Abelson, Cohen, Hovland, and Janis, are members of the Yale Psychology Department. The present locations of the other authors are as follows: Field is a graduate student in Social Relations at Harvard; Elaine Graham is

v

on the staff of the Bank Street College of Education; King is with the Personnel Assessment Branch of the U. S. Naval Medical Research Laboratory at New London; Lesser is on the faculty of Hunter College; Harriet Linton is on the faculty of the Research Center for Mental Health at New York University; Rife is a student at the Harvard Medical School.

Most of the research focuses on the personality attributes of persons who are moderately persuasible, in contrast to those who are resistant to all attempts at persuasion or those, at the opposite extreme, who are indiscriminately gullible. In these studies, emotional factors, symptoms of personal adjustment, sex differences, and differences in intelligence are systematically analyzed in relation to degree of persuasibility.

Thus this volume presents a series of interrelated investigations, all bearing on a common set of problems. Except for editorial work to provide some uniformity of format, each study is presented in the author's own style. Inevitably there is considerable variation in the type of presentation used by the different authors and in their emphases. However, an attempt has been made to provide guideposts that will indicate some of the interrelations between the studies. There is an introductory analytic essay by the editors which gives the general framework of the problem of persuasibility and specifies how each of the individual contributions to the volume fits into the framework. Following the presentation of the original research investigations, to which most of the volume is devoted, there is a summary chapter in which the editors attempt to extract the common threads and to piece together the over-all pattern that emerges from the various studies. In a final postscript chapter, we present a new set of theoretical categories that seems to be useful for integrating and analyzing the relevant findings on personality differences in responsiveness to social influence.

The editors are indebted to the authors of the individual chapters for their patience and indulgence in accepting criticisms and suggestions. In the evaluation of the materials and in suggestions for presentation, the editors benefited from the wise and incisive criticisms of Fred Sheffield and Leonard Doob. Their careful reading of the chapters helped greatly in the preparation of the entire volume.

We are indebted to Rosalind L. Feierabend for drafting portions of the summary chapter and for suggestions for styling of other chapters as well. Her skillful but gentle rewording has greatly increased the book's readability.

The financial support which enabled these studies to be done is gratefully acknowledged. Our thanks go to the Rockefeller Foundation, for general support of the Yale program, and especially to Leland C. DeVinney, of their Social Science Program, who has continually given us encouragement. Appreciation is also expressed to the United States Public Health Services for their support of the studies by Abelson and Lesser.

The arduous task of preparing the typescript was capably performed by Patricia Stannard with generous assistance from Kristine Christensen and Jane Olejarczyk. Throughout all phases of publication the staff of the Yale University Press has been most helpful. The authors are particularly indebted to Jane Olson, whose imaginative suggestions and conscientious styling were indispensable.

CARL I. HOVLAND
IRVING L. JANIS

New Haven, Conn.
December 31, 1958

CONTRIBUTORS' ACKNOWLEDGMENTS

IN ADDITION to those who contributed to the book as a whole, there were a number of individuals who were of particular assistance to the authors of the individual chapters. Their contributions are here gratefully acknowledged.

Chapters 2 and 3:

Appreciation is expressed to the Social Science Research Council for the award of an undergraduate research stipend to Field. Special thanks are due Robert P. Abelson for advice on problems of statistical analysis and for valuable suggestions concerning the formulations of the factor analysis findings. The authors also wish to express their thanks to John Forsythe, Lawrence Hilford, and Joyce Montgomery, who assisted the authors in administering the tests, and to Eileen Beier, who carried out the factor analysis computations. The research data were obtained from the Milford High School, Milford, Connecticut, and the authors are deeply grateful to Herbert R. French, principal, and to the social science faculty for their helpful cooperation.

Chapter 4:

The research in this chapter is based on two dissertations submitted in candidacy for the degree of Doctor of Philosophy at Yale University. The writers are indebted to Leonard Doob and Irvin L. Child, chairman of their theses committees, and to Carl Hovland, Seymour Sarason, Harold H. Kelley, and

Robert P. Abelson, the other members of their committees, for their advice and encouragement. They are particularly indebted to H. A. Witkin for the use of the facilities of his laboratory and to him, Helen B. Lewis, Max Hertzman, Marie Jahoda, Robert R. Holt, David Riesman, and Nathan Glazer for their advice and criticism on various aspects of the study.

Chapter 5:

The author wishes to express his indebtedness to Edwin Thomas, Ezra Stotland, Alvin Zander, and Gerald S. Blum for their collaborations and criticisms at various stages of the research.

Chapter 6:

The authors wish to express their appreciation to Dr. Edgar C. Yerbury, Superintendent of the Connecticut State Hospital, Middletown, and to Jules Holzberg, Director of the Psychology Department in the same institution, for their helpful cooperation which enabled us to carry out this study with hospitalized patients. We also wish to thank the staff of the Children's Center, Hamden, Connecticut, for permitting us to include young men from that institution in our study. We are indebted to Leonard Doob and Fred Sheffield for detailed criticisms and suggestions which were extremely valuable in redrafting our research report.

Chapters 7, 8, and 9:

The authors are indebted to many people whose kind co-operation enabled them to collect the data. They wish to thank particularly the administrators and teachers in several schools in New Haven, Connecticut, and in Uniondale, New York. The administrators and school principals include: J.

Allen Hickerson, Lois King, Kay James, John J. Forester, Margaret Fitzsimons, Helen Rakieten, May White, John Wesolowski, Mary Griffin, Pearl Rosenstein, Mary Matthews, and Philip Cosgrove. The teachers include, among others: Doris Maiorano, Agnes Healy, Ruth Curtis, Elizabeth Hunter, Ebba Olsen, Myra Foster, Ruth Bolan, Eileen Egan, Constance Hakkerup, Adrienne Mantis, Cathleen Schaefer, Mildred Isherwood, Jean Dowd, and Elizabeth Pearson. School Psychologist Harry J. Popper, Jr., has also offered considerable assistance.

There were a number of student assistants whose participation in the research was invaluable. We are indebted to Roger Porr, Jerrold Post, Irma Ember, Russell Sardo, Willa Abelson, Elizabeth Parnes, Jean Sayers, and most especially to Cynthia Fox and Donald Clark, whose contributions were tantamount to co-authorship of a few portions of this report.

Chapter 10:

Thanks are extended to the author's advisory committee, Carl Hovland, Leonard Doob, Fred Sheffield, and Seymour Sarason, for their invaluable help and criticisms during the preparation of the Yale doctoral dissertation on which this chapter is based.

CONTENTS

xiii

CHAPTER 1

An Overview of Persuasibility Research

IRVING L. JANIS AND CARL I. HOVLAND

THEORISTS AND RESEARCH INVESTIGATORS in many different
areas of human behavior—attitude change, group dynamics,
psychotherapy, hypnosis, and social perception—share a common interest in understanding the *predispositional* factors
which underlie responsiveness to one or another form of
social influence. While these researchers have approached
the study of predispositional factors from widely different
points of emphasis, many of their findings converge on a few
basic variables which have been designated as "persuasibility
factors."

Several studies of personality factors in relation to individual differences in persuasibility were reported by Hovland,
Janis, and Kelley in 1953. Since that time further studies have
been conducted to provide a more systematic analysis of the
personality correlates of persuasibility and also of the course
of its development from childhood through adolescence. The
present volume reports these newer investigations.

DEFINITION OF PERSUASIBILITY

By "persuasibility factor" is meant any variable attribute
within a population that is correlated with *consistent individual differences* in responsiveness to one or more classes of in-

1

fluential communications. The meaning of the key terms in this definition will become somewhat clearer if we consider a brief schematic analysis of the communication process involved in successful persuasion.

Whenever an individual is influenced to change his beliefs, decisions, or general attitudes, certain identifiable external events occur which constitute the *communication stimuli,* and certain changes in the behavior of the person take place which constitute the *communication effects.* Communication stimuli include not only what is said, but also all of the intentional and unintentional cues which influence a member of the audience, including information as to who is saying it, why he is saying it, and how other people are reacting to it.

The observable communication effects could be said to subsume all perceptible changes in the recipient's verbal and nonverbal behavior, including not only changes in private opinions or judgments but also a variety of learning effects (e.g. increased knowledge about the communicator's position) and superficial conformist behavior (e.g. public expression of agreement with the conclusion despite private rejection of it). However, our main interest centers upon those changes in observable behavior which are regarded as components of "genuine" changes in opinions or in verbalizable attitudes. This requires observational methods which enable us to discern, in addition to the individual's public responses, those indications of his private thoughts, feelings, and evaluations that are used to judge whether the recipient has "internalized" the communicator's message or is merely giving what he considers to be a socially acceptable response.

We use the term "attitude change" when there are clearcut indications that the recipient has internalized a valuational message, as evidenced by the fact that the person's perceptions, affects, and overt actions, as well as his verbalized judgments, are discernibly changed. When there is evidence of a genuine change in a *verbalized belief or value judgment,* we use the term "opinion change," which usually constitutes one component of attitude change. Almost all experiments on the effects of persuasive communications, including those reported in the present volume, have been limited to investigating changes in opinion. The reason, of course, is that such changes can readily be assessed in a highly reliable way, whereas other components of verbalizable attitudes, although of considerable theoretical interest, are much more difficult to measure.

Neither "opinion change" nor "attitude change" is used to refer to those instances of surface conformity in which the person *pretends* to adopt a point of view that he does not really believe. Thus, the area of opinion change with which we are concerned includes studies dealing with what has been referred to as "internalization" and "identification," but excludes those dealing with "compliance" (cf. Kelman, 1959).

Figure 1 gives a schematic outline of the major factors that enter into attitude change. The observable communication stimuli and the observable effects are represented as the two end-points of the communication process. These are the antecedent and consequent events that are observable; they constitute the empirical anchorage for two main types of constructs which are needed in order to account for the inter-relationships between the communication stimuli and observable effects: *predispositional factors* and *internal mediating processes.* Predispositional factors are used to account for *individual differences in observable effects when all communication stimuli are held constant.* Constructs referring to internal, or mediating, processes are used in order to account for the differential effects of different stimuli on a given person or group of persons. In other words, internal-processes constructs have been formulated primarily to account for the different effects attributable to *different types of communications* acting on the *same people;* whereas, predispositional constructs are needed to account for the different effects observed in *different people* who have been exposed to the *same communications.*

Hovland, Janis, and Kelley (1953) have reviewed and an-

Figure 1. Major Factors in Attitude Change Produced by Means of Social Communication

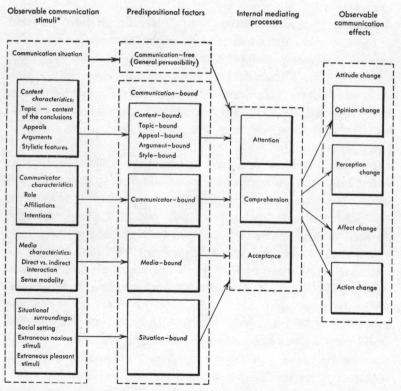

* The categories and subcategories are not necessarily exhaustive, but are intended to highlight the main types of stimulus variables that play a role in producing changes in verbalizable attitudes.

alyzed the experimental evidence on the effects of low vs. high credibility sources, strong vs. weak fear-arousing appeals, one-sided vs. two-sided presentation of arguments, and other such variations in communication stimuli. From such studies it has been possible to formulate a number of generalizations concerning the conditions under which the probability of opinion change will be increased or decreased for the *average* person or for the *large majority* of persons in any audience. Such propositions form the basis for inferences concerning the mediating processes responsible for the differential effectiveness of different communication stimuli.

Mediating processes can be classified in terms of three aspects of responsiveness to verbal messages (see Hovland, Lumsdaine, and Sheffield, 1949; and Hovland, Janis, and Kelley, 1953). The first set of mediating responses includes those which arouse the *attention* of the recipient to the verbal content of the communication. The second set involves *comprehension* or decoding of verbal stimuli, including concept formation and the perceptual processes that determine the meaning the message will have for the respondent. Attention and comprehension determine what the recipient will *learn* concerning the content of the communicator's message; other processes, involving changes in motivation, are assumed to determine whether or not he will accept or adopt what he learns. Thus, there is a third set of mediating responses, referred to as *acceptance*. Much less is known about this set of responses, and it has become the main focus for present-day research on opinion change. At various points in this volume, and especially in the last chapter, we shall return to the distinction between attention, comprehension, and acceptance, in order to discuss the implications of these constructs for research on predispositional attributes.

Two major classes of predispositions can be distinguished.

One type, called "topic-bound," includes all of those factors which affect a person's readiness to accept or reject a given point of view on a particular topic. The other main type, called "topic-free," is relatively independent of the subject matter of the communication. In the discussion which follows, we shall first make some comments about the nature of topic-bound predispositions and about the more general class of "content-bound" factors, including those referred to as "appeal-bound," "argument-bound," and "style-bound." Then we shall attempt to extend the analysis of predispositional factors by making further distinctions, calling attention to a number of content-free factors that are nevertheless bound to other properties of the communication stimuli. These various types of "communication-bound" factors will be contrasted with the unbound or "communication-free" factors to which our research efforts in this volume have primarily been directed.

TOPIC-BOUND PREDISPOSITIONS

Topic-bound factors have been extensively studied by social psychologists and sociologists over the past twenty-five years, and many propositions have been investigated concerning the motives, value structures, group affiliations, and ideological commitments which predispose a person to accept a pro or con attitude on various issues. The well-known studies of authoritarian personalities by Adorno, Else Frenkel-Brunswik, and others (1950) have provided a major impetus toward understanding attitude change on specific issues, such as racial prejudice, in relation to unconscious motives and defense mechanisms. Some findings which bear directly on topic-bound predispositions have been reported by Bettelheim and Janowitz (1950): Anti-Semitic propaganda (in the form of two fascist pamphlets) was most likely to be approved by men who either had already acquired an intolerant ideology toward Jews or who had acquired a tolerant ideology but were insecure personalities with much undischarged hostility. Another pioneering study in this field is that of Smith, Bruner, and White (1956); these authors conducted a small series of intensive case studies for the purpose of determining the personality functions served by holding certain flexible and inflexible opinions about Soviet Russia and communism. Many other studies have been made concerning the personality correlates of readiness to accept favorable or unfavorable communications about specific types of ethnic, national, and political groups (Hartley, 1946; Sarnoff, 1951).

Some recent studies of topic-bound predispositions deal with relatively general factors that are not limited to the modification of attitudes toward only one type of social group. For instance, Weiss and Fine (1955, 1956) investigated the personality factors which make for high readiness to accept a message advocating a strict, punitive stand toward social deviants. The findings suggest that persons who have high aggression needs combined with strong extrapunitive tendencies will be prone to adopt a strict, punitive attitude toward anyone who violates social norms. In order to test this hypothesis in its most general form, it would be necessary to use many different communications to determine whether the specified personality attributes are correlated with attitude change whenever a punitive stand is advocated toward any type of social deviant. If the hypothesis is confirmed, we shall be able to speak of a very general type of topic-bound predisposition.

This example highlights the fact that the difference between topic-bound and topic-free is not necessarily the same as the dimension of specificity-generality. Some topic-bound predispositions may be very narrowly confined to those communications expressing a favorable or unfavorable judgment toward a specific trait of a particular person (e.g. the members of an organization, after having been embarrassed by the gauche manners of their highly respected leader, would be disposed to reject only those favorable statements about him which pertain to a limited aspect of his social behavior). Other topic-bound predispositions may be extremely general (e.g. certain types of persons may be inclined to accept any comments which express optimism about the future). A topic-bound predisposition, however, is always limited to one class of communications (a narrow or a broad class) which is defined by one or another characteristic of the *content of the conclusion*.

Similar restrictions hold for some of the topic-free factors. For example, Hovland, Janis, and Kelley (1953) point out that many topic-free factors may prove to be bound to specific characteristics of the communication:

> Some of the hypotheses concerning topic-free predispositions deal with factors which predict a person's responsiveness only to those persuasive communications that employ certain types of argumentation. Investigations of topic-free predispositions ultimately may reveal some that are associated primarily with the nature of the communicator, others that are associated with the social setting in which the communication takes place, and perhaps still others that are so broad in scope that they are relatively independent of any specific variables in the communication situation.

Thus, for any communication, we assume that there are likely to be several different types of personality predispositions, topic-bound and topic-free, whose joint effects determine individual differences in responsiveness. The essential point is that, by also taking account of topic-free factors, it should be possible to improve predictions concerning the degree to which members of the audience will be influenced by persuasive communications. Such factors have generally been neglected in analyses of audience predispositions [p. 176].

In the discussion which follows, we shall attempt to trace the implications of the distinction—which we now believe to be extremely important—between topic-free factors that are bound in some nontopic way and those that are completely unbound. A suggested list of bound predispositions is provided in the second column of Figure 1. We shall briefly consider those topic-free factors which are bound to other features of the communication situation before turning to a detailed examination of the unbound, or communication-free, factors.

Content-Bound Factors

The content of a communication includes appeals, arguments, and various stylistic features, as well as the main theme or conclusion which defines its topic. The effectiveness of each of these content characteristics is partly dependent upon certain predispositional factors which we designate as "content-bound."

Appeal-bound factors. In the content of many communications one finds appeals which explicitly promise social approval or threaten social disapproval from a given reference group (see Newcomb, 1943). Responsiveness to these social incentives partly depends upon the degree to which the person is motivated to be affiliated with the reference group (see Kelley and Volkart, 1952). Personality differences may also give rise to differences in responsiveness to special appeals concerning group consensus and related social incentives (Samelson, 1957). Different types of personalities may be expected to have different thresholds for the arousal of guilt, shame, fear, and other emotions which can be aroused by special appeals. For example, Janis and Feshbach (1954) have found that certain personality factors are related to individual differences in responsiveness to fear-arousing appeals. Experimental studies by Katz, McClintock, and Sarnoff (1956, 1957) indicate that the relative effectiveness of rational appeals, and of self-insight procedures designed to counteract social prejudices, depends partly upon whether the recipient rates low, medium, or high on various measures of ego defensiveness.

Argument-bound factors. Many variables have been investigated which involve stimulus differences in the arrangement of arguments and in the logical relationship between arguments and conclusions. Cohen, in Volume 1 of the present series (1957, Ch. 5), presents evidence indicating that predispositional factors play a role in determining the extent to which an individual will be affected by the order in which information is presented. Individuals with low cognitive-need scores were differentially influenced by variations in order of presentation while those with high scores were not. One would also expect that individual differences would affect the degree to which a person will be influenced by such variations as the following: (1) The use of strictly rational or logical types of argument vs. propagandistic devices of overgeneralization, innuendo, *non sequitur,* and irrelevant *ad hominem* comments. (2) Explicitly stating the conclusion that follows from a set of arguments vs. leaving the conclusion implicit. (A comparison of effects for subjects with high and low intelligence is presented in Hovland and Mandell, 1952.)

Style-bound factors. Differences in social class and educational background probably account for some of the individual differences in responsiveness to variations in style—for example, a literary style as against a "folksy" approach. Other

variations in treatment that may be differentially effective
are technical jargon vs. simple language; slang vs. "pure"
prose; long, complex sentences vs. short, declarative sentences. Flesch (1946) and other communication researchers
have presented evidence concerning individual differences
in responsiveness to such stylistic features.

Communicator-Bound Factors

The effectiveness of a communication depends on the recipient's evaluation of the speaker (see, e.g., Hovland and
Weiss, 1951–52). The phase of the problem which has been
most extensively studied is that concerned with the authori-
tativeness of the communicator. That personality differences
in the recipients are associated with the extent to which particular communicators are effective is clearly shown in a
study by Berkowitz and Lundy (1957). Their college-student
subjects who were more influenced by authority figures
tended to have both higher self-confidence and stronger authoritarian tendencies (high F-scale scores) than those who
were more influenced by peers.

The affiliation of the communicator is also an important
factor, in interaction, of course, with the group membership
of the recipient. Thus the communicator who is perceived
as belonging to a group with which the recipient is also
affiliated will be more effective on the average than a communicator who is perceived either as an outsider or as a
member of a rival group (Kelley and Volkart, 1952; Kelley
and Thibault, 1954). When, for example, a speaker's affiliation with a political, social, religious, or trade organization
becomes salient to the audience, persons who are members
of the same organization will be most likely to be influenced
by the speaker's communication.

Finally, the intent of the communicator is perceived differently by different members of the audience, with a conse-

quent influence on the speaker's effectiveness. A number of studies have shown that the fairness and impartiality of the communicator is viewed quite differently by individuals with varying stands on an ideological issue, and this in turn is related to the amount of opinion change effected. For a discussion of this problem see Hovland, Harvey, and Sherif (1957).

Media-Bound Factors

It seems probable that some persons will be more responsive to communications in situations of direct social interaction, whereas others may be more readily influenced by newspapers, magazines, radio programs, television, movies, and mass media in general. (See the discussion by Lazarsfeld, Berelson, and Gaudet, 1944, concerning the psychological differences between propaganda emanating from mass media and from informal social contacts.) Other media characteristics that may evoke differential sensitivities involve variations in the sense modalities employed: e.g. some people may be more responsive to visual than to auditory media. There is some evidence that individuals with less education may be more influenced by aural presentations (e.g. by radio and lectures) than by printed media (see summary of studies by Klapper, 1949). However, few systematic studies have been made as yet on the relation between predispositions and media characteristics.

Situation-Bound Factors

While no systematic studies can be cited, there are indications that some persons tend to be more influenced when socially facilitative cues accompany the presentation of a persuasive communication (e.g. presence of others, applause). The experiments by Asch (1952) and other investigators contain some indirect implications bearing on individual differences in responsiveness to an expression of consensus on the part of others in the audience. Research by Razran (1940) and an unpublished study by Janis, Kaye, and Kirschener indicate that some people are affected by the pleasantness or unpleasantness of the situation in which a communication is received. For example, the effectiveness of persuasive messages was found to be enhanced if they were expressed at a time when the subjects were eating a snack. We might expect to find some personality factors associated with low vs. high sensitivity to extraneous stimulation of this type.

Just as in the case of topic-bound factors, each of the above content-bound, communicator-bound, media-bound, and situation-bound factors may include some predispositions that are very narrow in scope (e.g. applicable only to communications which emanate from one particular communicator) and other predispositions that are broadly applicable to a large class of communications (e.g. to all communications emanating from purported authorities or experts). It is the predispositions at the latter end of the specificity-generality continuum that are of major scientific interest, since they are the ones that increase our theoretical understanding of communication processes and help to improve predictions of the degree to which different persons will be responsive to social influence.

PREDICTIVE VALUE OF UNBOUND PERSUASIBILITY FACTORS

Unbound persuasibility factors, on which this volume is primarily focused, involve a person's general susceptibility to many different types of persuasion and social influence. We assume that these factors operate whenever a person is exposed to a persuasive communication and that they do not depend upon the presence or absence of any given type of content or on any other specifiable feature of the communication situation. Thus unbound factors are communication-free, and this differentiates them from even the most general of the bound factors.

One long-range product of research on bound and unbound persuasibility factors might be conceived of as a set of general formulae which could be used to predict, within a very narrow range of error, the degree to which any given person will be influenced by any given communication. The formulae would be multiple regression equations and would specify the personal attributes $(X_1, X_2, X_3, \ldots X_n)$ that need to be assessed in order to make an accurate prediction concerning responsiveness to a given class of communications (Y_A). More than one regression equation would presumably be necessary in order to take account of the major bound personality factors; i.e. certain attributes might have high weight for one type of communication (Y_A) but low or zero weight for other types $(Y_B, Y_C, Y_D,$ etc.). This way of looking at persuasibility research helps to clarify the essential difference between bound and unbound factors. Unbound factors would enter with a sizable weight into *every one* of the regression equations, irrespective of the type of communication for which predictions are being made $(Y_A, Y_B, \ldots Y_Z)$. Bound factors, on the other hand, would have *varying* weights, ranging from zero in some regression equations to very high weights in others.

The concept of a set of multiple regression equations highlights the descriptive character of persuasibility factors. They are, in effect, individual traits whose consequences are directly measurable by observing changes in verbal behavior and in overt nonverbal behavior. They enable us to estimate the probability that a given individual will change his opinions or attitudes in response to a given class of communications. The unbound predispositions are communication-free factors which permit estimates concerning the probability of change in response to any communication, i.e. they purport to apply universally to all communications.

It should be noted, incidentally, that a given attribute (e.g. degree of motivation to conform to the demands of others) might turn out to be partly bound as well as unbound. That is to say, the attribute may be a communication-free factor because it enters into every regression formula with a substantial weight but, at the same time, it might be partly bound in that the weight may be much higher in a regression equation that applies to one particular class of communications (e.g. those which contain arguments and incentives appealing directly to the recipient's social conformity motives).

It should also be borne in mind that a seemingly unbound factor might actually be bound in a rather subtle or unexpected way. During the early stages of research, a given persuasibility factor may seem to be unbound, since it consistently enables better-than-chance predictions for a wide variety of communications differing in topic, communicator characteristics, media characteristics, and so forth. Subsequent research, however, might reveal that the factor is bound to some very broad category (e.g. it may apply to one-way mass-media situations but not to direct interpersonal relationships in which two-way communication takes place). Although more limited in its scope than had at first been apparent, the factor might, nevertheless, remain a valuable predictive attribute for an extremely wide range of communication situations. This example again points to the need for regarding "bound" and "unbound" as end-points of a continuum rather than as a dichotomy, since there may be wide variation in "degree of boundedness."

Some bound factors may apply to such small or trivial classes of communications that they are of little value for predictive or theoretical purposes, whereas other bound factors may pertain to extensive and socially significant classes of communication. Certain bound factors may conceivably turn out to be almost as broad in scope as the unbound ones and may permit the formulation of some general laws of persuasibility with relatively few limiting conditions. Thus, the quest to discover unbound persuasibility factors need not be regarded as having failed in its scientific purposes when the investigator discovers instead a set of bound factors. If they are sufficiently broad in scope, they may help to formulate general propositions concerning the type of person who will be influenced by various kinds of social communications.

In line with this conception, we regard the purpose of the persuasibility research represented in this volume to be that of *discovering and assessing both unbound factors and bound factors of broad scope.* The ensuing discussion of the measurement of persuasibility refers to unbound factors only, but it should be understood that the same considerations apply to the discovery of the broadest of the bound factors.

MEASUREMENT OF PERSUASIBILITY

The preceding discussion has several implications for the measurement of general persuasibility factors. As we are seeking to discover communication-free factors, we must build into the measures some way of eliminating as much as possible those content-bound, communicator-bound, media-bound, and situation-bound factors that might drastically limit the scope of the findings. Consider, for example, the measurement of audience reactions to a typical magazine article presenting arguments and appeals advocating a pro-United Nations attitude. Wide individual differences might range from minus scores (for persons who were negatively influenced) through zero scores (for those who remained uninfluenced) to positive scores (for those who were influenced in the direction advocated by the communicator). To what extent could these scores be relied upon to predict the reactions of these same people to other communications? Obviously, the individual differences in responsiveness to any single communication of this kind would be heavily determined by narrow topic-bound factors such as the person's initial attitude toward the UN and the degree to which he values national autonomy as against international cooperation. Moreover, individual reactions to the communication would also depend on the arguments used, the affiliations and intentions of the communicator, and other narrowly circumscribed stimulus factors that affect some highly specific predispositional tendencies (content-bound, communicator-bound, media-bound, and situation-bound factors) which are confounded with the general persuasibility factors. Thus, one would have little confidence in predicting, on the basis of opinion-change scores for the pro-UN communication, the reactions of these same people toward communications on other topics, such as the harmful effects of alcohol, the value of learning to play a musical instrument, and the desirability of having a town manager rather than a mayor.

The above example points up the problem of obtaining a relatively "pure" measure of general persuasibility in which general factors will not be overshadowed by and confounded with interacting specific factors. Two methods of solving this problem have been attempted. We shall call one the method of *systematic variation* and the other the method of *exclusion*.

Systematic Variation

If the systematic-variation method were used to its fullest extent, the subject would be exposed to a large cross-sectional sample of social communications representing a wide range of topics, appeals, arguments, communicator characteristics, media characteristics, and situational contexts. Essentially an analysis-of-variance design, it would attempt to separate the variance attributable to bound factors from the variance attributable to unbound factors responsible for consistent individual differences in general persuasibility. Execution of a design of this sort would require a long-term panel study to obtain opinion-change measures from the same persons for a sample of perhaps several hundred diverse communications. This version of the method of systematic variation does not seem feasible, but a close approximation might be a design similar to that of the OSS program of personnel assessment during World War II, in which a group of men were given a concentrated barrage of assessment tests during a three-day period at an isolated house in the country. However, a "weekend in the country" procedure would obviously run the risk of adding an element of artificiality which might invalidate the findings.

More feasible are the *small-scale applications* of this method. An example is the persuasibility test described by Janis and Field in Chapter 2, which includes ten communications representing a wide range of topics, appeals, and sources. The adequacy of any such small-sample version of the method is partly dependent on the extent of variation the investigator is able to introduce.

The Exclusion Method

The exclusion method attempts to eliminate the necessity for exposing subjects to a large number of communications. It reduces the variance attributable to arguments, appeals, and other bound factors by employing skeletal communications from which everything has been excluded except the source and the conclusion. An example of the "stripped-down" communications used to measure general persuasibility in young children will be found in the studies by Abelson and Lesser (Chapters 7, 8, and 9). In a study of older children

(Chapter 10), King also used the exclusion method; his communications consisted merely of check marks to show the
opinions held by various sources (peers, teachers, parents,
and experts). It is conceivable that similar methods, perhaps
including some ambiguous stimuli of the kind used in projective personality tests, would be useful in measuring general persuasibility tendencies in adults.

Both the exclusion and the systematic variation methods
require the same precaution with respect to eliminating the
"initial opinion artifact," which is discussed by Abelson and
Lesser (pp. 146–8). Also, in order to avoid stimulating
spurious social compliance, the test administrator must set
up conditions which permit the respondents to feel free to
express their true opinions.

Assessment of Consistency

Implicit in the above discussion of the measurement of
general persuasibility factors is the assumption that such
factors will, in fact, be found to exist. But it is an empirical
question, of course, whether there are individual differences
in responsiveness to different types of communications of
such consistency that one or more general persuasibility factors can be extracted.

Some preliminary results on this question were reported
by Ferguson (1944), based on actual exposure of subjects to
a series of communications. Subsequent evidence by others,
using less direct methods (Fiske, 1949; Richards and Simons,
1941; Layman, 1940; Brogden and Thomas, 1943), also suggests that there are consistent individual differences—that
some persons regularly tend to accept the conclusions put
forth in diverse communications whereas other persons regularly tend to reject them. Nevertheless, the evidence repre-

sented by these studies is not crucial and could be interpreted in other ways.

In their survey of this literature, Hovland, Janis, and Kelley (1953) conclude:

> Until data are available from more comprehensive research, one cannot be at all confident about the existence of unitary predispositional traits on which accurate predictions can be based as to how people will respond to various persuasive communications presented in diverse communication situations. Ideally, further research on this problem should secure data on actual changes induced by exposure to communications, as in the case of Ferguson's study, but employing a large series of communications which vary not only in subject matter but also with respect to media, type of appeals used, arrangement of arguments, and other stimulus characteristics. The scanty evidence already available, however, suggests that at least in some types of communication situations people show fairly consistent tendencies to be highly influenced or to remain uninfluenced by each of a series of discrete communications on different topics.

> Probably there is no single general factor, in the sense that every individual can be assigned a single score which will represent his degree of susceptibility to any and all situations where changes in attitudes or opinions are elicited. On the other hand, the opposite assumption of complete specificity seems to be unwarranted. That is to say, the available evidence apparently contradicts the assumption that individuals exhibit completely unrelated degrees of susceptibility that are unique to each opinion topic or to each communication situation. Consequently, there is reason to expect that a number of more or less general factors will eventually be isolated,

some of which may apply to a fairly broad range of communication situations. . . .

"Persuasibility" [is used] as a generic term to refer to any topic-free aspects of responsiveness to persuasive communications, without prejudging the question of which components, if any, form unitary variables. For the present we must expect that whatever indices of persuasibility are used will be relatively impure measures, representing (to unknown degrees) various general and more specific predispositional tendencies. But this limitation does not necessarily preclude the possibility of finding significant relationships between personality factors and objective measures of persuasibility [pp. 178–9].

The study by Janis and Field reported in Chapter 2 was designed for the purpose of obtaining systematic evidence on the consistency of individual differences in persuasibility. Further evidence bearing on general persuasibility factors comes from the series of studies reported by Linton and Graham in Chapter 4. Their results suggest that there may be more than one general factor underlying susceptibility to social influence.

THEORETICAL APPROACHES

Persuasibility factors, whether general or specific, bound or unbound, are essentially descriptive traits. Such factors refer to the observable degree to which an individual is susceptible to one or another (or all) forms of social influence. The central research problems with respect to the predispositional aspects of opinion change consist of: (1) isolating and developing methods for assessing each of the major persuasibility factors and (2) studying the underlying causes that explain or specify the conditions under which each persuasibility factor will be strong or weak. The first task has been discussed in the preceding section; we turn now to the second task, that of accounting for the strength of general persuasibility factors.

There are numerous theoretical approaches to this problem, but they can all be classified as either *genetic* or *dynamic* explanations. Genetic explanations are those which attempt to explain *how a person becomes what he is.* Dynamic explanations, on the other hand, are not concerned with the past history of the individual but, rather, focus on the underlying motives, defenses, anticipations, attitudes, and other latent attributes that may explain *why the person behaves as he does at the present time.*

The Genetic Approach

In current psychological theory, there appear to be two main sources of genetic concepts that pertain to susceptibility to social influence: learning theory and psychoanalysis. Some genetic propositions can be derived from the learning theory formulations presented by Hull (1952), Dollard and Miller (1950), Tolman (1951), and other behavior theorists who specify either reward or incentive as a necessary condition for the acquisition of verbal habits. The principles of learning theory, however, have rarely been applied specifically to the acquisition of persuasibility attributes by young children and to the persistence or change of such attributes during the subsequent stages of individual development. Some preliminary genetic formulations, using certain of the concepts of contemporary learning theories, will be found in the theoretical analysis presented by Abelson and Lesser in Chapter 7.

Freud and other psychoanalysts have seldom discussed the problem of persuasibility in normal persons, but some of their developmental constructs might prove a useful source of theoretical assumptions concerning the psychogenesis of compulsive conformity, hostility toward authorities, fear of being manipulated by others, hypercritical attitudes toward prestigeful communications, and defensive attitudes of negativism toward all hidden or open persuaders. Thus, for example, Flugel (1945) has discussed some of the psychogenetic determinants of a general tendency to reject and resist all communications which either refer to prohibitions or suggest restrictions upon personal freedom. Flugel links a generalizable rejection tendency with "the lost feeling of infantile omnipotence" which supposedly develops from the child's first feeding frustrations (not being given the breast or bottle when it is wanted). Certain frustrations are assumed to inflict deep wounds in the young child's feeling of omnipotence: "Every subsequent prohibition may reopen [the first wound] by painfully reminding us of the obstacles to our desires. The feeling can be restored only if we satisfy ourselves in spite of a continuing prohibition, the mere removal of which could not produce this satisfaction" (Flugel, 1945, p. 197).

Certain psychoanalytic constructs concerning the genesis of hysteria have been thought to be applicable on the assumption that hysterical neurotics are generally much more persuasible and suggestible than other people (Weinberg, 1952, p. 157). Other genetic concepts, stemming from Freud's theories and from the psychoanalytically oriented research of Else Frenkel-Brunswik, are employed by Hoffman (1953) in his discussion of compulsive conformity.[1] Compulsive conformity, he claims, originates in childhood experiences with parents who are punitive and dominantly overprotective:

1. Hoffman's (1953) own empirical research on the TAT responses of "compulsive conformers" does not provide an adequate test of any of the genetic

The child's aggressive responses to such frustrating parental stimuli, whether directed toward the parents or displaced, are punished in such a way as to produce anxiety and feelings of guilt over the aggressive impulses. . . .

The reaction formation against hostile impulses toward the parents may involve turning them toward the self and, in combination with such guilt-producing cultural demands as "honor your father and your mother," lead to overconcern for the well-being of the parents, overidealization of them, submission to their demands, and overinterjection of their attitudes and values. Partly as a result of this process of reaction formation and partly in response to continuing pressure from without, the individual may develop a very positive attitude toward, and a strong need to conform to all forms of authority [p. 384].

Although psychoanalytic concepts have influenced various theorists in the field of opinion-change research, very little evidence is available, as yet, for evaluating the validity of the psychogenetic constructs for explaining individual differences in persuasibility within the normal range of adult personalities.

The Dynamic Approach

Whereas psychoanalytic concepts of psychogenesis have not as yet had much influence on persuasibility research, the situation is quite different for psychoanalytic formulations bearing on personality dynamics, emotional conflicts, ego defenses, and various unconscious processes that influence

---

propositions he formulates. Rather, his findings deal with attitudes of overidealization toward parent figures and repressed hostility and guilt, all of which are dynamic factors pertaining to the current personality make-up of adults who display strong conformist tendencies.

everyday behavior in adult life. In fact, psychoanalytic theory appears to be a major source of the dynamic hypotheses which occupy the attention of many research investigators studying the personality determinants of individual differences in general persuasibility. Thus, for example, psychoanalytic constructs concerning repression, denial, projection, and rejection are employed by Cohen in his discussion of the social influence exerted in direct interaction by persons of low and high self-esteem (Chapter 5). Various psychodynamic concepts are also introduced by Janis and Field (Chapter 3) into their discussion of findings bearing on the relation of self-esteem to measures of persuasibility obtained by exposing adolescents to mass-type communications. Psychoanalytic concepts pertaining to defense mechanisms are used by Janis and Rife in their analysis of comparable data from emotionally disturbed patients (Chapter 6) and by King in his discussion of persuasibility in children (Chapter 10).

Various neo-Freudian concepts evolved by Erich Fromm and David Riesman, concerning the role of internal moral or superego standards and social anxiety, have also been adopted by some investigators. An example of this type of theoretical influence will be found in the discussion of personality correlates of conformity behavior by Harriet Linton and Elaine Graham (Chapter 4).

Although learning theory and Freudian and neo-Freudian concepts have influenced the thinking of research workers in this field, the theoretical issues have not been clearly drawn and many of the inferences derived from the popular usage of such concepts as "drive," "reward," "defense," "incentive," "unconscious conflict," and "inner- vs. other-directedness" are ambiguous and even potentially contradictory. The research findings available so far have not led to any great sharpening of theoretical constructs and they frequently lend themselves to alternative interpretations. In other words, research in this field has not yet reached the stage where precise theoretical questions can be put to the data; thus none of the existing studies can be regarded as *crucial* research with respect to testing rival theories.

In this volume we shall try to take stock of the empirical findings that have grown out of the studies on persuasibility conducted at Yale and elsewhere, looking toward theoretical integration and toward evolving a set of constructs that will be useful for future research. In the final two chapters we shall present a summary of the preliminary product of our efforts in this direction.

PART ONE

*Persuasibility and
Its Personality Correlates*

A Behavioral Assessment of Persuasibility: Consistency of Individual Differences

IRVING L. JANIS AND PETER B. FIELD

A NUMBER of recent investigations (Ferguson, 1944; Hovland, Janis, and Kelley, 1953; Janis, 1954, 1955; Janis and Feshbach, 1954) have been concerned with individual differences in responsiveness to persuasive communications and have raised the possibility that there may be a general factor of susceptibility to persuasion, or "persuasibility." The latter term does not refer to attitudes predisposing the individual to accept or reject communications which favor a *particular type of conclusion*, but rather to those attitudes or personality factors leading to low or high resistance to a *wide variety of persuasive communications on many diverse topics*. The existence of one or more general factors of susceptibility to persuasion would imply that some individuals tend to be indiscriminately influenced by the many persuasive communications to which every modern urban community is

Reprinted with minor editorial revisions from *Sociometry*, 1956, *19*, 241–59, by permission of the publishers.

continually exposed, while other individuals tend to be generally unresponsive to such communications.

Previous studies bearing on general persuasibility have been limited in scope and in generality because of their use of a small number of communications, relatively homogeneous in argumentation and in type of persuasive appeal. An initial study by Janis (1954) used three communications which dealt with different topics, but which were relatively homogeneous in that they all advanced predictions of future events and used logical argumentation rather than other possible persuasive appeals (e.g. fear-arousing appeals or prestigeful endorsements). A second study by the same author (1955) used five communications which were heterogeneous in content, but all of them were again limited to predominantly logical argumentation. Both studies were conducted with male college students and the results supported the conclusion that there are consistent individual differences in persuasibility which are related to personality factors such as feelings of personal inadequacy.

One of the main questions which the present investigation was designed to answer is: Are individual differences in susceptibility to persuasion consistent enough to warrant the assumption that there is a more or less general factor of persuasibility? To help answer this question we have developed a test for assessing a person's susceptibility to persuasion, modeled after the behavioral measures of persuasibility used in Janis' earlier studies. The method consists of three steps: first, the subjects are given an initial opinion test; next they are exposed to a series of persuasive communications; then they are given a postcommunication opinion test to determine the degree to which their opinions change in the direction of the communicators' conclusions.

The new test of general persuasibility to be described here differs from the ones used in the earlier studies in the following important respects: the series of communications is much larger and represents a much wider variety of topics and of persuasive appeals. By administering the new test to a large sample of subjects, it was possible to examine the consistency of opinion changes in response to the various communications. If specific content-bound predispositions are the only major factors which determine individual differences in responsiveness to persuasive communications, correlations close to zero should be found among the resulting opinion changes. A different prediction follows from the hypothesis that there is a general factor (or set of factors) underlying individual differences in susceptibility to persuasion. According to this hypothesis, the resulting opinion changes will be positively intercorrelated: those persons who are most strongly influenced by any one of the persuasive communications should show a tendency to be most strongly influenced by each of the others, irrespective of the subject matter.

The present chapter will be devoted to describing and discussing the evidence pertaining to test reliability and the consistency of individual differences in persuasibility. Chapter 3 will deal with additional evidence bearing on potential *sources* of consistent individual differences—sex differences, IQ differences, and various motivational factors that predispose a person to high or low susceptibility to persuasive communications.

METHODS AND PROCEDURES

The Persuasibility Test

The new test of persuasibility (see Appendix A) consists of three components: (1) the Initial Questionnaire, designed to measure initial opinion on fifteen items; (2) Booklet I, containing five persuasive communications on five topics, each of which is followed by the three pertinent questions from the Initial Questionnaire; and (3) Booklet II, a second series of five persuasive communications on exactly the same topics as the first series, but taking diametrically opposite positions to those taken in the first series. After each communication in Booklet II the subjects are given the same opinion questions they had answered earlier in the Initial Questionnaire and in Booklet I. Thus, at three different times the subjects are asked to express their opinions: first, before any communication is presented; a second time, after reading the initial set of communications (Booklet I); and a third time, after reading an opposing set of communications (Booklet II).

The persuasibility scores obtained from the test are based on a total of 30 questions (3 questions for each of 10 communications). The method of scoring will be described below.

In Booklet I, the articles present various types of arguments and persuasive appeals in support of the following main conclusions:

1. The U. S. Civil Defense organization should be greatly expanded—to include 25 million men and women.

2. An effective cure for cancer can be achieved within one or two years if an all-out research effort is made; about 50 per cent of all medical research specialists should concentrate on this task.

3. General Von Hindenburg, president of the German Republic after the First World War, was a democratic leader and a great statesman.

4. Radio stations should (and soon will) cut down on the amount of classical music they dish out, because it is dull stuff, strictly for the long-haired highbrows and stuffed shirts.

5. Jack O'Keefe, a corny comedian who is trying to break

into TV, is not worth watching and his TV show will be a complete flop.

In Booklet II, the same types of argumentation and persuasive appeal are used to support the opposite conclusions —e.g. the Civil Defense organization should be cut down to about 2000 well-trained people so that our main defense effort can be concentrated on using our air power; a cure for cancer cannot be expected for at least 30 years and it would be a mistake to take scientists away from other, more promising tasks to work on this one; and so on.

In addition to the wide diversity of topics covered in each booklet, there is a wide variety of special persuasive appeals. An attempt was made to include representative examples of major types of persuasive appeals currently found in mass communications, ranging from the logical argumentation employed in the communications about cancer research to the hyperbolic, stereotyped language in the comments about the television comedian. Table 1 summarizes the topics and the main types of appeals.

In selecting the communication topics, care was taken to avoid such possible confounding dimensions as a consistent "liberal" or "intellectual" position, or a consistent tendency to believe the good or the bad about people. Moreover, it was for the purpose of avoiding correlations with specific ideological predispositions that we included the subjects' opinion changes in response to the communications in both booklets (presenting *both the pro and con position* on each issue) in arriving at the over-all persuasibility score. A person agreeing with both the pro and con communications on a given issue would be likely to do so not because of some specific preference for one side of the issue, but rather because of a general tendency to accept the communications regardless of the initial attractiveness of their conclusions. Thus, the inclusion of opposing communications in the persuasibility test should help to insure that positive correlations among opinion changes will not be attributable to a tendency to accept either all pro or all con communications, or to accept a given set of

TABLE 1. *Subject Matter and Special Appeals Used in the Persuasibility Test Communications*

Topic	COMMUNICATOR'S POSITION: Booklet I	Booklet II	Special appeal used in pro and con communications
1. Public participation in civil defense effort	Pro	Con	Fear-arousing threat statements (e.g. danger of unpreparedness, destructiveness of atomic warfare)
2. Expansion of cancer research	Pro	Con	Logical arguments and specialized information (citing expert scientific opinion)
3. General Von Hindenburg	Pro	Con	Stereotyped characterizations (overidealized hero or exaggerated villain)
4. Classical music	Con	Pro	Social incentives (predictions that the given preference will be a means of attaining social approval)
5. A new television comedian	Con	Pro	Hedonic incentives (predictions that the given choice will lead to enjoyment or nonenjoyment)

ideologically related opinions, but will reflect a more general persuasibility tendency.

We attempted also to vary the degree of structuring with respect to the subjects' previously formed opinions and amount of prior knowledge. The communications range from those on which the subjects could be expected to hold definite initial opinions (e.g. preference for classical music) to those on which they could have no previous opinions (e.g. the fictitious television comedian). One assumption tested in this study is that, if a general factor of susceptibility to persuasion is present, consistent individual differences should be found on all topics, but should show up most strongly on the *unstructured* topics, i.e. those for which initial opinions are not based on familiarity with the nature of the issue or on prior information about the pros and cons. For instance, with high school students it could be expected that opinion changes on Von Hindenburg and the fictitious television comedian would be the most sensitive indicators of any general persuasibility tendency.

Every one of the ten communications, whether pro or con, took a sufficiently extreme position to ensure that practically none of the subjects would initially agree with the position advocated by the communication. It should be noted that any communication which yielded complete acceptance or complete rejection would not have been satisfactory for our purposes, because it could not be used to study individual differences in susceptibility to persuasion. The communications and questions were repeatedly revised on the basis of successive individual and group pretests so that (1) the communications would be intelligible and interesting to high school student subjects and (2) the questions could differentiate subjects who were influenced by the communications from those who were not.[1] From a preliminary analysis of the changes in opinion produced by the communications in a sample of 100 cases, it was found that on all 30 postcommunication questions a significant degree of change occurred.

Procedures for Investigating Consistency

The persuasibility test was administered to approximately 185 high school juniors in history classes. The Initial Ques-

1. The three questions included for each communication were to some extent redundant, but not completely so because they covered somewhat different aspects or implications of the main conclusion. The specific questions are shown in Appendix A, pp. 282–5.

tionnaire and Booklet I, including the second questionnaire, were administered successively in the same session; Booklet II, including the third questionnaire, was administered a week later. For each class, the regular teacher introduced the experimenter as a member of a university research organization "which is conducting studies in this and other high schools throughout the state." The experimenter administered the Initial Questionnaire and then gave a standardized introduction, explaining the material in Booklet I.

The subjects were informed that the articles were written by reporters and presented their opinions on controversial, newsworthy topics. Each communication in both booklets was headed "Opinions in the News" and had a by-line designed to impress upon the reader the fact that the communication had been written by a reporter. The students were told that the experimenter wanted to know whether they agreed or disagreed with the articles, and they were instructed to express their own personal opinions on the questions following each article. They were also assured that their answers would be kept strictly confidential and would not be seen by the teacher or by anyone else at the school. In order to avoid implicit or explicit pressure for opinion change, the following instructions were given orally by the experimenter, immediately after the subjects had finished filling out the Initial Questionnaire:

Now I am going to ask you to read some articles on the topics that I have just asked you about. I would like you to answer some more questions about your opinions after you have read these articles.

I am giving you the articles to show you what some other people are thinking about these matters. You are perfectly free to agree or disagree with these articles, of course. After you have read each article you will be asked whether you agree or disagree with it. Remember, I want to know what you think, so give me your own personal opinion.

The articles that you're going to read have been taken from a professional news service. This news service brings together articles about opinions in the news today.

There are many different opinions about these different subjects. The reporters who wrote the articles you're going to read have put down their own points of view. There are other people, of course, who think differently about these topics. For instance, my own personal views do *not* happen to agree with certain of these articles, although there are some other articles with which I am inclined to agree.

Now if I showed these articles to a lot of people in [name of city]—including for instance all the teachers in this high school—I would get a good deal of disagreement. The average person would probably agree with some of the articles and disagree with others. These articles are on matters of opinion, you see, and some people have one opinion while others have a different opinion about each topic. So feel free to decide *for yourself* whether you agree or disagree with each of these articles.

Please read these articles the same way you would read an article in a magazine or a newspaper, and then answer the questions about your own opinion.

Similar instructions were used when Booklet II was administered, one week after Booklet I.[2] Three weeks later a

2. The introduction for Booklet II included the following:
"I have come here today to ask you to read some more News Service articles of the same kind you read before. You remember that last week you read some articles in which newspaper reporters expressed their opinions about topics in the news today. As you were told last week, there are many different

self-rating questionnaire was administered by the high school teachers. This questionnaire asked the subject to rate himself on his general susceptibility to influence by mass communications (newspaper articles, radio and television programs) and his tendency to conform with the opinions of his friends.

Scoring of the Persuasibility Test

A persuasibility score was assigned to each individual to represent his opinion changes in response to the communications in the two booklets. This score was the sum of the number of questions on which the subject changed from his Initial Questionnaire position in the direction advocated by any given communication. (About 3 per cent of the subjects failed to answer 3 or more questions out of the 30 and were eliminated from the sample; scores for subjects with one or two no-answer responses were prorated.) Changes in the negative direction (i.e. opposite to that advocated in the communica-

---

opinions on these topics. Today you will read some articles by some other reporters who take a different point of view on these matters.

"The Opinion News Service gives a chance for many different viewpoints to be expressed, and so they often put out articles by writers who take opposite points of view on the same topics. I am going to ask you to read these new articles and then answer the same questions as before, after you've read the other side of the story and after you've had a chance to see what some of the different opinions are on these topics.

"Let me remind you that you are perfectly free to agree or disagree with these articles, and you will be asked whether or not you do agree with each article after you have read it.

"As I mentioned last week, if I showed any of these articles to people here I would probably find a good deal of disagreement. Some people would agree and others would disagree with each one. As for myself, I agree with some of the articles and disagree with some others.

"Remember, you should decide *for yourself* whether you agree or disagree with each of these articles. Please read the articles in the same way you would read an article in a magazine or newspaper, and then answer the questions about your opinions.

"And remember, all your answers will be kept strictly private in our study and none of your teachers will see any of your answers."

tion) rarely occurred and did not exceed 10 per cent on any item; they were counted the same as no change, or zero. This method of scoring does not reflect magnitude of change: a change of one unit or many units is scored as 1. The main reason for adopting this procedure is that there is no simple way to equate the *magnitude* of change on one question with that on another, especially since about half the questions required the subjects to express their opinions as quantitative estimates, while the other half required the students to place a check mark opposite one of the verbal answer categories presented in a standard check list.

Since only the direction of the change was counted, the scores on the persuasibility test vary from zero to 30, representing the number of items on which the subject changed his opinion in the direction of a conclusion advocated by one of the communications he had just read. The response to each question in Booklet I was examined in relation to the response given to the same question on the Initial Questionnaire. For each item on which the subject changed in the direction of the communication, he was given a score of 1; for each item on which he showed no change or a negative change, he was given a score of zero.

The scoring of the opinion changes following Booklet II was somewhat more complicated. A simple scoring of change in the direction of the second communication might involve a serious methodological error. On the basis of prior studies of the stability of opinion changes produced by persuasive communications (Hovland, Janis, and Kelley, 1953), it is expected that, as a result of forgetting and other processes, opinions would tend to regress (from their level immediately following Booklet I toward their original level) during the week that intervened between Booklet I and Booklet II. In other words, if the identical questions had been asked a week later, even without any intervening opposing communications, there would probably have been a change away from the position expressed immediately after exposure to Booklet I. Such a change could give rise to spurious scores that do not reflect accurately the change in response due solely to the persuasive communications in Booklet II. In order to minimize this source of error, the criterion of change after Booklet II was defined as a shift from the answer given on the Initial Questionnaire. If the individual had shown a positive change following the Booklet I communication, then, following the Booklet II communication, he had to change all the way back to his original position, or beyond, to be scored as having changed in the direction of the latter communication. Consider, for example, an individual who changes his opinion twice on the following question: "What is your own opinion as to how much time the average radio station should devote to classical music each week?" Let us say that he changes from 30 to 15 hours after reading the con communication in Booklet I, and then changes to 25 hours on the same question after reading the pro communication in Booklet II. The change following Booklet I would be scored as 1, but the change following Booklet II would be scored as zero because the individual did not return to his initial opinion. He would have to change back to 30 hours or more to receive a positive score on the question in Booklet II.

RESULTS

Split-Half Reliability

The reliability of the persuasibility test was investigated in a subsample of approximately 100 cases, constituting about two-thirds of the total sample to which the test was administered. The subsample was a stratified random sample, including approximately equal numbers of male and female subjects. The split-half reliability was determined by giving each subject one persuasibility score on the 15 odd items and another on the 15 even items. Just as with the total scores based on all 30 items, the subtest scores represent the number of items on which the individual showed an opinion change (from the precommunication test to the postcommunication test) in the direction advocated by one or another of the communications. The raw reliability coefficient was found to be .69; the estimated value of the reliability coefficient is .81 when corrected by the Spearman-Brown formula. This finding indicates that the persuasibility scores are sufficiently reliable for making group comparisons.

Item Analysis

The internal consistency of the persuasibility test was studied in the same subsample of approximately 100 cases. Table 2 gives the results of an item analysis. It shows the results of plotting the changes on every item against the sum of the positive changes (or the total persuasibility score). The dichotomization of the total score was at the median; the dichotomization of item scores was between a change in the direction of the communication and no change or negative change.

Additional evidence of internal consistency is presented in Table 3, which shows tetrachoric correlations for each persuasibility subscore (on each communication of the persuasibility test) plotted against every other subscore on the test. Since there were three opinion questions for each communication, the scores for each communication ranged from zero (no positive change on any of the three questions) to 3 (positive change on all three questions). Dichotomizations were made so as to yield a split as close as possible to the median; the best split was found to be between scores of zero or 1 vs. 2 or 3.

Both the item analysis (Table 2) and the table of tetrachoric

TABLE 2. *Item Analysis of the Persuasibility Test: Chi Square for Score on Each Item vs. Sum of Persuasibility Scores for Booklets I and II*

Topic	Item	Chi square (1 df)	Confidence level (two tails)
BOOKLET I			
1. Pro civil defense	1	7.28	<.01
	2	5.84	.02
	3	5.92	.02
2. Pro cancer research	4	1.64	.20
	5	2.64	.11
	6	0.37	>.40
3. Pro Von Hindenburg	7	8.40	<.01
	8	5.73	.02
	9	12.35	<.01
4. Con classical music	10	3.36	.08
	11	2.51	.12
	12	5.91	.02
5. Con TV comedian	13	15.98	<.01
	14	37.35	<.01
	15	25.10	<.01
BOOKLET II			
1. Con civil defense	16	4.19	.05
	17	6.08	.02
	18	5.77	.02
2. Con cancer research	19	9.28	<.01
	20	3.22	.08
	21	7.88	<.01
3. Con Von Hindenburg	22	12.76	<.01
	23	21.62	<.01
	24	5.79	.02
4. Pro classical music	25	2.48	.13
	26	0.01	>.40
	27	5.81	.02
5. Pro TV comedian	28	4.50	.04
	29	11.72	<.01
	30	0.81	>.35

Note: N = approximately 100, with an occasional decrement of one to four because of no-answer responses.

correlations (Table 3) clearly show a strong positive relationship among changes on the various topics comprising the persuasibility test. In Table 3, 39 out of 45 correlations are positive. Only 6 are negative, all very small and nonsignificant. The item analysis in Table 2 shows that 23 out of 30 questions are positively related to the total score at the .10 confidence level (two-tail) or better; 11 out of 30 are significant at the .01 confidence level. Only 3 of the 30 items are very

TABLE 3. *Tetrachoric Correlations among Persuasibility Subscores from Each Communication in the Persuasibility Test*

	I–1	I–2	I–3	I–4	I–5	II–1	II–2	II–3	II–4	II–5
I–1 Pro civil defense	—	–.06	.50	.25	.22	.38	.05	.34	.21	.33
I–2 Pro cancer research		—	–.05	.10	.07	–.12	.14	–.12	.17	.16
I–3 Pro Von Hindenburg			—	.25	.31	.28	.05	.47	.25	–.07
I–4 Con classical music				—	.44	.09	.05	.15	.23	.13
I–5 Con TV comedian					—	.50	.30	.52	.22	.27
II–1 Con civil defense						—	.29	.49	–.08	.02
II–2 Con cancer research							—	.30	.15	.27
II–3 Con Von Hindenburg								—	.02	.27
II–4 Pro classical muisc									—	.33
II–5 Pro TV comedian										—

Note: $N =$ approximately 100, with an occasional decrement of one to four because of no-answer responses.

weakly correlated (above the .20 confidence level), but each of these was retained in the test because the very same question in the other booklet yields a significant relationship with the total score. No items correlated negatively with the total score.

The results indicated that, for our sample of high school students, the persuasibility test has a relatively high degree of internal consistency. The findings support the general hypothesis that there are consistent individual differences in the opinion changes elicited by a series of diverse communications.

Factor Analysis

A centroid factor analysis was computed from the array of tetrachoric correlations shown in Table 3 and the results are shown in Table 4. The proportion of the communality which enters into the first centroid factor is .60; this supports the assumption that the persuasibility test scores are determined

TABLE 4. *Factor Analysis Results for Persuasibility Sub-scores (Based on data in Table 3)*

CENTROID FACTOR MATRIX (UNROTATED)

	I	II	III	Communality (h^2)
I–1 Pro civil defense	.58	.31	.24	.49
I–2 Pro cancer research	.10	—.41	.04	.18
I–3 Pro Von Hindenburg	.53	.41	.38	.59
I–4 Con classical music	.45	—.19	.26	.31
I–5 Con television comedian	.71	—.03	—.17	.53
II–1 Con civil defense	.50	.39	—.32	.50
II–2 Con cancer research	.40	—.15	—.35	.30
II–3 Con Von Hindenburg	.63	.30	—.29	.57
II–4 Pro classical music	.39	—.32	.28	.33
II–5 Pro television comedian	.43	—.29	—.06	.27

ROTATED OBLIQUE FACTOR MATRIX

	A	B	C
I–1 Pro civil defense	.05	.56	.47
I–2 Pro cancer research	.40	—.31	—.10
I–3 Pro Von Hindenburg	—.06	.62	.62
I–4 Con classical music	.40	.06	.26
I–5 Con television comedian	.41	.33	.00
II–1 Con civil defense	—.06	.59	—.02
II–2 Con cancer research	.34	.07	—.28
II–3 Con Von Hindenburg	.09	.57	.01
II–4 Pro classical music	.48	—.08	.21
II–5 Pro television comedian	.48	—.04	—.07

CORRELATIONS BETWEEN FACTOR AXES

	A	B	C
A	—	.42	.00
B	.42	—	—.42
C	.00	—.42	—

to some degree by a single general factor. Three factors were found necessary, however, to account satisfactorily for the entire set of intercorrelations. These three factors were rotated obliquely and a clear, simple structure emerged. On two of the rotated factors, denoted A and B, pro and con communications on the same topic had similar loadings: either both were high positive or both were close to zero. This result—the clinging together in the factor space of pro and con communications on the same issue—is in accord with the assumption that individual differences in opinion change are partially determined by factors other than the predisposition to develop a pro or con attitude on the issue. The analysis indicates that there is a tendency for individuals to change either *both* ways on a given topic or *neither* way. Factors A and B constitute two correlated clusters each showing this tendency. For factor A, both pro and con communications on the following topics have high positive loadings (.35 or above): cancer research, classical music, and the television comedian. Other loadings are negligible. For factor B, the four highest positive loadings occur on the following: the pro and con communications on Von Hindenburg and civil defense.

As a preliminary interpretation of the difference between factors A and B, it is plausible to suppose that factor A topics have directly favorable or unfavorable implications for the individual, while factor B topics are on more remote, impersonal political issues. A more extensive factor analysis using a much larger number of topics would be needed to test this possibility. In any case, factors A and B correlate .42 with each other, and thus may be construed as variations on a single theme, whatever their individual interpretations. That theme is a general persuasibility factor which can be visualized as lying between factors A and B.

Factor C, which accounts for the least variance of the three factors, has high loadings on only two communications: pro civil defense and pro Von Hindenburg. The con versions of these communications have negligble loadings, as do all other communications. Factor C is thus a more specific, content-bound factor than either A or B. Factor C correlates .00 with factor A and —.42 with factor B. No explanation is offered for factor C.

Self-Ratings

The personality inventory, a 130-item questionnaire which was administered three weeks after the final part of the persuasibility test, included the following three questions for the purpose of obtaining the subjects' own self-ratings on susceptibility to *influence by mass communications:*

1. Do you usually agree or disagree with the articles that you read in newspapers and magazines?

   Agree with practically *everything* I read; Agree with *most* of the things I read; Agree with *about half* and *disagree* with half; Disagree with *most* things I read; Disagree with practically *everything* I read.

2. Nowadays when the American people listen to the radio or look at television, they see or hear a great deal of advertising, publicity, and information that attempts to influence their opinions and attitudes. As compared with the average person of your own age, how much are your own ideas likely to be influenced by the things you hear or see on the radio or television?

   Much *more influenced* than the average person; Somewhat *more influenced;* Slightly *more influenced;* About the *same;* Slightly *less influenced;* Somewhat *less influenced;* Much *less influenced.*

3. Consider all the magazine articles and newspaper columns presenting a specific point of view which you may have read during the past year. About how many of them may have influenced your opinions?

Practically none of them; Very few; Some; A fairly large number; Most of them; Practically all of them.

The answer to each question was given a score ranging from zero, or not influenced, to 5, highly influenced (the extreme categories in question 2 being combined). The subject's total score for the entire cluster was obtained by adding together the score values for his answers to all three questions.

The same scoring procedure was used with another cluster dealing with susceptibility to *influence by friends*. The following eight questions were included in this cluster, each of which was accompanied by a self-rating check list of five categories:

1. How often do you change your opinion if you discover that most other people you know do *not* share your point of view?

2. When one of your friends wants to convince you of his point of view, does he usually have a hard time or an easy time?

3. As compared with the average person of your own age, how much are you usually influenced by the ideas expressed by your friends?

4. As compared with the average person of your age, how strongly do you usually hang on to your own opinions or beliefs at times when your friends are trying to get you to change your mind?

5. How easy is it for your friends to get you to do what they want?

6. When other people criticize your ideas or object

to your opinion, how often do you end up feeling that that they are right and you are wrong?

7. How often do you become uneasy when the opinions of one of your friends is different from your own on some important topic?

8. How often do you feel sure you know what is right or wrong about the ideas expressed by the people you know?

TABLE 5. *Correlations (Pearsonian r) between Persuasibility Test Scores and Self-Ratings on Susceptibility to Social Influence*

Persuasibility test scores correlated with:	Females (N = 96)	Males (N = 86)
Self-ratings on responsiveness to persuasive mass communications	.06 (p > .25)	.26 (p = .02)
Self-ratings on responsiveness to influence of friends	.11 (p > .25)	.10 (p > .25)

Note: p values are for two tails.

Table 5 shows correlations between total persuasibility scores (sum of the positive opinion changes shown on the 30 questions in Booklets I and II) and each of the two clusters of self-ratings on susceptibility to influence. These correlations are based on a total sample of 86 males and 96 females, who answered all the pertinent questions.

The correlation between the persuasibility test scores and self-rating scores on susceptibility to influence by mass communications is significant at the .02 level for males, but the correlation is close to zero for females. The difference between the correlation for males and for females is not significant (p = .18, determined by Fisher's z-transformation formula). The fact that the persuasibility test scores of the female subjects bear no relationship to their self-rating scores indicates that the two procedures do not measure the same thing. In the case of the male subjects, however, there is some degree of overlap, since the persuasibility test scores make possible better-than-chance prediction of what a subject will say about his responsiveness to mass communications in general.

The second correlation, between persuasibility and the subject's own evaluation of his susceptibility to influence by friends, shows no strong relationship for either males or females, although the trend is in the expected (positive) direction.

Discussion

Consistency of Individual Differences

The null hypothesis tested in the present study is that changes in opinion resulting from persuasive communications are wholly content-bound and are always highly specific to the subject matter of each particular communication. According to this hypothesis, the opinion changes produced by any two communications arguing unrelated cases on unrelated issues would generally be unrelated, and opinion changes following two opposing communications would be negatively related. In the light of the data presented in Table 3 and the factor analysis results in Table 4, the null hypothesis is inadequate. We found a strong positive relationship between changes in opinion on unrelated topics (e.g. between pro civil defense and pro television comedian) and also a strong positive relationship between changes in opinion following opposing communications on the same topic (e.g. between pro civil defense and anti civil defense). The latter type of relationship was found in the case of every one of the five topics, and in four of the five instances the positive correlation is large enough to be regarded as statistically

significant. The hypothesis that opinion change is exclusively
determined by topic-bound predispositions fails to explain the
positive relationships among opinion changes on diverse and
opposing communications.

The factor analysis yielded two common persuasibility
factors that were positively correlated. This finding suggests
that persuasibility may be determined by a general factor
combined with one or more group factors that are less limited
in scope than the highly specific factors underlying susceptibility to influence on particular topics.

Some further implications concerning the nature of the
general persuasibility variable can be gleaned from an examination of the individual differences in opinion changes
produced by different communications. On page 35 we gave
a rationale for predicting that opinion changes in response to
the Von Hindenburg and television comedian communications would be the most sensitive indicators of general persuasibility. As stated previously, we expect specific content
predispositions to be less important as determinants of change,
in comparison with any general persuasibility factor, when
the persuasive communications touch upon unfamiliar topics
or issues about which the individual has not yet developed
any strong, precommunication interests and motivations.
Since Von Hindenburg is virtually an unknown figure to
present-day American high school students and since the television comedian is fictitious, it was predicted that these two
topics would have the highest loadings on any general factor
of persuasibility. The results of the factor analysis, shown in
the table of tetrachorics, largely substantiate this prediction.
In column one of the Centroid Factor Matrix in Table 4, it
will be noted that the first communication on the television
comedian had the highest loading on the first (unrotated)
centroid factor, and the second communication on Von Hindenburg had the next highest loading. The other communica-

tions on Von Hindenburg and the comedian also showed high loadings on this factor. Moreover, among the ten communications included in the persuasibility test, the three highest communalities (h^2 in the Centroid Factor Matrix) are those for the two communications on Von Hindenburg and the first communication on the television comedian. The reliability and internal consistency of the persuasibility test could probably be improved by using more communications on unstructured attitudes of this sort in place of the ones that had the lowest factor loadings.

The only communication with a very small loading on the first (unrotated) centroid factor is the first communication on cancer research. This communication is unique in that the opinion changes it elicited have only a very small, nonsignificant correlation with the opinion changes evoked by each of the other nine communications (see Table 3). Individual differences in response to this communication, which was by no means overwhelmingly accepted, were not strongly related to those observed on the other nine communications. Perhaps the explanation lies in the scientific nature of the subject matter. Scientific reports, even in popularized form, may be perceived by many laymen as unquestionably authoritative and therefore as noncontroversial. This type of communication therefore might not be comparable to the others in the test; acceptance of this particular communication may be related more closely to other attitude or ideological variables (e.g. attitude toward science).

The lack of relationship to the rest of the persuasibility test was not apparent, however, in the second communication on cancer research. The explanation of this may be that the diametrically opposite position of the second communication made the subjects aware for the first time that the issues pertaining to research on a cure for cancer are genuinely in the realm of controversy. In the second booklet, then, this topic may have lost the distinguishing qualities of a scientific communication, and the determinants of individual differences in reaction to this communication may then have become similar to those for other controversial topics. In any case, the reliability and the internal consistency of the persuasibility test would be improved if this topic were eliminated.

Relationship of the Persuasibility Test to Self-Ratings

The correlations between self-ratings on susceptibility to influence and the behavioral measures obtained from our persuasibility test give some pertinent information concerning the equivalence or nonequivalence of the two measures. A significant correlation was found between persuasibility test scores and self-ratings on influence by mass communications for the male sample. This finding gives some weight to the assumption that both measures are tapping a common persuasibility tendency. Nevertheless, we cannot overlook the fact that in Table 5 there is only one significant correlation —and it is not a very large one—while the other three are too small to approach statistical significance. It is apparent that the persuasibility test is measuring something quite different from what is measured by the self-ratings on susceptibility to influence.[3] The findings in Table 5 suggest that it will not be an easy task to devise a simple, self-rating test to replace the more cumbersome and time-consuming procedure of exposing each subject to a series of persuasive communications.

If we were to assume that the self-rating scores concerning the influence of friends have some degree of face validity, it

3. Perhaps the main reason for the low correlations is that the self-rating scores have low reliability. It should be noted, however, that the self-rating score on influence by mass communications, based on only three items, yielded the one significant correlation, whereas an approximately zero relationship was found for the self-rating score concerning the influence of friends, which was a more reliable measure, based on eight items.

would follow that persuasibility, as measured by our behavioral test, is not equivalent to general amenability to social influence. This possibility raises the complex problem of the generality vs. specificity of various forms of suggestion and social influence (see Allport, 1954). It remains for further research to determine whether susceptibility to influence by formal communications of the type presented in our test is predictive of responsiveness to any of the various forms of social pressure or suggestion in direct interpersonal interaction.

Generality of the Findings

The generality of our present findings is limited by the fact that the experimental communications were delivered to high school students in a classroom setting. From the outset, we were aware of the possibility that their opinion changes might sometimes represent merely a superficial conformity with a point of view attributed to the school authorities or to a prestigeful experimenter. We attempted to minimize this possibility by emphasizing the fact that none of the teachers would see the subjects' answers and by including an explicit statement by the experimenter to the effect that he personally was inclined to agree with some of the communications and not with others. In order to obtain a mental set comparable to that in everyday experience with persuasive communications, the subjects were instructed to read the articles as they would articles in a magazine or newspaper. Nevertheless, in spite of all these precautions, generalization beyond the classroom setting may not be justified. It is conceivable that opinion changes in response to the persuasive communications received at home via television, radio, and other media do not correspond closely to the opinion changes measured by a persuasibility test administered in a classroom setting. Obviously, replications with samples of other populations are needed before we can determine whether or not the persuasibility findings that emerged from out study of high school students hold true for the entire population of modern urban society.

CHAPTER 3

Sex Differences and Personality Factors Related to Persuasibility

IRVING L. JANIS AND PETER B. FIELD

In the preceding chapter, we described a test of persuasibility affording a behavioral measure of susceptibility to influence by persuasive communications. Evidence was presented concerning test reliability and the consistency of individual differences among a large group of adolescent subjects. The study reported in the present chapter is focused on potential *sources* of individual differences in persuasibility.

Hypotheses

Previous research by Janis (1954) on the relationship between personality factors and susceptibility to persuasion has shown that among male college students high persuasibility is positively correlated with personal adjustment factors indicative of low self-esteem (such as feelings of social inadequacy, inhibition of aggression, and depressive affect). Low persuasibility was found to be positively correlated with factors indicative of neurotic defensiveness (such as neurotic anxiety and obsessional symptoms). Subsequent evidence (Janis, 1955) failed to confirm at a statistically significant level the inverse relation between persuasibility and neurotic defensiveness. This second study did, however, provide some substantial support for the positive relationship between persuasibility and low self-esteem. Self-ratings on fear of social disapproval and fear of failure in test situations were found to be positively related to persuasibility.

A search through the social-psychological literature revealed that a number of additional studies had reported findings on personality correlates of various aspects of conformity behavior that may be related to general persuasibility. In these studies, personality correlates similar to low self-esteem were noted (see Hochbaum, 1954; Asch, 1948; Berkowitz and Lundy, 1957; Crutchfield, 1955; Maslow, 1939).

One purpose of the present study was to investigate further the *low self-esteem* and *neurotic defensiveness* hypotheses. It was also designed to explore two additional hypotheses, which were suggested by clinical, impressionistic observations and by indirect correlational data (Hovland, Janis, and Kelley, 1953, pp. 192–212): (1) Persons capable of reacting with *rich fantasy responses*—e.g. vivid imagery and intense emotional empathy—tend to be relatively more persuasible than others. (2) *Hostile* personalities—characterized by hyperaggressive behavior, argumentativeness, and suspiciousness—tend to be relatively less persuasible than others. Differences in general intellectual ability, as measured by a group intelligence test, were also investigated. Finally, a sex comparison was made to test further the hypothesis (derived from earlier studies of suggestibility) that females in our society tend to be more persuasible than males (Terman, Johnson, Kuznets, and McNemar, 1946).

Methods and Procedures

As a behavioral measure of susceptibility to persuasion, the previously described test was administered to 185 subjects, almost all of whom were high school juniors. (For details of the procedure see above, pp. 31–40.) In addition, a person-ality-inventory questionnaire was given which contained a series of self-rating items designed to assess the subject's level of anxiety, self-esteem, hostility, richness of fantasy, and re-lated variables pertinent to the hypotheses stated above. The personality inventory was isolated as much as possible from the persuasibility test. It had a different format, was given three weeks after the latter, and was administered by high school teachers rather than by the research personnel. The students were told that their school was participating in a state-wide survey of students' health and adjustment; they were assured that neither the teacher nor anyone else at the school would be permitted to see their answers. The "Health and Adjustment" questionnaire contained numerous filler questions on personal hygiene habits along with the key items on personality factors. Most of the latter questions were adapted from other personality inventories and a few were specifically constructed to test the hypotheses under investigation.

Altogether there were 88 items in the personality question-naire and, on the basis of the authors' a priori judgments of their manifest content, they were sorted into nine clusters. (For the items included in each, see Appendix A.) The split-half reliability estimates [1] for the nine clusters are shown in Table 6.

The school records for each subject were made available to the experimenters and provided data on age, IQ, and other

1. Because each scale has relatively few items, two separate estimates of reliability were obtained for each cluster by splitting the halves in different ways. The two correlation coefficients for each cluster were transformed to Fisher z's and combined to form a single estimate of reliability. In the case of two clusters (suspiciousness and obsessive-compulsive symptoms) there were so few items that all possible ways of splitting the halves were used; the total possible intercorrelations were obtained, transformed into Fisher z's, and then averaged to obtain single estimates of the split-half reliability.

TABLE 6. *Split-Half Reliabilities for Nine Clusters of Self-Ratings from the Personality Questionnaire*

	No. of items in cluster	Split-half reliability estimate	Reliability estimate based on Spearman-Brown formula
1. Feelings of social inadequacy	23	.83	.91
2. Social inhibitions	11	.48	.65
3. Test anxiety	8	.83	.91
4. Richness of fantasy	11	.64	.78
5. Argumentativeness	6	.50	.67
6. Hyperaggressiveness	10	.70	.82
7. Suspiciousness	4	.63	.77
8. Obsessive-compulsive symptoms	5	.55	.71
9. Neurotic anxiety symptoms	10	.64	.78

background factors for the 86 males and 96 females who completed the entire battery of tests in the study.

Results and Discussion

Sex differences. The persuasibility test data were first analyzed to determine if there were any consistent sex differences.[2] The mean score for males was significantly lower than that for female subjects (Table 7). The fact that the boys were less persuasible on the average than the girls prob-

2. The data were also initially analyzed for classroom differences, inasmuch as the test had been administered in eleven classrooms within the same high school. No sizable or consistent differences were found with respect to the persuasibility test scores or the self-rating personality scores. Consequently, we concluded that there was no need to use a classroom-by-classroom breakdown in the analysis of relationships between persuasibility and personality variables.

ably should be interpreted in the light of sociological evidence on differentiated sex roles in our society, particularly with respect to intellectual independence and docility in many activities of everyday life (see Diggory, 1953; and Parsons, 1953). Our results on sex differences in persuasibility indicate that it is necessary to consider separately the male and female subsamples when studying the correlations between personality factors and persuasibility.

TABLE 7. *Differences between Males and Females in Persuasibility Scores*

	Males (N = 86)	Females (N = 96)
Mean	10.7	12.2
S.D.	4.5	3.8
t test	2.40	
p value	.02	

Intelligence and other background factors. Scores on the persuasibility test were investigated in relation to scores on the Otis Mental Ability Test. The Beta form of the Otis IQ test had been administered to the vast majority of students in our sample as part of a routine testing program two years prior to the present study, and the Gamma form had been administered to the remaining small percentage of students at irregular later dates. The correlation results were as follows: $r = .11$ for males (N = 82) and $r = .10$ for females (N = 86). Neither correlation is significantly different from zero (p > .25 for r = .11). This outcome agrees with previous empirical findings by Hovland, Lumsdaine, and Sheffield (1949), who reported an absence of any over-all relationship between intelligence and susceptibility to influence by propaganda and orientation films among army personnel. Their explanation was that two opposing abilities are correlated with intelligence: (1) the ability to comprehend arguments and to draw valid inferences from a communication, which inclines the person to be influenced and (2) superior critical ability, which inclines the person to be unimpressed by many persuasive appeals. The two abilities would often tend to operate in opposite directions and would therefore mask any consistent positive or negative relationship between intelligence and susceptibility to persuasion.

Since there is no significant relationship between intelligence scores and persuasibility scores, the personality correlates described in the sections which follow cannot be accounted for simply by mutual correlations with intelligence. A further implication of the negligible relationship between intelligence and persuasibility is that we succeeded in constructing communications that were not accepted or rejected by our high school subjects on purely intellectual grounds.

Hypothesis 1—Feelings of social inferiority. Inferiority feelings were measured in three ways in the personality questionnaire. One measure consisted of the total score on *feelings of inadequacy* from 23 items which asked the subjects to give self-ratings on anxiety in social situations, self-consciousness, and feelings of personal worthlessness. (For the exact wording of the questions see Appendix A, pp. 300–1.) A second set of items dealt explicitly with *social inhibitions*. This cluster included 11 self-rating items concerning social avoidance behavior and the preference for being alone (pp. 301–2).[3] There were also 8 questions on *test anxiety*

3. Originally we felt somewhat uncertain as to whether the social inhibitions cluster was related to inferiority feelings because of the possibility that this cluster might measure a different variable, such as asocial (or "schizoid") withdrawal tendencies. But we found that the correlation between scores on social inhibitions and scores on personal inadequacy was .45 for both males and females, which is significant at beyond the .01 level. Moreover, scores on social inhibitions had only very low, nonsignificant correlations with scores on argumentativeness and hyperaggressiveness. Therefore we were led to regard it as a supplementary measure of inferiority feelings.

(adapted from the scale developed by Sarason and Mandler, 1952), which were assumed to give additional indications of the subject's lack of self-confidence (see p. 302). Excessive anxiety about performance on examinations suggests a low evaluation of one's own intellectual capabilities or a high expectation of failure in competition with one's peers. If our assumption is correct, there should be a significant positive correlation between test anxiety and feelings of social inferiority. For the male sample, feelings of inadequacy and for the male sample (p < .01) and .51 for the female sample (p < .01).

Every question in the three clusters had a check list of five possible answers, to each of which was assigned a score ranging from 0 (no feelings of inferiority) to 4 (very high feelings of inferiority). The subject's total score for each cluster was obtained by adding together the score values for his answers to all the questions in the cluster.

Table 8 shows the correlation between total persuasibility score and each of the three scores bearing on feelings of inferiority. For the male samples, feelings of inadequacy and

TABLE 8. *Pearsonian Correlations between Persuasibility and Nine Self-Rating Personality Clusters*

	Males (N = 86)	Females (N = 96)
1. Feelings of social inadequacy	.27 (p < .01)	.03 (p > .25)
2. Social inhibitions	.18 (p = .05)	—.09 (p > .25)
3. Test anxiety	.11 (p > .20)	.03 (p > .25)
4. Richness of fantasy	.21 (p = .03)	.01 (p > .25)
5. Argumentativeness	.19 (p = .05)	.02 (p > .25)
6. Hyperaggressiveness	.16 (p = .08)	—.08 (p > .25)
7. Suspiciousness	.10 (p > .25)	—.07 (p > .25)
8. Obsessive-compulsive symptoms	.08 (p > .25)	.01 (p > .25)
9. Neurotic anxiety symptoms	.04 (p > .25)	—.04 (p > .25)

Note: p values are for one tail.

social inhibitions are positively related to persuasibility at beyond the .05 confidence level. The test-anxiety cluster yields a correlation in the expected direction, but it is not significant. These findings are similar to Janis's findings (1954, 1955) from studies of male college students. Thus, for the male sample, the present data constitute a replication of the previous findings and provide some additional support for the self-esteem hypothesis. However, the correlations are not of high magnitude, and hence only a small proportion of the variance in persuasibility scores is accounted for by the self-esteem factor, as measured by the self-ratings.

For the female sample, the self-esteem hypothesis is not supported: the correlation between persuasibility and the three clusters bearing on inferiority feelings was found to be close to zero. (See pp. 65–8 below for a discussion of this and other differences noted in the correlations from the male and female samples.)

Hypothesis 2—Richness of fantasy. The theoretical derivation of the fantasy hypothesis stems directly from an analysis of persuasibility by Hovland, Janis, and Kelley (1953). They postulate that a major mediating mechanism in opinion change is the anticipation of rewards and punishments offered implicitly or explicitly by the communicator for acceptance of his conclusions. These authors state (pp. 203–4) that any individual who has "difficulty in anticipating accurately the rewarding or punishing situations depicted in persuasive communications" will tend to be relatively unpersuasible.

It was felt that useful indicators of a person's capacity for fantasying anticipated rewards and punishments might be provided by self-ratings dealing with imagery and empathic responses to symbolic representations. Thus, as a crude measure of richness of fantasy, a series of 11 questions was devised to determine the subject's evaluation of the vividness of his daydreams, his ability to imagine future events, and the intensity of his emotional response to fictional accounts of dramatic events (see p. 303).

The total scores for richness of fantasy based on the self-ratings were correlated with the persuasibility test scores. Table 8 shows a significant correlation for males ($r = +.21$, $N = 86$) but an approximately zero correlation for females ($r = .01$, $N = 96$). The fantasy hypothesis, then, is but partially supported; it is borne out by the data for the males only, and the size of the correlation is small though statistically significant.

Hypothesis 3—Interpersonal aggressiveness. Three measures of aggressiveness were employed, based on self-ratings from the personality questionnaire: (1) hyperaggressiveness, (2) argumentativeness, and (3) suspiciousness (pp. 303–5). In Table 8, the fifth, sixth, and seventh rows show the correlations between persuasibility scores and each of the three measures of aggressiveness. The hypothesis that there is an inverse relationship between persuasibility and interpersonal aggressiveness is not supported by any of the correlations.[4]

4. We used an additional measure of interpersonal aggressiveness, a "Judgment of Motives" test which was developed by the authors for the specific purpose of assessing suspiciousness and related personality tendencies. In this test, the subjects are asked to read a series of paragraphs about ambiguous social situations, each of which is described in detail. The subject is told to imagine himself as actually experiencing the events and then to write down whatever he thinks would be the most likely explanation of the motives of the other person involved.

The test stimuli consist of eight paragraphs describing the following situations: (1) A friend unexpectedly gives you a valuable gift. (2) After engaging you in conversation a cashier shortchanges you. (3) You wake up in a hospital remembering only that everything went black at a time when you were resting in a city park. (4) Your new supervisor fails to answer your questions about how to do your work. (5) A doctor prescribes a new, expensive treatment for a minor ailment. (6) A pawnbroker asks to talk privately with you. (7) You experience violent cramps after eating dinner at the house of someone with

Two of the male correlations (hyperaggressiveness and argumentativeness) indicate a trend in the direction opposite to that predicted. These findings suggest a slight tendency for the more persuasible male subjects to believe that they have such unfavorable personal characteristics as excessive argumentativeness and aggressiveness. Perhaps those persons who report themselves as feeling inferior are in general somewhat self-derogatory; they not only admit having feelings of personal inadequacy but criticize themselves for being too aggressive as well. This assumption is partially supported by the positive intercorrelations among the self-rating clusters. For instance, we found—again unexpectedly—that there was a significant positive correlation between scores on inadequacy feelings and scores on argumentativeness: Pearsonian $r = .39$ for the males and .20 for the females. Self-ratings on inadequacy feelings were also positively correlated with self-ratings on hyperaggressiveness: Pearsonian $r = .31$ for males and .41 for females. All four p values are below .05.

Hypothesis 4—Neurotic defensiveness. Two measures of acute neurotic symptoms were employed: (1) self-ratings on obsessive and compulsive symptoms and (2) self-ratings on symptoms of severe neurotic anxiety such as insomnia, nightmares, intense feelings of apprehensiveness, and frequent bodily manifestations of an excessive autonomic excitation

---

whom you had a quarrel many years ago. (8) Someone telephones you, introduces himself as a representative of a television research agency, and asks on what nights you are regularly at home.

The responses were scored according to the degree of suspiciousness and the degree to which the subject perceived or failed to perceive cues indicating possible manipulative or hostile intent. The Pearsonian correlation coefficients between scores on this new new test and scores on the persuasibility test were close to zero: —.04 for the male sample and —.07 for the female sample (p values > .25). Thus, the quasi-projective test, like the self-rating inventory, failed to support the hypothesis that hyperaggressive, suspicious persons are more resistant to persuasive communications than others.

(p. 305). Table 8 shows very low correlations between persuasibility scores and the scores from these two clusters. The results do not support the hypothesis that acute symptoms are correlated with low persuasibility; neither measure indicates any definite trend. It should be noted that Janis's second study (1955), in which the neurotic-defensiveness hypothesis was examined, did not confirm his earlier findings that had given some initial support to this hypothesis. The negative evidence from the present study reduces further the validity of the neurotic-defensiveness hypothesis.

Magnitude of the correlations. When all the data in the foregoing sections are examined, it becomes apparent that the magnitude of the correlations between the persuasibility scores and the personality questionnaire scores is consistently low. The hypotheses tested are either unconfirmed or confirmed only partially, and, although some correlations are statistically significant, the largest is only .27. The weakness of the correlations cannot be explained simply by the low reliability of the instruments, because the split-half reliabilities of the persuasibility test and of the personality subscales are sufficiently high to yield substantial intercorrelations. This important aspect of the findings is discussed in detail in Chapter 11, in a review of all the studies reported in this volume. There the editors discuss factors which may obscure genuine personality-persuasibility relationships, such as the low validity of the self-descriptive personality ratings.

Differences between male and female subsamples. One of the most striking features of the data is that the significant correlations come from the male sample whereas no significant relationships are obtained from the female sample. In two instances, involving fantasy and social inhibitions, there are differences between the male and female correlations which approach significance at the .06 and .08 levels, respectively (based on Fisher's z test, with two-tail p values). The other relationships show nonsignificant differences in the same direction. The general pattern of the male vs. female differences suggests that persuasibility may prove to be more predictable as a function of personality factors for adolescent males than for adolescent females.

It is also noteworthy that the results in Chapter 2 showed a marked sex difference with respect to the relationship between persuasibility test scores and the self-ratings on susceptibility to influence by mass communications, derived from the personality inventory. This relationship was significant for the male sample but approximated zero in the female sample (see Table 5).

Our present results suggest that sex is a significant factor in persuasibility and that different generalizations concerning personality correlates of persuasibility may be required for males and females. (See the summary of findings from other studies on pp. 238–40.) Further data are needed to determine whether the pattern of sex differences observed for the high school students holds for other sectors of the population, especially among other age groups and educational levels. In this connection it should be pointed out that the sex differences we have observed are similar to those reported by Witkin and his collaborators (1954) on the basis of their investigations of perceptual and cognitive phenomena. These studies obtained perceptual judgments of the spatial environment from men and women at a time when they were exposed to misleading visual cues. Witkin et al. found that the female subjects were more readily influenced by the misleading cues than were the male subjects and thus were higher in "perceptual-field dependence." Moreover, women were found to be less self-consistent than men, i.e. the correlations among judgments in various perceptual-field tasks tended to be lower for the female sample than for the male sample.

That Witkin's tests of perceptual-field dependence may be tapping some of the same predispositional factors that enter into persuasibility is suggested by two additional findings: (1) low self-confidence and other indicators of low self-esteem are positively related to high perceptual-field dependence (Witkin et al., 1954) and (2) scores on Witkin's perceptual-field tests are positively correlated with persuasibility, as measured by amount of opinion change following exposure to two different persuasive communications (Linton and Graham in Chapter 4). (See the discussion of these interrelationships below, pp. 77ff., 93ff.)

If studies of the relationship between persuasibility and personality factors continue to show marked differences between males and females, it may be useful to assume that there are at least two broad classes of predispositional variables affecting an individual's persuasibility. One class involves personality factors, while the other concerns cultural sex-typing influences which produce more or less stereotyped differences between male and female role behavior in our society. We have already referred to this cultural difference in discussing the fact that on the average the females in our sample were significantly more persuasible than were the males. To this might be added the further assumption that cultural determinants of persuasibility tend to be relatively stronger in females than in males.

Perhaps in future investigations some indications concerning the influence of socially prescribed sex roles may be obtained by comparing those females who adhere most closely to the role prescriptions with those who tend to be relatively deviant. If "tomboys" and "masculine" women show essentially the same pattern of correlations between persuasibility and personality factors as we have found in our male sample, our tentative assumption concerning the cultural sources of sex differences in persuasibility could be regarded as something more than merely a speculative *ad hoc* explanation. In any case, replications of the present findings are obviously needed before the generality of the observed relationships can adequately be specified.

CHAPTER 4

Personality Correlates of Persuasibility

HARRIET LINTON AND ELAINE GRAHAM

THE STUDY REPORTED here attempts to identify variables related to change of opinion in response to persuasive communications and to describe a fundamental pattern of personality characteristics that seem to predispose a person to accept or resist persuasion, influence, suggestion, and conformity in many kinds of situations. To this end a wide range of measures was used to tap various levels of personality organization, such as perceptual behavior, attitudes toward the self and the world, response to personality test material, and response to different kinds of social influence.

PROCEDURE

Subjects. The subjects were 52 male students in their first semester at Brooklyn College. All were volunteers and none had taken any courses in psychology. The socioeconomic status of their families, as judged by their parents' occupations, covered a wide range; the parents of about half were skilled workers, and only a fifth of the subjects came from families of the professional class. In the majority of cases at

This study was done while the first author was a Public Health Research Fellow of the National Institute of Mental Health.

least one parent was foreign-born—in most cases from eastern Europe. Approximately 85 per cent were Jewish.

Measures. The entire array of measures used in the study is briefly presented here. Each will be discussed below in more detail, and more complete descriptions are available elsewhere (Graham, 1955; Linton, 1952, 1955).

An opinion-change test, in which changes induced by authoritative-sounding communications were recorded, was used as the measure of persuasibility. The test is similar to that described in Chapter 2, but included fewer communications.

A test of response in an autokinetic situation was the only other direct measure of social influence. It differs from the opinion-change test in that the source of influence was a peer who was present in the situation.

The tilting-room–tilting-chair test (Witkin et al., 1954) was used to study dependence on the external field in perceptual behavior. It measures the extent to which a person relies on the external field as against his bodily sensations in determining orientation in space.

The Witkin version of the embedded-figures test (1950) was also employed to evaluate perceptual-field dependence. This test is adapted from Gottschaldt and is primarily a problem-solving task.

An inner-directed vs. other-directed (ID-OD) questionnaire was designed to evaluate the relative importance for a person of personal goals and standards as opposed to conformity and adaptation to the group.

Items from the authoritarian personality questionnaire (Adorno et al., 1950) were used to measure attitudes toward authority and associated personality trends.

A personality questionnaire was used to investigate the subject's consciously held and publicly stated picture of himself.

A human-figure-drawing test (developed by Karen Machover, 1949) was used to study the self-image by means of projective procedures.

The Rorschach test was used to investigate personality patterns.

The Opinion-Change Test

Persuasibility by written communications was measured by the opinion-change test. The following three questions (originally employed by Hovland and Weiss, 1951–1952) were included in a questionnaire administered during one of the early experimental sessions:

1. Do you think that the number of movie theaters will increase, decrease, or remain the same by 1955? [The testing was done in the fall of 1951.]

2. Do you believe that a practicable atomic-powered submarine can be built at the present time?

3. Do you believe that cold-preventive drugs, like antihistamines, should continue to be sold without a doctor's prescription for them?

Opinions were rated as to the degree of certainty on a four-point scale: Very certain, Certain, Uncertain, Very uncertain. The issues were intended to be ones on which most subjects would have opinions, but not opinions of central importance.

At a later session (from one day to one week later) the subjects were asked to read articles on the same three topics, and were told:

> These are excerpts from recent magazine articles. I'd like you to read them carefully, the way you would read an article in a magazine. Sign your name at the end of each one to indicate you have read it. When you are through, you'll be asked some questions about your re-

actions to the articles. You'll be able to keep the articles
to refer to, if you wish, so don't try to memorize them,
just read them to get the meaning.

The articles were designed to sound impartial, while con-
cluding by taking a definite stand on the issue. The article
on movie theaters was attributed to *Fortune* magazine, that
on atomic-powered submarines to Dr. J. Robert Oppen-
heimer, and the article on antihistamines to a *New England
Journal of Biology and Medicine*.

Immediately after reading the articles, the subjects were
given a questionnaire which began: "Before you give us
your opinions of the articles themselves, we'd like to know
your *own* opinions on these topics." The three questions
asked previously were then repeated; they were followed by
five questions about the subject's interest in the topics and
his opinion of the articles.

Scoring. In evaluating the degree of opinion change for
each issue, it was necessary to take the subject's initial position into account, since this limited the amount that he
could shift in the direction favored by the article. Since certainty of opinion was rated on a four-point scale, the total
range of opinion possible (from "No, very certain" to "Yes,
very certain") covered an eight-point scale. If, for example,
the article favored a "No" position, and the subject's initial
position was "Yes, very certain," seven units of change (to
"No, very certain") was possible; if his initial position was
"No, very uncertain," only three units of change in the direction favored by the article was possible. For each issue,
therefore, the influence of the article was measured by a
fraction whose numerator was the number of scale positions
the subject changed in the direction favored by the article
and whose denominator was the number of units of change
possible in that direction; if the subject's opinion changed in
the opposite direction a minus sign was used.

The response to the article on movie theaters was inconsistent with a priori requirements and with the response to the other two articles.[1] Accordingly it was eliminated, and responses from the other two articles (atomic submarines and antihistamines) were combined to obtain a total opinion-change score. This score is expressed as a percentage based upon the number of scale positions changed (summed for the two issues) divided by the number of units of change in the advocated direction possible (also summed for the two issues). Subjects for whom the denominator was less than four were omitted: 47 of the 52 subjects in the original sample were retained. The scores ranged from +100% to —100%, with a mean of 25.15% and a sigma of 39.30%. Ten subjects had negative change scores.

Preliminary analysis of the data showed that many of the relationships were not linear; while subjects with high positive change scores generally differed from subjects with low positive or zero change scores in the expected directions, those with negative change scores did not follow many of the predictions for nonchangers and seemed to be a special group. It seemed appropriate, therefore, to divide the sample into three groups:

Changers: 18 subjects with high positive change scores (36% to 100%).

---

1. The sources for the three communications were intended to be of high credibility. They were so regarded in the case of the atomic submarine and antihistamine, but in the case of the movie theaters the *Fortune* source was regarded as trustworthy by only 64 per cent of the subjects who were classified as highly predisposed to change. (By contrast, 83 per cent of the low-predisposition subjects considered it trustworthy.) The difference between evaluations by our Brooklyn students and those of the Yale students used by Hovland and Weiss (1951–1952) concerning this source is sociologically interesting. A second consideration for eliminating this issue was that there was a significant interaction between predispositional factors and evaluation of the source. Subjects whose personality and behavior pattern would lead to a prediction of high persuasibility were more likely to have a low opinion of the source. Thus cancellation of relationship could be brought about by two opposed effects.

Nonchangers: 21 subjects with low change scores ranging from $+33\%$ to -8%.[2]

Negative changers: 8 subjects with negative change scores $(-9\%$ to $-100\%)$.

Predictions

Predictions about differences between opinion changers and nonchangers are based on the broad hypothesis that a person's response to persuasive communications is but one reflection of a more general tendency to accept or reject influence. It was therefore predicted that, compared with nonchangers, changers would: (1) be more influenced in the autokinetic situation and show the other reactions typical of subjects who are influenced; (2) be more field-dependent in the perceptual tasks; (3) tend to be "other-directed"; (4) give more authoritarian responses to the authoritarian questionnaire; and (5) receive more of the signs in the human-figure-drawing and Rorschach tests found in the study by Witkin et al. (1954) to be associated with perceptual-field dependence.[3]

In testing the above predictions, p values were based on one tail of the probability distribution.[4] No predictions were made for the personality questionnaire, and two-tail tests were therefore used. Where the groups are compared on individual signs or items, chi-square is used. Where they are compared on scaled measures, t tests are used.

2. Two of these subjects have negative scores. One of them follows the special pattern found in the negative changers and the other does not. The decision to place them with the nonchangers was motivated by a desire to keep the negative-change group as pure as possible and rationalized on the grounds that such a small negative change would be likely to occur as a chance fluctuation around a true zero score.

3. The one exception to this is the *Hd* Rorschach sign; the opposite prediction was made because of the relationship previously found by Linton (1954a) between this sign and the autokinetic test.

4. Where chi-square is used, a one-tail test is made by dividing the tabled p values in half.

The predictions that were made for negative changers derived from the assumption that change of opinion in a direction opposite to the view supported by the communications represents an active (though not necessarily conscious) resistance to authority. The authors felt, furthermore, that such a negativistic reaction to influence reflected a fear of being controlled and a suspiciousness of the motives of others that might be rationalized by the use of projection. These notions led to the predictions that negative changers would: (1) not be influenced in the autokinetic situation, making their own judgments and actively resisting the confederate; (2) express little authoritarian submission but much cynicism and projectivity in the authoritarian questionnaire; (3) have strong, assertive human movement (i.e. lack *M-type* sign) in the Rorschach test, and project hostile facial expressions onto human figures. These predictions were tested by means of one-tail tests; all other differences between negative changers and other subjects were evaluated by two-tail tests.

RELATIONSHIPS BETWEEN OPINION CHANGE AND OTHER VARIABLES

Autokinetic Influence

The autokinetic situation was the only other test of social influence in the present study. The subject was asked to judge the apparent movement of a point of light in a dark room. The judgment is a difficult one and Sherif (1935, 1936) and others (e.g. Kelman, 1950) have found that it can be modified by the influence of other persons. A confederate [5] presented as a fellow student gave "judgments" of the distance the light moved that averaged 5 inches greater than those given by the subject in a preliminary series.

5. The authors wish to thank Arthur Shaw for his skillful performance in this role.

Subjects were categorized as influenced or not influenced by the confederate (see Linton, 1954b, for scoring technique). Since both tests measure social influence, it was predicted that opinion changers would be most likely to be influenced in this situation and that nonchangers and negative changers would resist influence. A comparison of opinion changers with nonchangers and negative changers shows that changers were significantly ($p < .02$) more likely to be influenced by the confederate. Fifty per cent of the changers were influenced, in contrast to 26 per cent of the nonchangers and none of the negative changers; the lack of influence found in the negative changers is significant at the .05 level (two-tail) when they are compared with the other two groups. Eight subjects in the sample actually decreased their autokinetic judgments after hearing the confederate; they were all nonchangers or negative changers in the opinion-change test (p of their difference from changers $< .01$).

After the test, subjects were interviewed about their reactions to the task and to the confederate, and three variables were scored from the interviews. Each variable was found to predispose a subject to accept or reject influence. (1) Measures of *coping* ability and activity (in the period before the confederate gave his response) were based on the subject's reports of active efforts to form some basis for judgment, his reports of being upset by the dark room, and the experimenter's observations of his handling of his body when being led into the room blindfolded. Poor coping ability was significantly (.05 level) more frequent among opinion changers. (2) Some subjects reported a *negativistic* reaction, that is, a conscious concern over the danger of being influenced and the exertion of deliberate efforts to resist influence, such as "not listening" or making up their minds before the confederate spoke. Both nonchangers and negative changers were significantly (.01 level) more likely than changers to make such efforts. (3) Some subjects were *responsive* to the confederate, that is, they reported that when they heard his "judgments" they felt that he must be right or was in some way better qualified to judge than they, and these subjects were more likely to be influenced by him. This tendency was found to be unrelated to opinion change in the written communication test.

Perceptual-Field Dependence

Influencibility in the perceptual sphere is measured by Witkin's tilting-room–tilting-chair test and his version of the Gottschaldt embedded-figures test (Witkin, 1950, and Witkin et al., 1954). In the tilting-room test the subject's chair is tilted and the room is also tilted. He is required to determine the upright in two ways: (1) by adjusting the room until it seems upright to him while his chair remains tilted (*series 1a,* body and room initially tilted to the same side; *series 1b,* body and room initially tilted to opposite sides) and (2) by adjusting his chair until he feels that his body is upright while the room remains tilted (*series 2a,* both on same side; *series 2b,* body and room on opposite sides). In the embedded-figures test he must find geometric figures hidden in more complex figures whose lines are distracting.

Both situations measure the extent to which performance is affected by the surrounding perceptual field. In the tilted room visual cues are pitted against the bodily cues that would lead to an accurate adjustment; in the embedded-figures test the complex figure interferes with the finding of a simple figure which must be retained in memory. High scores (large deviations from the true upright in the tilted room, long solution time in the embedded-figures test) reflect much influence by external events (the "field") and constitute what Witkin has termed "field dependence." "Field independence," measured by accurate and quick performance in these tests, involves the ability to deal differentially with different aspects of a complex configuration utilizing the features relevant to the task at hand and discounting the irrelevant.

It was predicted that opinion changers would tend to be field-dependent and nonchangers would tend to be field-independent. The changers and nonchangers do differ in the predicted direction on all parts of the tilting-room test and on the embedded-figures test. In the tilting-room test the difference is greatest on series 1a (.02 level) and almost as great for series 2a (.025 level); there is a moderate difference on series 2b (.05 level), and only a slight difference on series 1b (not significant). On the tilting-room index, composed equally of the four series, changers are more field-dependent than nonchangers at the .01 level. In the embedded-figures test, the changers take longer to find the figures, significant at the .01 level. When the two groups are compared on a Perceptual Index, composed of the tilting-room score and the embedded-figures score, the difference is significant at the .001 level.

The negative opinion-changers cannot be characterized as either dependent or independent of the field. On the Perceptual Index their scores cluster around the middle of the distribution; they are significantly (.02 level, two-tail test) more independent than the changers, and nonsignificantly more dependent than the nonchangers. When the experimental situations are analyzed separately, however, it appears that in the embedded-figures test they do as poorly as the changers (difference from nonchangers significant at .02 level), while they do almost as well as the nonchangers in the tilting-room test (difference from changers is significant at .02 level). A possible interpretation would be that the negative changers cannot discount the irrelevant aspects of the stimulus field directly (as the nonchangers can) and are disoriented, but they are able to overcome the field influence and achieve a correct solution. This may make them take longer to find the hidden figures (since time to reach a correct solution is the score, accuracy is not a variable), but may enable them to make rather accurate adjustments in the tilted room, where time is not scored.

In summary, the opinion changers are highly affected by the interfering aspects of the stimulus field and do not overcome interference successfully; the nonchangers show the least interference effect; the negative changers are affected by the interference but show an ability to overcome this influence.

Inner- vs. Other-Directed Values

The ID-OD questionnaire originally developed by Graham (1955) and based on the distinction between *inner-directed* and *other-directed* character, developed by David Riesman (1950), was among the related measures used in connection with the opinion-change investigation. The attempt to use sociocharacterological concepts for individual psychological measurement necessitated some rather far-reaching modification and redefinition of Riesman's terms. First of all, since the intention was to develop a questionnaire, Riesman's concepts were modified to refer to an attitude or value continuum, rather than to a characterological distinction based upon character mechanisms, patterns of behavior, or source of standards and values—all far more recalcitrant to measurement.

Second, in developing a scale for present-day adolescents, it was not possible to define "inner-direction" in the nineteenth-century Protestant terms which were appropriate for Riesman's sociohistorical theory. "Inner-direction," as it is here redefined for purposes of the questionnaire, is a value system which stresses personal goals and standards as against group conformity and adaptation. Thus, the inner-directed value pattern contains a large admixture of what Riesman would call "autonomy" rather than inner-direction.

The translation of Riesman's concepts into value terms made possible the development of a series of alternate-choice questions which present hypothetical dilemmas, to which the subject might choose an inner-directed or an other-directed solution. For example:

> Since the age of 13, Stewart—now a high school senior—has set his heart on becoming a great chemist. He daydreams about it frequently and reads all he can about famous chemists and chemistry. Recently, a close friend of his advised him to forget about his ambitions for the future and concentrate more on making a success of the present. He pointed out that if Stewart were more sociable and really gave some time and energy to it, he could easily be among the real leaders in his class—in extracurricular activities and general popularity.
>
> Do you think Stewart should follow his friend's advice?
> _____yes
> _____no

A long questionnaire, with 80 items of this type, was administered to 38 of the 47 subjects for whom attitude change scores and other experimental and personality measures were available. The ID-OD score is based upon the 28 items that correlate best with the total score for the 80 items. High scores refer to the "other-directed" end of the continuum. The range of scores shows an approximately normal distribution, and yields an odd-even reliability coefficient of .79.

A cluster analysis was made of the original 80 items in order to see whether they fell into separate groups which might represent different dimensions of inner- vs. other-directed attitudes. The analysis yielded four clusters which can be regarded as subscales. The fact that reliabilities for the subscales are higher than for the general questionnaire suggests that they are measuring more homogeneous attitude dimensions.

On the basis of the content of the items comprising each subscale, they appear to be dealing with the following attitude factors:

Subscale A. A hardheaded, practical orientation (ID) vs. a rather global, unrealistic interest in "warmth" and "sincerity" (OD).

Subscale B. Work-oriented values such as efficiency, control, competence, and meeting high personal standards (ID) vs. needs for friendship, popularity, intimacy, group adjustment and cooperation, and a responsiveness to social pressure on the basis of these needs (OD).

Subscale C. Concern with self, with inner drives and preferences which may be unconventional, with strivings toward creative achievement and personal recognition, and with independence from social restrictions (ID) vs. needs for security, social approval, participation in the community, and a responsiveness toward conformity pressures on the basis of these needs (OD).

Subscale D. Concern with ideas and principles, as against people, and an intellectualized approach to human problems (ID) vs. concern for people and for adjustment in concrete, short-run situations (OD).

On the basis of their value content, subscales B and C would appear closest in essence to Riesman's general distinction between inner- and other-direction, although they involve somewhat different aspects of these clusters. Thus the low end of subscale B appears more clearly inner-directed while that of subscale C seems to stress "autonomy." Subscales A and D, on the other hand, appear to deal with aspects of inner- as against other-direction which are less centrally concerned with self-determination as opposed to social conformity.

Scores on the general ID-OD questionnaire and on each of the subscales were compared for changers, nonchangers, and negative changers. It was predicted that the opinion-changers would tend to accept other-directed values, and that the nonchangers would tend towards inner-direction and autonomy; no prediction was made for negative changers. Changers proved to be significantly more other-directed than nonchangers on the total ID-OD scale (.02 level), on subscale C (.01 level), and on subscale D (.05 level). The two groups are not significantly different on subscales A and B, which, in contrast to subscales C and D, are less concerned with intellectuality and ideology, and may therefore be less relevant to persuasibility or resistance to reasoned argument.[6] Negative changers do not differ significantly from either the changers or the nonchangers.

The distribution of scores for changers and nonchangers shows that persuasibility vis-à-vis the authoritative-sounding communications in the opinion-change test does not in all cases accompany a conforming other-directed value pattern; it is rather that the acceptance of certain inner-directed values [7] appears incompatible with persuasibility in this particular kind of influence situation. The personal attitudes and values tapped by the questionnaire may be operating directly in the communication situation, making for resistance on the part of the inner-directed individual. It seems

6. Perhaps an even more important factor is that a kind of tough realism (or pseudo-realism) characterizes *inner-direction* on subscales A and B, particularly the former, and it was independently found in the present study that on the F scale it is the *changers* whose ideology includes an admiration for external power and strength.

7. This is not true of influence in the autokinetic situation, which shows a much lower, nonsignificant relationship to the ID-OD questionnaire.

more likely, however, that these value choices are closely related to underlying personality characteristics which also operate in certain situations where the external influence is actually present.

Personality Measures

AUTHORITARIAN-PERSONALITY QUESTIONNAIRE

The questionnaire of authoritarian attitudes consisted of 55 appropriate items selected from three of the scales presented in *The Authoritarian Personality* by Adorno, Frenkel-Brunswik, et al. (1950). Since 85 per cent of the students at Brooklyn College are Jewish, items expressing anti-Semitic attitudes were omitted because they could be expected to be both nondiscriminating and offensive to the subjects.

No significant differences were found between the opinion-change groups in their total scores on this test; that is, they do not differ in over-all authoritarian trends as measured by the questionnaire. Significant differences are found, however, when the items are grouped according to the dimensions along which they were originally organized.

Sixteen items of the fifty-five came from the Politico-Economic Conservatism (PEC) scale and the Ethnocentrism (E) scale, but no predictions were made for them and no significant differences between groups were found. Thirty-nine items from the F (Fascism) scale were grouped according to the variables that comprise the hypotheses on which the F scale is based (Adorno et al., 1950, pp. 224ff.). Many items exemplify more than one variable, but each was put into the category that seemed closest to its meaning. Results for the total test and for the various subtests are given in Table 9.

Authoritarian submission. It should be noted that all the items from this group used in the present study deal with the importance of uncritical love for parents and respect for parents and other authorities. It was predicted that opinion changers would have the highest scores, nonchangers intermediate scores, and negative changers the lowest scores. The changers and nonchangers have virtually identical means,

TABLE 9. *Comparison of Opinion-Change Groups on Authoritarian Questionnaire*

	MEAN SCORES		
Scale	Changers	Nonchangers	Negative changers
Over-all score	22.36	20.95	21.00
I. PEC items	1.67	1.81	1.88
II. E scale items	3.78	4.33	3.25
III. F scale items	16.92	14.81	15.88
1. Authoritarian submission	2.56	2.43	1.13 ‡
2. Authoritarian aggression	1.44	1.19	.81
3. Anti-intraception	3.61 ‡	2.43	3.13
4. Power, toughness	3.17 *	2.48	2.69
5. Cynicism	1.78	1.86	3.25 †
6. Projection	1.25	1.48	1.69

Note: Groups compared are specified in text.
  * $p < .05$, † $p < .02$, ‡ $p < .01$, based on t tests.

but the negative changers do have low scores, as predicted: they are significantly lower than the other two groups combined at the .01 level.

Authoritarian aggression. This subscale measures a tendency to condemn and punish people who violate conventional values, and consists of items prescribing harsh treatment for such deviates as conscientious objectors, homosexuals, sex criminals, and the feebleminded. The prediction was that opinion changers would score highest, but no prediction was made for the relative scores of nonchangers and negative changers. The changers do have the highest mean score; the negative changers have the lowest mean score, and the mean of the nonchangers is midway between the other two groups. The difference between the changers and negative changers is significant at the .10 level; there are no significant differences on any of the six individual items.

Anti-intraception. These items measure opposition to subjective, introspective, and intellectual values, and a preference for doing rather than thinking. The prediction was that opinion changers would show the most anti-intraception and nonchangers the least; no prediction was made for negative changers. The prediction is supported at the .01 level, and the mean for the negative changers is between the two other groups but significantly different from neither.

Power and toughness. These items reflect a preoccupation with and admiration for strength, and a tendency to categorize in terms of strong-weak and dominance-submission dimensions. The prediction that changers would have higher scores than nonchangers is supported at the .05 level. The negative changers, for whom no prediction was made, have a mean score between those of the other two groups, significantly different from neither.

Destructiveness and cynicism. The items used in this group express the view that human nature is rapacious and the world a place of inevitable conflict. While the "authoritarian aggression" items express a displacement of aggression onto deviates felt as moral indignation, these items express a view of "the way things are" that purports to be objective and is not moralized. Since a cynical view of other people's motives would be expected to produce opposition to their arguments, it was predicted that the negative changers would accept many of these items. The prediction is supported at the .02 level; opinion changers and nonchangers have virtually identical scores, while negative changers have higher scores.

Projectivity. Since projection in its most extreme form, paranoia, is clinically associated with some forms of resistance to social influence, it was tentatively predicted that negative changers would accept these items most often, nonchangers an intermediate amount, and changers the least. The means of the three groups are arranged in the predicted order, but only the difference between changers and negative changers is significant at the .10 level.

Other items. Three variables in the original F scale were eliminated since they overlapped other scores. These were: *Rigid adherence to conventional middle-class values, Superstition and stereotypy, and Exaggerated concern with sexual matters.*

Opinion change is, then, unrelated to total score on the authoritarian questionnaire, but it is clearly related to certain components of this score. It is, furthermore, related to all the subscales that represent variables considered by the authors of *The Authoritarian Personality* to reflect personality trends predisposing a person to be authoritarian or not; it is unrelated to the two scales (Politico-Economic Conservatism and Ethnocentrism) that reflect social attitudes directly. Each opinion-change group has a special pattern of scores on the subscales and each tends to score in the authoritarian direction on some subscales and in the nonauthoritarian direction on others, leading to the lack of difference in total test scores. For each group, however, the pattern is meaningful and seems consonant with that group's performance in the opinion-change test. It appears, then, that in a population of this sort knowledge of how authoritarian-oriented a person is does not help to predict his response to communications from sources such as the scientific authorities used in the opinion-change test, but that an understanding of the pattern of his relationship to authority does.

PERSONALITY QUESTIONNAIRE

Each subject was given a check-list personality inventory of 84 items intended to reveal those consciously held feelings about himself that he is willing to state publicly.

When the groups are compared on individual items, they are found to differ considerably more than would be expected by chance, and the pattern of differences appears rather consistent with the information provided by the other tests. Thirty-three items (or 39 per cent) show differences between groups that are significant at the .10 level, twelve of those at the .05 level or better. The opinion changers' responses describe them as feeling inadequate and unassertive, and give some evidence of the use of repression as a defense. The non-changers' responses suggest independence of thought combined with social maturity, feelings of adequacy, and a direct, nonobsessional approach to life. The negative changers report themselves at odds with society, express negative feelings about authority figures, indicate physical inferiority and phobic reactions, and tend to show considerable hostility and conflict.

HUMAN FIGURE DRAWING

Subjects were instructed: "Draw a person—the whole person, not just the face." When they completed their drawings —a male figure in most cases—they were told to draw a person of the opposite sex. The drawing of a human figure is presumed to tap the subject's self-image, particularly its unconscious components (Machover, 1949), more directly than any of the other techniques (in contrast to the personality questionnaire, which elicits only the conscious components of the self-image). It also reflects his conception of the opposite sex and, to some extent, his comparative conceptions of the two sexes.

The human-figure drawing test was scored for 38 dichotomous categories selected from the longer list developed by Karen Machover to investigate persanality correlates of field dependence in the study by Witkin and his collaborators (1954). The particular items in the present study were selected primarily for the ease with which they could be scored objectively from the published descriptions and also to eliminate duplications. Six subscales were then developed by grouping the items so that items within a scale would tend to intercorrelate highly and would correlate less strongly with items in the other scales. This was done before examining the relationships of the items to opinion change. The items are all oriented so that the score was associated with field dependence in Witkin's sample.

The prediction was that opinion changers would receive more signs than nonchangers; no prediction was made about negative changers. The mean number of signs for changers is 15.56, compared to 11.60 for nonchangers and 10.75 for negative changers. The difference between changers and each of the other two groups is significant at the .05 level. Sixteen items (42 per cent) taken individually yield group differences significant at the .10 level or better, twelve of these at the .05 level.

Scale A includes eight items that seem to reflect weakness, dependency, and disproportion, particularly of the male figure.[8] It was found that opinion changers had the largest number of these signs and negative changers the fewest, with nonchangers intermediate. The difference between changers and negative changers is at the .10 level. Nonchangers show some disproportion, but not weakness or dependency.

Scale B consists of six items that deal with the amount of elaboration of the torso, and subjects receiving the most signs draw the torso like an empty shell, indicated only by an outline. The items in this scale are all interpreted by Machover as reflecting aspects of bodily consciousness or

8. The interpretation of each scale is based primarily on the meaning of the individual items; in addition, for each scale, drawings of subjects high on that scale and not high on others were examined, and the outstanding impression from these drawings was incorporated into the interpretation of the scale.

concern (high score: lack of this). Changers have the largest number of signs and negative changers the fewest, with the difference between them significant at the .10 level; non-changers have intermediate scores.

Scale C is made up of six items dealing with sexual differentiation, sexual elaboration, and sensuous attributes. High scores indicate that a drawing is not only sexless, but has a wooden facial expression as well, and gives an impression of over-all lifelessness. Opinion changers receive the largest number of these signs and nonchangers the fewest, with the difference significant at the .05 level; negative changers have intermediate scores.

The remaining three scales were unrelated to opinion change. High scores on scale D indicate that the female figure is hostile and stronger than the male figure; scales E and F contain items that are considered to reflect different forms of anxiety. Of the seven items that were not included in any of the scales, three show significant differences between changers and the other two groups. These three items are all attributes of children's drawings and may therefore be assumed to be signs of immaturity; the changers show more of them than either nonchangers or negative changers.

In summary, the drawings of opinion changers tend to be disproportionate and weak, to lack elaboration of the body and sensuous or sexual features, to lack male-female differentiation, and to show other signs of immaturity. The nonchangers draw stronger figures, with some elaboration to the body and appropriate secondary sex characteristics and male-female differentiation, and in general their drawings are more mature. The negative changers draw strong, well-proportioned figures, with much elaboration suggestive of heightened bodily consciousness, with sensuous attributes and other signs of maturity, but somewhat lacking in sexual differentiation.

THE RORSCHACH TEST

The Rorschach test was taken by 41 subjects: 16 changers, 19 nonchangers, and 6 negative changers. The protocols were scored on 12 dichotomous signs previously found to relate to field dependence [9] as well as to several other variables that seemed relevant to opinion change.

Of the single signs, the *M-type* sign yielded the greatest difference between groups; it is given to subjects whose human movement responses reflect passivity or a low energy level. Higher scores are most frequent among the changers (.01 level). Both nonchangers and negative changers produce predominantly strong, assertive *M*. Evidence suggests that *M* content reflects attitudes toward the self (Hertzman and Pearce, 1947, and Klopfer et al., 1954). Hence, we may say that the changers express a weaker and more passive self-concept than the other groups.

More *Hd* (parts of human figures) is produced by both nonchangers and negative changers than by changers (.05 level, whether *Hd* is considered in relation to amount of *H* —whole human figures— or in relation to total number of responses). Various interpretations of *Hd* may be made (cf. Klopfer et al., 1954), depending on its context. A frequent interpretation, low self-esteem, seems untenable for the nonchangers and negative changers because of the strong self-image indicated by their lack of the *M-type* sign.[10] The nonchangers not only emphasize *Hd* but also produce more anatomical content than other subjects (.10 level). This pattern, in the context of an essentially strong self-concept, suggests

9. The dichotomous signs were based on those originally developed by Hertzman for the study of field dependence by Witkin et al. (1954); the criteria for several of the signs were modified for the present study, and four new signs were added (for modifications and additions, see Linton, 1954a).

10. The combination of much *Hd* and assertive *M* occurs in 44 per cent of nonchangers and negative changers, but is found in none of the changers (difference between changers and others at .01 level, two-tail test).

that nonchangers tend to be preoccupied with themselves and their bodies, and probably have an overly analytical and critical attitude toward themselves. The negative changers do not produce much anatomical detail, and other features of their protocols suggest that for them Hd is more likely to reflect a critical attitude toward others.[11]

The three groups show certain differences in form level, which is a measure of the accuracy of fit of the responses to the blots and the degree of organization of parts of the blot into meaningful larger concepts. Form level is considered to reflect contact with reality and intellectual performance (Klopfer et al., 1954, pp. 587f.). Although the differences are significant when the total test is considered, they are most significant for the cards with color or strong shading; the differences emerge most strongly, then, under emotional impact, and indicate the degree of control under such stimulation. The negative changers have the highest average form level (.10 level, two-tail test), are more likely to have some very superior responses (.02 level), and produce no vague or inaccurate responses. This suggests not only high ability, but strong controls consistently maintained. Nonchangers produce some very superior responses also, but under the impact of color or shading they produce some vague and inaccurate ones (.10 level); since their average form level is adequate this means that their performance is more variable in form quality than that of other subjects. Inspection of the responses of poor form level shows that, while some reflect poorly con-

11. In the sample studied by Witkin et al. (1954) a predominance of Hd was associated with field dependence. The reversal of that finding in the present sample may be due to the age difference between the two samples. His male subjects average 21 years of age, while the present sample was made up of freshmen averaging 17 years, who were therefore presumably more deeply enmeshed in the problems of adolescence. It is conceivable that Hd in the younger group represents, at least in part, an adolescent anxiety about the self and a tendency to self-examination, while in a somewhat older group it is more indicative of low self-esteem and a disintegrated self-image.

trolled disturbance, others indicate a capacity for free and playful fantasy. The form level of the changers is uniformly adequate but unimaginative, with few responses of either poor or very superior quality.

The variability in form level and occasional fantasy produced by the nonchangers is accompanied by a greater variety of content (.02 level, two-tail test) than that produced by other subjects. This suggests a more flexible approach and a wider range of ideas and interests.

The ratio between human movement responses and weighted sum of color (ΣC) responses ("experience type") is taken to indicate the balance between a person's inner resources and his responsiveness to the environment. Changers and nonchangers do not differ significantly; the negative changers, however, were most likely to have a markedly introversive experience balance (.02 level, two-tail test), i.e. many M signs in combination with a low ΣC. This suggests a well-developed inner life and a reduced involvement with the outer world; such a person "tends to restructure the world in terms of his own values and needs. He reads much of his own interpretation into reality" (Klopfer et al., 1954, p. 371). The tendency to project suggested by this finding (and also by the authoritarian questionnaire) is supported by the fact that all the negative changers attribute some facial expressions to the figures (vs. 46 per cent of the other subjects; the difference is significant at .02 level): the facial expressions seen by negative changers are generally hostile and sinister.

In summary, the protocols of opinion changers reflect a weak and passive self-image. They do not show the gross signs of disturbance found in the other groups, but appear to be generally passive and unimaginative.

The protocols of the nonchangers indicate that they have a self-image that is essentially strong, but are much given to self-examination. They cannot always control the impact of emotional stimuli. The wide range of content and form quality suggests, among other things, that these adolescents have a richer fantasy life than subjects in the other two groups and, perhaps, more creative potential.

The protocols of the negative changers indicate that they also have a strong self-image, but tend to be hypercritical and to project hostility onto others. They are introversive, guided to a great extent by their own values and needs, and tend to give comparatively little weight to environmental demands. They can, however, meet objective demands—their consistently high form level reflects high achievement, strong controls, and resistance to emotional pressures.

DISCUSSION

The relationships presented above between persuasibility and the other variables indicate that a person's response to a persuasive communication is not an isolated act but is rather part of a complex pattern of attitudes, ways of perceiving, and ways of dealing with the world and the self. Since the elements of this pattern have been presented piecemeal, it may be helpful at this point to summarize the information about each of the opinion-change groups. Table 10 summarizes the results of the various analyses presented above.

Opinion Changers

The person who is easily persuaded is likely to guide his behavior by external standards in other situations as well, to have values that favor conformity, to have an immature and weak concept of himself, to be unimaginative, and to have a limited range of interests. The projective tests (Rorschach and human figure drawing) reflect weakness, passivity, immaturity, and little awareness of sexuality. More overt signs of disturbance appear in the figure drawing, where subjects

TABLE 10. *Summary of Results for Changers, Nonchangers, and Negative Changers*

Test	Changers	Nonchangers	Negative changers
Autokinetic situation	Do not form own basis for judging	Form own basis for judging	Form own basis for judging
	Do not deliberately resist confederate's influence	May deliberately resist confederate's influence	May deliberately resist confederate's influence
	Are influenced by confederate	Little influenced	Not influenced
Perceptual measures	Field-dependent throughout	Resist influence of field throughout	Tilting room: accurate (independent)
	—	—	Embedded figures: long solution time (field-dependent)
Inner-other direction	Need for social approval, participation and security; succumb to peer-group conformity pressures	Concern with self-expression, creative strivings, personal achievement, freedom from social restrictions; resist peer-group pressures	No trend
	Ideological focus on people and adjustment in short-run situations	Ideological focus on ideas and principles	
Authoritarian questionnaire	High respect for parental authority	High respect for parental authority	Reject parental authority
	Harsh condemnation of social deviates	—	Nonpunitive toward social deviates
	Anti-intraceptive values	Intraceptive values	—
	Admiration for power	Little admiration for power	Moderately low admiration for power
	—	—	Cynical
	Little projection	—	Tend to project
Personality questionnaire	Feel inadequate and inferior	Feel adequate	Feel physically inadequate
	Little assertiveness	Wish for assertion and independence	Rebellious toward authority and convention
	—	—	Expressions of hostility

Test	Changers	Nonchangers	Negative changers
Human figure drawing	Weak, dependent male figure	Moderately strong male figure	Strong male figure
	Lack bodily consciousness	—	Much bodily consciousness and concern
	Lack sexual features and differentiation, lack sensuous elements	Have sexual features sensuous attributes	Lack sexual differentiation but have sensuous elements
	Childish-looking drawings	Quite mature-looking drawings and differentiation,	Quite mature-looking drawings
Rorschach	Weak, passive self-image	Strong, active, assertive self-image	Strong, active, assertive self-image
	Not critical of self or others	Much self-analysis, self-concern	Hypercritical
	Form quality adequate but unimaginative	Form quality variable, some very high, may become poor under emotional stimuli	Form quality consistently high, unaffected by emotional stimuli
	—	—	Markedly introversive
	Little facial expression	—	Project hostile facial expressions
	Limited content range	Content very varied, imaginative	—

must create their response with no external stimulus to guide them, than in the Rorschach, where they produce unimaginative responses which conform adequately to the blots.

Both personality and authoritarian questionnaires support the impression gained from the projective material that these individuals are not given to self-analysis, prefer to avoid thinking about their problems, and are likely to use repression as a characteristic defense. They apparently lack, therefore, strong sources of direction within themselves and they come to terms with life by valuing and relying on external sources of direction. The high value they place on support from authority is shown in the relevant subscales of the authoritarian questionnaire, and the value they place on peer-group support is indicated by the ID-OD questionnaire.

Their actual reliance on external supports is seen in all

the experimental situations where influence is exerted. In the tilting-room test they cannot use bodily cues effectively and are strongly influenced by visual stimuli. In the embedded-figures test they have difficulty because of the complexity of the figure. In the autokinetic situation they are disoriented, do little to form their own judgments, and readily accept the confederate's statements. It is not surprising, therefore, that in the opinion-change test they are easily influenced by articles attributed to sources they respect.

Nonchangers

The person who is comparatively unaffected by the persuasive communications is likely to be little affected by external standards in other kinds of situations, to have a mature and strong self-image, to value subjective feelings and have a relatively rich inner life, to examine himself and his role in life to an extent that may include marked self-criticism, and to be independent without being rebellious. As Table 10 shows, both projective tests reflect a highly differentiated concept of the self as strong and competent, and the figure drawings show more sexual awareness than is found in the other groups. Both tests show a somewhat variable control (especially when compared with negative changers), particularly in the more emotionally stimulating parts of the Rorschach.[12] The Rorschach protocols of the nonchangers are more imaginative than those of the other groups.

12. Since the personality picture presented by the nonchangers' protocols is, in general, healthier by clinical standards than that found in either of the other groups, some comment is in order about the signs of disturbance that are present. The areas in which they show more overt disturbance than one or both of the other groups are: some disproportion in the figure drawing, excessive Hd and anatomy, and the impairment of form-quality under the impact of color or shading in the Rorschach. In the context in which they occur, they suggest some disharmony in the self-concept, a somewhat obsessive self-examination, and an openness to emotional experience against which defenses are limited. In view of the fact that the subjects are 17 years old, these trends seem to the authors to indicate a process of emotional reorganization

In the personality questionnaire they demonstrate self-assurance, a desire for independence, and dislike of opposition combined with some evidence of tact in social relationships. The evidence of tact and their respect for parental authority (expressed in the authoritarian questionnaire) suggest that their wish for independence does not imply rejection of their backgrounds or hostility toward others.[13] In the authoritarian and ID-OD questionnaires they show that they value subjective feelings, ideas and intellectual activity, self-expression and creative achievements, and they say that they would try to live by these values in the face of opposing conformity pressures and social restrictions.

Their behavior in the experimental situation shows competence and independence of judgment. In the tilting-room test they discount visual stimuli and respond appropriately to bodily cues. In the embedded-figures test they perform analytically. In the autokinetic situation they are self-assured and form their own basis for making judgments; when the confederate's statements are introduced they do not lose confidence and their judgments are little affected.

Negative Changers

The pattern for the negative changers suggests that they are engaged in a struggle to win out over what they perceive as hostile, potentially engulfing forces. The authoritarian questionnaire, personality questionnaire, and certain features of the Rorschach test show that they perceive the world as a

---

and a search for self-definition that is appropriate in late adolescence. The other data available for nonchangers makes it seem likely that, of the three groups, they are the most likely to emerge as self-sufficient, well-integrated, and flexible adults.

13. In spite of the fact that changers and nonchangers express respect for parental authority to an equal degree, in their choice of an adult career changers tend to follow their parents' wishes while nonchangers do not. One probable reason for this difference is the fact that changers are less likely to have any clear preference of their own.

hostile, destructive place in which they are threatened by annihilation; they consider themselves at odds with society and strongly reject parental or other authority (but they do not necessarily reject the peer group, as shown by the ID-OD questionnaire).

The self-image that is reflected in the projective tests is strong, active, and assertive, although the figure drawing suggests much concern with the body. In the personality questionnaire they are likely to report that something is wrong with their bodies, and phobic tendencies are also evident. They maintain an image of themselves as strong people, apparently, by projecting feeling of inadequacy and other unacceptable impulses onto physical symptoms, feared objects, and forces of chaos and hostility which they then attribute to the world and other people. They also seem deficient in the warmer aspects of human relationships and emotions; this is indicated by the lack of response to color in the Rorschach and the asexuality of their figure drawings (an unusual feature in drawings that are otherwise mature and well-integrated).

In the experimental situations, there is evidence that they are affected by the sources of influence but actively try to cope with the tasks and fight against being influenced (rather than being relatively unaffected, as are the nonchangers). In the perceptual tests, the long time it takes them to find the embedded figures shows that the distracting elements of the complex figure affect them strongly, but their accurate adjustments in the tilted room demonstrate their ability to overcome external interference. In the autokinetic situation they are unaffected by the initial lack of external support and form their own basis for judging movement, but when the confederate's statements are introduced they show signs of temporary disorientation. They resist his influence, however, and none of them change their judgments to conform to his. In the opinion-change test the fact that they change their opinions strongly suggests that they are affected by the communications, but they react negatively. It is the quality of active resistance to an influence that affects them which differentiates them from the changers, who do not resist the influence, and from the nonchangers, who are relatively unaffected by it.

The present study supports the idea that there exists an underlying tendency in a person which affects his perception, his cognitive processes, his attitudes and values, and his social behavior. This tendency, which might be termed "self- vs. field-orientation," predisposes the person to rely either on sources of direction within himself or to be easily influenced by external factors. Furthermore, the strength or weakness of inner resources seems to be an important determinant of the direction of this tendency.

Other studies of the personality predispositions underlying field dependence (Witkin et al., 1954) and social conformity (Linton, 1954a, 1955) have pointed to the fact that susceptibility to influence in these situations is related to two main areas of personality functioning: the underlying attitudes toward the self and the quality of a person's reactions to the environment—his ability to cope with it and his responsiveness to its emotional and personal aspects.

In this study, it is the personality patterns having to do with attitudes toward the self which appear to be of primary importance; personality measures relating to reactivity or minimal adequacy vis-à-vis the environment do not differentiate between the opinion-change groups.[14] Unlike those who are susceptible to influence in the autokinetic situation, opinion

14. In one sense, the lack of correlations between coping and responsiveness on the one hand and opinion change on the other can be understood simply as an outcome of the fact that the opinion-change experience is a nonstress, impersonal situation which does not require active manipulation of the environment or include a direct interpersonal element; thus the simpler coping and responsiveness tendencies of an individual could be expected to play a relatively unimportant role.

changers do not appear to be emotionally more responsive, or less controlled in their emotional reactivity, than are those in the nonchange group. Neither are they less responsive, as the other-directed individual tends to be in comparison to the inner-directed. In terms of coping, the opinion changer can generally cope with the task at hand adequately if not imaginatively when prescribed pathways are available. In situations where there are no external guides (e.g. the auto-kinetic situation *before* the confederate, the human figure drawing), the coping of the opinion changer is relatively inadequate. In addition, he does not reach high levels of performance in situations which require creativity, originality, or analytic ability; this level of coping implies a degree of inner strength which is evidently unavailable to him.

The question arises, however, as to why the self-attitudes of the individual should prove to be of such central importance in relation to susceptibility to influence on issues which were chosen because of their lack of personal importance to the individual. It should be emphasized that the communications used in the present study are attributed to scientific authorities and deal with the practical applications of science. Since most of the subjects were pre-science students this material may have been particularly salient for them although still not of deep personal significance, and it is possible that different material might yield different results. On the basis of these results, however, it appears that for those who are characterized by self-awareness and independence, an opinion which they hold—no matter how unemotionally —is integrated with their egos in such a way as to lead to resistance to change. Those with weaker and more passive egos may also be said to treat these opinions as they do more important and personal feelings and thoughts; such thoughts and feelings are not invested with drive or with clarity, and therefore the individual is relatively open to influence from external sources possessing an authoritative aura and tone.[15]

In summary, the relationships found in this study indicate that persuasibility is not an isolated phenomenon, but is rather the product of certain underlying attributes of the personality. Personality patterns apparently make a person more or less susceptible to influence in a wide variety of situations, whether the influence arises from the structure of the external field, from another person, or from a written communication.

15. Similarly, the negative changers, who seem engaged in a struggle to defend themselves against hostile inroads from the outside world, overreact in their defense of these opinions.

CHAPTER 5

Some Implications of Self-Esteem
for Social Influence

ARTHUR R. COHEN

RESEARCH ON THE RELATIONSHIP between personality and persuasibility has indicated the general importance of self-esteem
as a determinant of the individual's responsiveness to influence
from both mass media and social interaction. Evidence presented in the preceding chapters by Janis and his co-workers
indicates that people of high and low self-esteem, as measured
by feelings of personal adequacy, differ in their responsiveness
to persuasive communications: those with low self-esteem are
more persuasible than those of high self-esteem, who are
better able to resist influence in mass-communication situations. Also, the author observed (1959) that individuals of
different degrees of self-esteem tend to differ in their reactions
to the threatening exercise of power over them, these
tendencies centering around their vulnerability to an experimental situation. Those with high self-esteem appeared to
repudiate the power situation with greater ease and were
more self-protective and self-enhancing, whereas those with

The studies referred to in this chapter were carried out at the University of
Michigan under USPH grants M-659 and M-701C.

low self-esteem seemed to be more dependent upon the situation and more vulnerable to its pressures.

The present chapter continues the discussion of self-esteem, focusing on some of the relationships of this personality factor to social influence. An attempt will be made to show how these relationships can be accounted for in terms of some basic personality mechanisms.

A person's self-esteem affects the evaluation he places on his performance in a particular situation and the manner in which he behaves when in interaction with others. Self-esteem concerns the amount of value an individual attributes to various facets of his person and may be said to be affected by the successes and failures he has experienced in satisfying central needs. It may be viewed as a function of the coincidence between an individual's aspirations and his achievement of these aspirations.

Self-esteem, then, may be defined as the degree of correspondence between an individual's ideal and actual concepts of himself. If a person has set certain ideals for himself, the degree to which he has met these ideals should result in feelings of success or failure. And feelings of success and failure experienced in any given situation should generalize to his entire self-percept. Thus, a discrepancy between ideals and actual attainment points to a state of motivation within the individual in which need satisfaction has not occurred. It is possible to think of ideals and attainments as centering around a range of specific needs and to think of success and failure in terms of these needs. For example, if a person has failed to meet certain of his achievement standards, we may speak of a level of aspiration for achievement which has not been attained and expect resultant feelings of failure. When an individual's needs are aroused, his ideals with regard to these needs become salient, and the degree to which he feels that these ideals can be or have been met should affect his experience of success or failure. If we determine this sequence for a variety of needs operating in a variety of situations, we will have a good indication of the individual's general self-esteem.

Since an individual's experience with a variety of needs in a variety of situations contributes to his over-all level of self-esteem, persons of low self-esteem should suffer characteristic failure experiences whereas those with high self-esteem generally should be more successful in meeting their aspirations. This implies that persons with high self-esteem would differ from those who are low in self-esteem in their reactions to an immediate experience relevant to their need satisfaction. Individuals with high self-esteem might be expected to react to new situations with expectations of success since characteristically they have been successful in the past in meeting their needs. Those with low self-esteem, characteristically expecting failure, may be more vulnerable to the effects of failure experiences, thereby reinforcing the general discrepancy between self-ideals and self-percept. Persons of low self-esteem may allow their attitudes about themselves and others to be more affected by what other persons communicate to them concerning their performance and responsibilities.

These considerations generate a number of very broad hypotheses. First of all, we may expect that, since persons of high self-esteem appear to be less susceptible to events in mass-communications and power situations, they may, in general, be less susceptible to interpersonal influence in social interaction. We may also expect persons with high self-esteem to be less susceptible to influence from those of low self-esteem than vice versa. In addition, it may be inferred that persons of high self-esteem may exert more influence attempts than persons of low self-esteem when they interact.

Since people with high self-esteem may protect themselves from negative self-evaluation and may be less vulnerable to the impact of outside events, they may also be expected to be less affected by the communication of failure experiences and more responsive to success experiences than are persons of low self-esteem. Furthermore, they should be less responsive to the expectations for their performance communicated to them by their social group.

These broad hypotheses will be explored in the present chapter. Data from a number of studies which bear on one or another of the hypotheses will be cited. Some of the ways self-esteem and social influence are related will be discussed, and an attempt will be made to provide support for the relationships in some relatively basic personality mechanisms.

The Measurement of Self-Esteem

The instrument for measuring self-esteem (used in all the studies) was designed in accordance with the definition given at the beginning of this chapter. It was modeled after one used by the author (1953), who, in turn, was stimulated by Shapiro's (1952) use of an ideal-actual discrepancy measure in a study of determinants of friendship choice. The instrument is a modified Q-sort. The items are brief paragraphs, each describing a hypothetical situation in which a person faces a potential frustration of a need. Five representative need areas are included: achievement, autonomy, recognition, affiliation, and cognition. Each of these need areas is placed within three contexts: one of individual behavior and judgment, one concerned with interpersonal relations, and one in a more general group framework. This makes 15 hypothetical stories and permits a representative sampling of needs in situations.

After reading each paragraph, the subject indicates how the person would react by choosing among five behavioral alternatives. He is asked to note his reactions to each situation twice: once in terms of how a person *ideally* should behave and once in terms of how a person *actually* does behave. He is asked also to choose the behavioral items *most* and *least* descriptive of both the ideal and real behavior. The individual's self-esteem score is fixed by the pattern of agreements and disagreements between his choices for most and least on the ideal set and on the real set. On any one item the individual can obtain a score varying from $+2$ to -2. The responses are scored $+1$ for each occasion where the reaction selected as most descriptive of an actual solution is the same as that seen as most descriptive of an ideal reaction; also where the solution viewed as least descriptive of an actual reaction coincides with that regarded as least descriptive of an ideal reaction. A score of -1 is given for the coincidence of the least descriptive actual reaction with the most descriptive ideal reaction, and for the most descriptive actual reaction with the least descriptive ideal one. If no coincidence whatever occurs, no score is given. The person's total score indicating the over-all extent of agreement or discrepancy is obtained by summing algebraically across all items. The size of the discrepancy or agreement between his ideal and real choices of "most" and "least" is assumed to reflect the degree to which his ideals for meeting need satisfaction have been attained. It is thus assumed to provide a measure of self-esteem.

The instrument first developed by the author (1953) appeared to have some validity in terms of its correlation with other measures of self-evaluation (e.g. inferiority and ascendancy scales of the GAMIN). Data were secured from a sample of 198 workers in a large industry. The correlations were highly significant and ranged in the low .70s. The odd-even correlation for the first scale developed was .63; application of the Spearman-Brown formula yielded a reliability of .77. The distribution covered 70 per cent of the range of possible scores. On the basis of this measure successful predictions were made as to the degree of insecurity experienced by the subjects in a threatening power situation (Cohen, 1959).

With this assurance in the measure it was revised to include a better sample of needs and situations and given to a large group of Air Force personnel and 35 graduate students. A random sample of 60 subjects was drawn from the Air Force population and an odd-even correlation showed the revised instrument to be quite reliable: the odd-even correlation for the subsample was .84, and the Spearman-Brown formula brought a reliability coefficient of .91. In addition, a homogeneity analysis showed that all the needs and all the situations were working in a generally similar fashion to produce the over-all self-esteem score: when the individual was above the group median in self-esteem he scored in the same direction on each need and each situation. The same was true for those below the median in self-esteem.

On the basis of the results with this sample a second and minor revision of the instrument was undertaken in order to equate the popularity of items more adequately. The instrument was then given to 44 college fraternity men and to 175 undergraduate subjects participating in a group experiment. Time considerations necessitated the use of a short form of the instrument in the latter experiment. This appeared safe in light of the fact that scores on the items used were found to be significantly related to total scores on the larger instrument.

It should be understood that self-esteem is used in the present chapter as a preselected personality variable. All results dealing with the effects of self-esteem are based upon the measurement and identification of self-esteem groups before the application of any experimental stimuli or manipulations. Such a procedure, of course, allows some ambiguity of interpretation because of the possible correlation of self-esteem with other variables which could be responsible for the obtained results. Therefore any assessment of the present data should be made within this framework.

Research Evidence

Perceived social influence in social interaction. Theoretical considerations led to the expectation that persons of high self-esteem would exert more influence attempts than persons of low self-esteem in interactions between the two. Data bearing on this hypothesis were obtained from two experiments on self-esteem and interpersonal relations.

In one experiment, by Thomas and Burdick (1954), 30 members of a graduate course in social psychology were paired with each other according to their self-esteem levels. Those with high self-esteem were paired and those of low self-esteem were paired. Each subject was given general "case history" material, asked to assess it individually and then discuss it with his partner. After this discussion, each subject reassessed the material individually. Predictions were made concerning each subject's perception of the influence attempts exerted by his partner.

The data in Table 11 show that among the pairs of highs more attempts at influence were perceived than among the lows. On an a priori eight-point rating scale highs rated their

TABLE 11. *Self-Esteem and Rating of Partner's Attempted Influence within Each Pair*

(N = 15 pairs)

Self-esteem:	Low influence *	High influence
High-high pairs	4	5
Low-low pairs	6	0

* The mean of the two influence ratings made by the pair of subjects was taken as the perceived influence score. The data were then broken into the best median split.

partners higher in attempted influence than lows rated their partners (p < .05).

In another experiment (Cohen, 1956), 44 undergraduate members of a social fraternity were paired in terms of their defenses against common psychosexual conflicts and asked to interact around some common conflict-arousing content. Each member of a pair read a series of conflict-arousing "case history" accounts, made individual assessments and interpretations of the case histories, discussed the material with his partner and, finally, he and his partner together made a joint assessment and interpretation of the material. Predictions were made as to the quality of interaction and, specifically for the present purposes, as to the perception of mutual influence. Since the subjects had been measured for self-esteem as well as ego-defense before the conduct of the experiment, it was possible to study the influence which persons of high and low self-esteem perceived themselves to have exerted on the partner.

TABLE 12. *Self-Esteem and Perception of Own Attempted Influence*

(*N = 44 individual subjects*)

	Low influence *	High influence
High self-esteem	9	18
Low self-esteem	10	7

* Low and high categories were determined by making the best median split.

When the data from this experiment are examined (Table 12), it can be seen that persons of high self-esteem perceived that they made more efforts to exert influence than the lows perceived of themselves (p < .10). In sum, the data indicate that, both in terms of their own perceptions and in terms of their partners' perceptions, high self-esteem persons are seen to exert more attempts at influence in interaction situations.

Actual social influence in social interaction. It was further expected that persons of high self-esteem would be more resistant to social influence than persons of low self-esteem when they were paired with one another. They might also reasonably be expected to accomplish more influence than the lows. Data bearing on these hypotheses come from both interaction experiments.

In the experiment in which graduate students were paired with others of the same self-esteem level (Thomas and Burdick, 1954), actual influence accomplished was measured by the correspondence between content elements in the individual stories written after interaction. The data in Table 13 show that pairs of subjects of high self-esteem exhibited a greater degree of mutual influence than did pairs of persons with low self-esteem (p < .01).

TABLE 13. *Self-Esteem and Actual Influence within Each Pair*

(N = 15 pairs)

	Low content * *correspondence*	*High content correspondence*
Self-esteem groups		
High-high pairs	1	8
Low-low pairs	5	1

* Low and high categories were determined by making the best median split.

The ego-defense and interpersonal-relations experiment (Cohen, 1956) provides further data concerning the amount of influence accomplished by persons of different levels of self-esteem in mutual interaction. Actual influence was measured by comparing the contribution of the person's individual assessment of the material before interaction to the combined assessment he and his partner made after interaction. The data show that the low's interpretations of the task never dominated in the final joint assessment. In all nine pairs combining high and low individuals, the assessment made before interaction by the high contributed more to the final joint assessment than did the assessment by the low.

In these particular data, it is difficult to separate the amount of influence exerted from the amount of influence accepted, or accomplished. Taking the data in Tables 11 and 12 into account, it would certainly seem that highs attempt more influence than lows. But it is not clear from the present data whether the greater amount of influence accomplished by the highs is due to their more frequent attempts at influence or to the lows' greater responsiveness to influence attempts. However, the evidence does seem to support the general hypothesis concerning the differential effects of self-esteem on social influence and attitude change. Compared to persons of low self-esteem, those of high self-esteem appear to exert more influence and to be able to change their partner's viewpoints more readily when the two interact.

The communication of group expectations, success or failure, and self-evaluation. Theoretical considerations led to the hypothesis that people of high self-esteem would be less affected by failure experiences in their social group, and possibly more affected by success experiences. Data from an experiment performed on 175 male undergraduates are relevant here (Stotland, Thorley, Thomas, Cohen, and Zander, 1957). Through experimental manipulations, members of the subject's group presumably communicated to him that they had either high or low expectations as to the quality of his achievement on individual tasks. The tasks were described as either relevant or nonrelevant to the purposes of the group. Half the subjects within each of the four conditions were allowed to succeed and the other half were told that they had failed. Measures of self-esteem were available for all participants. The dependent variable of interest is the individual's attitude toward his performance on the task (his evaluation of his success or failure), measured by an eight-point a priori rating scale.

The data indicate that although there are no differences between those who succeeded on the task in terms of their final self-evaluation, members who received word that they had failed differed considerably in their self-evaluation according to their level of self-esteem. When all other variables were held constant the mean self-evaluation for the subjects with high self-esteem was 2.55; for the lows it was 1.75 ($p < .05$).

Furthermore, though self-esteem does not appear to serve as a referent when the task is relevant to the purposes of the group, it does appear to have·differential effects on self-evaluation when the task is nonrelevant. The data in Table 14 indicate that where the group communicates both high and low expectations and the person fails on a task, those

TABLE 14. *Mean Evaluation of Success on Task for Non-relevant Conditions*

($N = 86$)

| | WHEN COMMUNICATIONS FROM GROUP CREATE: | |
	High group expectations	*Low group expectations*
Failure		
Persons with high self-esteem	2.67	2.45
	$p = .05$	$p = .01$
Persons with low self-esteem	1.50	1.20
Success		
Persons with high self-esteem	4.82	5.25
	ns	ns
Persons with low self-esteem	5.11	4.59

with high self-esteem have higher evaluations of their performance than persons with low self-esteem. The difference between the means in the high-expectations condition is significant at the .05 level; in the low-expectations condition it is significant at the .01 level. Where the subjects succeeded there were no significant differences. Thus, under conditions of low task relevance, persons of high self-esteem protect themselves against poor evaluations more than do those of low self-esteem. We may infer from these data that persons of low self-esteem show a greater responsiveness to criticism of their performance and to failure experiences communicated to them by members of their social group: their attitudes toward their performance are more affected than are the attitudes of persons with high self-esteem.

The communication of group expectations, success or failure, and concern with the group's expectations. The above data suggest that persons of high self-esteem do not always rate their own performance better than do persons of low self-esteem. What role do the expectations communicated by the group play in this? The following data indicate that persons with high self-esteem, compared with individuals of low self-esteem, are less responsive to the expectations communicated by the group.

TABLE 15. *Mean Concern with Expectations Communicated by the Group for Nonrelevant Conditions*

$(N = 87)$

| | WHEN COMMUNICATIONS FROM GROUP CREATE: | |
	High group expectations	*Low group expectations*
Failure		
Persons with high self-esteem	2.83	2.91
	$p < .01$	ns
Persons with low self-esteem	4.63	2.70
Success		
Persons with high self-esteem	3.18	4.11
	ns	$p = .01$
Persons with low self-esteem	3.68	2.94

In the course of the experiment with undergraduates, ratings were obtained of the subject's concern with the expectations for performance communicated to him by the group. As may be seen in Table 15, persons with high self-esteem stated that they had relatively little concern for the group's expectations when they failed and the group's expectations were high, as compared with those of low self-esteem under the same conditions. The means are 2.83 for the highs and 4.63 for the lows; p is beyond the .01 level. In addition, subjects with high self-esteem said that they were most concerned with the group's expectations when they succeeded and the expectations were low. Their mean concern was 4.11 while that of the lows under the same conditions was 2.94. The difference is significant at the .01 level.

It appears that subjects with high self-esteem reacted to the group's expectations when these expectation levels were easy to reach and in fact had been reached, and were less responsive to the group's expectations when these were difficult to reach and they had failed to perform at the required level. Persons with low self-esteem showed the opposite trend: they became responsive to the group's wishes when these were difficult to achieve and were less concerned when these were easily available and they had succeeded. The results suggest that persons of high self-esteem better protect themselves against unfavorable evaluation by becoming unresponsive to the expectations communicated by their group when an unfavorable comparison with others would be likely.

Discussion

The results of these explorations indicate that differences in self-esteem are associated with considerable differences in individuals' responses to external pressures. Persons of high self-esteem dealt with their experiences in experimental interaction situations in a way that helped them to maintain their high self-esteem. They tended to respond to failure by evaluating themselves more highly than did individuals with low self-esteem. Furthermore, they became responsive to the group's expectations only when favorable self-evaluation was readily possible. Persons with low self-esteem reacted to their experiences in a way that made it difficult for them to improve their self-regard: they reacted strongly to failure and became responsive to the group's expectations when an unfavorable self-evaluation was most likely. Different levels of self-esteem appear to induce different patterns of protective reaction to experiences of failure.

Differential responsiveness to social influence was further indicated by the data on perceived and actual influence in the interaction experiment. Persons of high self-esteem exerted more influence upon those of low self-esteem when the two were in interaction. Subjects with high self-esteem were also seen to exert more influence and perceived themselves as attempting to exert more influence than did the lows.

It would appear that some construct centering around the idea of degree of openness to change and negative self-evaluation would allow these results to be meaningfully interrelated. Thus people of high self-esteem may be less willing or able to permit their self-picture and views of the social world to be vulnerable to influence from others. There is good evidence for this interpretation in studies dealing with the relationship between characteristic ego-defenses and self-esteem (Cohen, 1954). In these studies, using the Blacky Test (Blum, 1949) and its associated Defense Preference Inquiry (Goldstein, 1952), high self-esteem has been found to be associated with the preference for avoidance defenses against unacceptable impulses, while low self-esteem is associated with the preference for expressive defenses. Avoidance defenses (reaction formation and avoidance) may be said to block the expression of unacceptable impulses and therefore to permit the creation of a self-protective façade. The expressive defenses (projection and regression), on the other hand, permit the unacceptable impulse to gain some sort of outlet. In effect, people of high self-esteem, who appear to be less responsive to outside influence, are also characterized by a preference for ego-defenses which help them to repress, deny, or ignore challenging and conflictful impulses. Individuals with low self-esteem, who are more open to outside influence, show a preference for the more expressive defenses, those which allow them to play out their impulses; being inclined to "act out" they may be more dependent upon situations and events.

The picture of self-esteem which emerges is an exceedingly complex one, but one that can be based upon the notion of the self-system's degree of openness to change. Persons of high self-esteem appear to take on early in life a defensive mode which handles challenging experience by a strong self-protective façade. They repress, deny, ignore, or turn about their potentially disturbing impulses in contrast to persons who express these impulses more directly by projection or regression. There are significant consequences for the person depending upon his use of one or the other of these defensive modes. For one thing, projection and regression are primitive defenses which occur early in psychosexual development. Within the world of everyday adult reality they may cause difficulties. The individual may find it hard to effect some kind of need satisfaction for his strong drives, expressed as they are in a direct fashion. The avoider, on the other hand, uses defenses which are far more socially facilitative and he thus may indirectly experience impulse gratification. The relationships found by Blum (1954) between general psychosexual conflict and the use of projection, on the one hand, and relative lack of conflict and the use of reaction formation, on the other, attest to the plausibility of this line of reasoning. Further support for this interpretation is provided by evidence relating low self-esteem to underlying psycho-sexual conflict (Cohen, 1954).[1]

Secondly, the use of avoidance defenses permits the individual to organize a cohesive and encapsulated self-picture. After they have been developed as a means of handling inner impulses, avoidance defenses become behavioral modes themselves and determine the social reality to which the person exposes himself. Consequently, persons with avoidance defenses can turn away from experiences which reflect unfavorably on their self-picture. Such persons may emphasize enhancing experiences, thereby preserving an insulated but positive self-picture. Persons whose defenses are more expressive may not be able to deal so selectively with external stimuli. Perhaps their low self-esteem is even partly a consequence of their failure to live up to generally accepted moral standards concerning the expression of forbidden impulses.

This implies that the different self-esteem groups are differentially able to fulfill the important acquired motive of maintenance of self-esteem at the highest possible level. Through their use of avoidance defenses and their greater expectations of need satisfaction, the highs are able to maintain a high-level equilibrium in the structure of their organized self-picture, whereas the lows are more dependent upon experiential variations. Thus, the highs are much more

1. Throughout this chapter it has been assumed that self-esteem is on a continuum. High and low self-esteem are not pure types; for convenience of analysis the self-esteem continuum has been broken into two groups by a median split. Other data (Cohen, 1954) present a more differentiated picture. When a middle group is isolated, its members show a more socially adjusted picture than either the highs or the lows: they have least psychosexual conflict, prefer projection least, and use avoidance defenses most. By definition, the medium self-esteem group took a more moderate approach to their own self-judgment on the self-esteem questionnaire; they selected a differentiated pattern of aspirations and achievements, scoring high on some and low on others.

resistant to change which may disturb their self-picture, as well as to influence in general.

The notion of the structure of the self, self-concept, or self-picture is thought to represent a coordinating construct. By this is meant the general percept the individual has of himself and of his potentiality for success in meeting needs. Defenses may be utilized in the service of a good self-image and may also allow persons to succeed differentially. Furthermore, they may allow the individual to organize his self-structure so that he is less open to new information, new influence, or any other disturbance of his existing view of the relationship between himself and the world.

It is in this light that we may view the implications of self-esteem for general persuasibility and responsiveness to social influence. The substratum of characteristic ego-defenses in the service of a positive and stable self-picture is consistent with responses to a self-esteem questionnaire which measures the size of the gap between self-ideals and attainments. And both are consistent with responsiveness to influence and to the communication by the social group of criticisms and expectations for performance.

It is possible, then, that in a mass persuasion situation, once opinion change has occurred and new information or persuasion has been accepted, regression over time and under the pressure of ordinary events would take place differentially with regard to self-esteem. Persons with high self-esteem should be less likely to show boomerang and "sleeper" effects due to situational and interpersonal influence.

In the present data there appears to be evidence for the differential effect of interpersonal influence upon persons of different levels of self-esteem. The mediation of mass-communication effects by interpersonal processes is undoubtedly partly a function of the fact that persons of high self-esteem attempt more influence in regard to lows than vice versa, and in fact do influence them more. A central issue for research concerns the variables of attempted influence vs. resistance to influence. Depending on which of these tendencies is stronger, behavior will be quite different. In a sense, both tendencies are assumed to be strong among the highs. The difficulty becomes apparent when people of any given level of self-esteem are paired in interaction: highs are expected to be more influencing, but also more resistant to influence. Which factor will predominate? Present evidence makes it difficult to separate the conditions under which one or the other of the assumed tendencies will predominate. Future research might well be concerned with controlling each of these factors, to provide further information concerning the interaction between the two factors and self-esteem in determining actual influence accomplished.

A further implication of the differing reactions of highs and lows to experiences which potentially threaten the maintenance of their self-esteem concerns their susceptibility to influence in mass-communication situations. Communications and/or communicators who threaten an individual's general picture of himself may be expected to influence persons of different levels of self-esteem differentially. Such threatening appeals may be rejected more by those of high self-esteem than by those of low self-esteem. On the other hand, appeals which enhance an individual's self-picture might be accepted more by the highs than by the lows. Thus one determinant of acceptance of mass-communication appeals may be the differential responsiveness to threats of negative changes in the self-picture on the part of those with high and low self-esteem.

The group-expectations experiment provided interesting evidence that variation in behavior may be predicted as a function of variation in personality characteristics more often when influences from the group are weak than when they are pervasive. This finding would certainly suggest that, in both the mass-communication and interaction situations, there are some conditions within which personality variations remain poor predictors of environmental influence and acceptance of persuasion. Within other conditions, however, specific personality variations may be very important in understanding behavioral effects. Thus, social conditions within which pressure is strong might move everyone in the direction of intended influence, regardless of differences in personality; where pressure is weak and few explicit demands are made on the person, relevant personality characteristics might make for greater differences in behavior.

CHAPTER 6

Persuasibility and Emotional Disorder

IRVING L. JANIS AND DONALD RIFE

IN THIS CHAPTER a research investigation is reported dealing with sources of individual differences in persuasibility among young men who were institutionally confined because of severe emotional disorders. A group of 56 deviant personalities was studied for a twofold purpose: (1) to gain further understanding of the ways in which personality disturbances may interfere with an individual's "normal" processes of attending to, comprehending, evaluating, and being motivated to change his attitudes when exposed to persuasive communication; and (2) to check on the generality of several hypotheses drawn from the study of clinically normal persons reported in the three preceding chapters—notably those asserting an inverse relationship between persuasibility and (a) level of self-esteem, (b) strength of hostile tendencies, and (c) degree of constriction in empathic fantasy activity.

Neurotics, psychotics, and psychopathic personalities have often been studied for the purpose of gaining insight into personality dynamics that apply to more or less normal people. For example, observations of the behavior of anxiety hysterics have led to increased understanding of changes in interpersonal relationships at times when anxiety mounts to a high level; studies of depressed patients have illuminated

some of the psychological mechanisms people use in an effort
to cope with acute guilt and low self-esteem; comparisons of
different types of schizophrenic patients have shown alternative ways in which conflicts over interpersonal hostility may
be resolved and have suggested some of the emotional consequences of releasing and inhibiting hostile impulses toward
other people. (See Fenichel, 1945; White, 1956.) When inferences are drawn from such studies concerning psychological mechanisms that may account for individual differences
among the normal population, the assumption is made that
persons suffering from emotional disorders represent *extreme
variations* of the same personality variables that occur among
clinically normal persons. This constitutes the main working assumption of our study of abnormal personalities.

Methods and Procedures

The persuasibility test developed by Janis and Field
(Chapter 2, pp. 31–40) was administered to 40 young male
patients at a Connecticut state hospital for the mentally ill.
The subjects consisted of all testable patients from 14 to 24
years of age and a random sample of patients in the 25-to-35
age group. All varieties of emotional disorder were included,
and testability depended only upon the judgment of the hospital staff as to the patient's ability to read and comprehend
printed material and to cooperate with respect to filling out
questionnaires. According to the psychiatric records, the state
hospital sample consisted of 24 schizophrenics, 6 severe personality disorders ("psychopaths"), 5 neurotics, 3 chronic
alcoholics, and 2 brain syndrome cases.

In addition, adolescent male subjects from another institution were included. The additional subsample consisted of
16 psychopaths, schizoid personalities, and severe neurotics,
all of them boys of high school age (13 to 16 years old) confined in a private institution for emotionally disturbed chil-

dren. This subsample was combined with the state hospital cases, for purposes of investigating personality correlates of persuasibility, after it was observed that there were only negligible differences in the means and standard deviations on all the personality measures (described below) as well as on the persuasibility test. Thus, the combined sample consisted of 56 males whose ages ranged from 13 to 35 years.

Each patient was brought to the examiner's office for two separate testing sessions, usually along with two or three other patients who were tested at the same time. In the first session, the first half of the Janis and Field test was given: the subject filled out the initial opinion questionnaire containing the three key questions on each of five topics, and then was given Booklet I. After reading each of the five persuasive articles in this booklet, the subjects again answered the same key questions.

In the second session, held one week later, the remaining part of the persuasibility test was administered. At the beginning of the session, the subjects were given Booklet II, containing five persuasive articles which take the opposite position from those in Booklet I. The subjects again answered the same key opinion questions after reading each article. (See Appendix A, pp. 281–99.)

During the same session, following the persuasibility test, the subjects were given three additional tests. The first two were tests of comprehension and retention of the communication contents. They were presented as article-evaluation tests, and the subjects were told that their answers to the questions would help the investigator to determine whether the articles were clearly written. On the first test, which we call the *immediate recall test,* the subjects were asked to answer the questions in such a way as to indicate the conclusions and arguments that were put forth in the five communications in Booklet II, which they had just finished reading.

On the second test, which we refer to as the *delayed recall test,* they were asked to answer the same questions, but this time to indicate the conclusions and arguments that had been given in the communications in Booklet I, which they had read a week earlier.[1] The subjects had no advance knowledge that these recall tests would be given.

The final questionnaire was a self-rating personality inventory. In order to test the three hypotheses concerning the way in which persuasibility is related to self-esteem, to hostile tendencies, and to fantasy constriction, the same personality inventory questions were used as in the study by Janis and Field (Chapter 3).[2] Although this questionnaire followed the persuasibility test and the recall tests, an attempt was made to keep it as distinctive as possible by giving it a different format and by telling the subjects that it was part of a differ-

---

1. The questions on the recall tests consisted entirely of multiple-choice and short-answer items which were constructed in such a way that there could be only one correct answer for each communication, depending upon whether it was the article in Booklet I or in Booklet II. The following two examples serve to show the type of questions included in the recall tests:
  1. According to the article, how long will it be before there is a cure for cancer?
    The author said it will probably be about: _____ years.
  2. The author feels that an interest in classical music will:
    (1) Increase one's talents in other cultural pursuits such as art and painting.
    (2) Mark a person as a stuffed-shirt phony.
    (3) Make a person a professional musician.
    (4) Increase one's status and prestige among his friends.
    (5) Have no effect upon a person's life.
In the first example the correct answer is 1 to 2 years for the article in Booklet I and 30 years for the one in Booklet II. In the second example answer 2 is correct for the article in Booklet I, and 4 is correct for Booklet II. Thus the correct answer depends upon which article the subject is instructed to base his answer.
  2. The split-half reliabilities of the various personality clusters were reported earlier (see pp. 57–8) by Janis and Field, on the basis of their data from "normal" high school students. Because abnormal personalities are likely to have much more difficulty in interpreting questions about their personal feelings and in making the self-ratings required by such questions, it was felt to be essential to recompute the reliabilities for the present sample

ent survey, designed to cover health and adjustment among people in hospitals throughout the state.

Additional evidence concerning personality factors was obtained from the institution's case file for each patient. These files contained information about the individual's life history, summaries of the psychiatrists' diagnostic interviews, and records of deviant behavior directly observed by members of the staff. The material was analyzed systematically before scoring the persuasibility test, so that there could be no contamination from an a priori knowledge of the subject's test performance. Nor was there any possibility of the reverse type of contamination, because the persuasibility test was scored mechanically by clerical personnel who had no knowledge of the subjects.

The subjects were divided into three groups according to their persuasibility scores: (1) *high* persuasibility (the upper third of the distribution), (2) *medium* persuasibility (the middle third), and (3) *low* persuasibility (the lower third). The three groups were then compared with respect to personality factors which had been assessed (without knowledge of the patient's persuasibility score) on the basis of a careful

---

of institutionalized patients. The following results were obtained for the various clusters of items used in the present study:

	Split-half reliability (Pearson r)	Estimated reliability for total test (Spearman-Brown correction)
Self-esteem (feelings of personal inadequacy)	.86	.93
Hyperaggressiveness	.70	.82
Suspiciousness	.47	.64
Argumentativeness	.50	.67
Constriction of fantasy activity	.66	.80
Emotionality (see pp. 131 f.)	.79	.88

The split-half reliability of the persuasibility test was also recomputed for the present sample of mental patients and was found to be .64; the estimated reliability for the total test based on the Spearman-Brown formula is .78.

study of all pertinent observational reports in the institution's psychiatric records. The main personality deviations investigated were the following: social passivity, depressive symptoms, antisocial aggressive behavior, and paranoid symptoms.

Results and Discussion

Social passivity, depression, and feelings of inadequacy. According to the "low self-esteem" hypothesis, persons who are excessively timid, inhibited, guilt-ridden, and passive in their social relationships will tend to be more persuasible than others. In order to determine whether this hypothesis holds for persons with severe emotional disorders, the three persuasibility groups were compared with respect to the incidence of: (1) social passivity (timidity and inhibited aggression in social relationships) and (2) depressive symptoms (feelings of guilt, sadness, self-derogatory complaints, suicidal tendencies). The results in Figure 2 show that for both attributes the differences are in the predicted direction. For depressive symptoms, the differences are not large enough

Figure 2. Personality Disturbances (Assessed from Psychiatric Case Records) Related to Degree of Persuasibility
(Low: N = 18; medium: N = 18; high: N = 20)

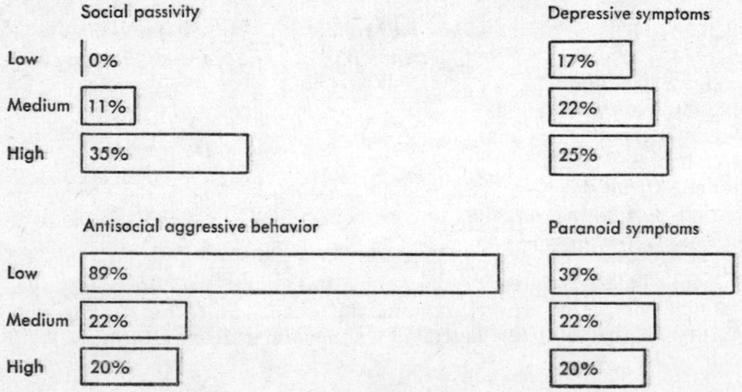

Social passivity

Low   0%
Medium   11%
High   35%

Depressive symptoms

Low   17%
Medium   22%
High   25%

Antisocial aggressive behavior

Low   89%
Medium   22%
High   20%

Paranoid symptoms

Low   39%
Medium   22%
High   20%

to be significant. But for social passivity the high persuasibility group differs markedly from the medium and low groups ($p < .10$ and $p < .05$, respectively). These findings partially confirm the specific predictions stated above.

The significant findings on social passivity derived from the psychiatric case records are supplemented by the objective questionnaire data, which also show that the inverse relationship between self-esteem and persuasibility holds for abnormal personalities. Self-esteem scores were obtained from a cluster of 23 self-rating questions concerning feelings of inadequacy and of social unacceptability (see pp. 300–1). The correlation between self-esteem scores and persuasibility scores ($N = 56$) proved to be —.66, which is significant beyond the .01 confidence level and is substantially higher than that obtained so far from any normal samples. For instance, the Janis and Field study of male high school students obtained an r of .21 for the same two measures, which is a significantly smaller correlation (C.R. based on Fisher's $z = 3.29$; $p > .01$).

The higher correlation for the sample of abnormal personalities is partly attributable to the fact that this group shows greater variance in self-esteem scores than the normal sample. For the abnormal group, the mean self-esteem score was 37.5 and the standard deviation was 17.14, whereas for the normal group the mean was 38.4 and the standard deviation was 12.28. The standard deviations are significantly different ($F = 1.95$; $p > .05$), although the means are not ($t = 0.41$; $p > .60$). This finding lends some empirical weight to the basic working assumption stated at the beginning of the chapter, namely, that personality differences in the population at large will sometimes be accentuated among abnormal patients and hence will be more readily observable. As measured by the scale used in the present study, the abnormal group showed a greater incidence of feelings of low self-esteem and also a greater incidence of feelings of high self-esteem, probably corresponding to the clinical differences between patients who are depressed and those who are euphoric or hypomanic. Thus, with a much greater spread in the self-esteem variable, the relationship between self-esteem and persuasibility emerges more clearly in the abnormal group than in the normal group, which has a more restricted range of self-esteem scores.

Antisocial aggressive behavior. Examination of the case records indicated that antisocial aggressive behavior had been recently manifested by about half of the emotionally disturbed patients in our sample. The vast majority of those who displayed such behavior proved to be in the low persuasibility group. Results in Figure 2 show that there is a marked relationship between antisocial aggressive behavior and degree of persuasibility. There is a 50.2 per cent difference between the low and medium persuasibility groups and a 59.0 per cent difference between the low and high groups, both of which are significant at beyond the .01 level.

Because there is no generally agreed-upon definition of antisocial behavior, especially in dealing with mentally ill persons, there is bound to be some ambiguity as to what types of action are included in this category. In order to help clarify the realm of behavior in the "antisocial" category, a series of illustrative examples is provided. The following statements were extracted from the records of the 16 patients in the low persuasibility group (89 per cent) who were judged to be displaying antisocial behavior.

Case 1. Frequently engages in physical violence against peers and teachers. Attacks other patients with physical violence at the slightest provocation. Reacts to disciplinary measures by aggressive retaliation.

Case 2. Was arrested by local police for molesting women on the street.

Case 3. Behaves in a belligerent, hostile manner in the hospital, constantly suspicious of hospital staff; refuses to cooperate with respect to the daily hospital routine.

Case 4. Foster parents unable to cope with disciplinary problem posed by this boy: steals, lies, cheats, and runs away from home. At institution is sullen, sulky, negativistic, and frequently expresses open hostility toward the staff.

Case 5. Has frequent temper tantrums and represents a constant disciplinary problem to institution staff because he reacts violently to criticisms or reprimands.

Case 6. Prior to committal, had engaged in violent behavior at a neighbor's house after using obscene language to neighbor's daughter. Displayed violent rage when brought to institution.

Case 7. Behaves in hostile manner at institution and threatens other patients with physical violence.

Case 8. Arrested for obtaining money under fraudulent pretenses and forging checks. Constant trouble with police. Expresses "sociopathic" attitude: says that other people are merely something to be used for obtaining his own satisfaction.

Case 9. Was hospitalized because of physical violence. Broke into a factory and assaulted the janitor. At institution expresses animosity toward his family and is hostile and negativistic toward the staff.

Case 10. Has frequent temper tantrums. Occasionally engages in violent fights with other patients.

Case 11. At school attacked others and on one occasion bit another boy. At the institution he behaves like a "tough guy"; displays outbursts of hostility.

Case 12. At home was constantly sullen, refused to go to work, wrote checks on his father's account, and was frequently hostile. At institution shows a sullen unwillingness to follow rules.

Case 13. Was hospitalized after threatening to kill his stepfather with a knife. At hospital refuses to conform and makes constant complaints about being persecuted by people upstairs.

Case 14. At home and in hospital frequently engaged in stealing. Often lies and is regarded by the staff as a disciplinary problem.

Case 15. Was hospitalized after creating disturbance in drunken state; went outside indecently dressed and struggled against police.

Case 16. Was hospitalized after belligerently accusing others of spying on him. At institution refuses to cooperate with staff and engages in violently destructive behavior.

Comparing the incidence of paranoid symptoms we find that the differences between the low persuasibility group and the other two groups are in the predicted direction, but are not large enough to be significant. However, for the joint occurrence of paranoid symptoms with antisocial behavior there is a significant difference between the low and high groups: the two symptoms occurred in 33.3 per cent of the low group, 22.2 per cent of the medium group, and 5.0 per cent of the high group.

The above findings suggest that a deviant personality with strong antisocial tendencies is likely to be relatively resistant to social communications which attempt to influence his beliefs and attitudes. Thus, a relatively low degree of persuasibility would be expected in persons who are generally hostile—hyperaggressive, suspicious, and quarrelsome—in their dealings with other people. But the personality inventory data from the present study, as well as from prior studies of normal samples, fail to bear out this implication. In order to test the "hostility" hypothesis, correlational data were obtained, based on the same three clusters of personality inventory items that were used by Janis and Field: hyperaggressiveness, suspiciousness, and argumentativeness (see pp. 303–5). No significant relationship was found between any of the three measures and the scores on the persuasibility test: the Pearsonian correlations were .08, .01, and .03 respectively.

The negative results may be attributable to the low validity of the self-ratings. In line with this interpretation, there is evidence which strongly suggests that the self-rating measures of interpersonal aggressiveness are obscured by extraneous personality tendencies which involve *readiness to admit negative emotional feelings* and which may have the opposite relationship to persuasibility. In order to obtain some data bearing on this possibility 12 items were selected from the personality questionnaire, comprising the questions on which the subjects most frequently admitted having strong negative emotions such as anger, irritability, anxiety, and feelings of discouragement. This set of items, which we shall refer to as the "emotionality" cluster, consists of the following:

1. How often do you feel cross or grouchy?

2. Some people feel so disgusted that they get angry about a lot of little things that ordinarily would not bother them at all. How often do you feel that way?

3. During the past three days, how many times have you argued or quarrelled with someone?

4. During the past three days, how often have you felt angry at someone?

5. How often do you lose your temper?

6. How often do you get so angry that you feel like smashing things?

7. Do you ever feel mean and full of hatred toward other people?

8. During the past three days, how often have you felt worried or upset?

9. When someone tells you about something unpleasant or dangerous that might really happen to you, how worried or upset do you usually feel?

10. When you are trying to win in a game or sport and you know that people are watching you, how rattled or flustered do you usually get?

11. Do you ever feel so discouraged with yourself that you wonder whether anything is worth while?

12. How often do you feel that you dislike yourself?

The emotionality cluster was scored the same way as the other clusters, high scores in this case representing high emotionality. The correlation (Pearson r) between these scores and persuasibility scores proved to be .26, which is significant at the .05 level. Thus, we can conclude that those persons who most readily admit having unpleasant emotional reactions (or who are least defensive) tend to be more persuasible than those who report less emotionality. This implies that the self-rating scores on aggressiveness, suspiciousness, and argumentativeness probably are not valid measures for testing the "hostility" hypothesis because those categories include many items in the emotionality cluster, which apparently involve a very different type of personality predisposition, at least among mentally ill patients. In any case, the findings based on the psychiatric observations indicate that if interpersonal hostility is assessed by observations of the patients' actual behavior, there is, in fact, the expected inverse relationship with persuasibility. The "hostility" hypothesis should therefore be carefully re-examined in subsequent studies of normal subjects, using direct behavioral observations to assess antisocial tendencies rather than self-rating questionnaires.

Cognitive capabilities. In order to be influenced by persuasive communications, a person obviously must have the ability and motivation to use the requisite cognitive skills. (See the discussion of cognitive factors in Chapter 12, pp. 257–68.) One essential cognitive function involves the capacity to anticipate the rewards and punishments that are conveyed by signs of the communicator's status or by his arguments and appeals. For those persons who are highly constricted in fantasy activity, any given persuasive communication would not be likely to evoke the requisite anticipations which foster acceptance and hence such persons would tend to be less persuasible than others. This is the hypothesis formulated by Janis and Field, which they investigated by devising a self-rating measure of rich vs. poor empathic fantasy activity. In Chapter 3 (see pp. 62–3), these authors report a significant correlation of $+.21$ with persuasibility scores for their sample of 86 normal male adolescents. We were able to replicate their finding in our study of abnormal male subjects. Using the same set of 11 questions on fantasy activity, we found that the correlation with persuasibility scores was .20 for the 56 institutionalized patients. This Pearson r approaches statistical significance at the .07 level, thus providing additional evidence suggesting that the relationship between richness of fantasy life and persuasibility may apply to a fairly wide range of personalities within the male population.

Additional findings bearing on cognitive capabilities were obtained from the recall tests. The scores were examined first in relation to persuasibility and then in relation to personality factors assessed by the self-rating inventory and by the psychiatric observations in the case records. As expected, scores on the delayed recall test were found to be positively related to the persuasibility scores based on Booklet I: Pearson $r = .24$, which is significant at beyond the 5 per cent confidence level. Similarly, scores on the immediate recall test were positively related to the persuasibility scores based on Booklet II: Pearson $r = .21$, which approaches significance at the 6 per cent confidence level.

Thus, each recall test contributes to the prediction of persuasibility for the particular set of articles to which the test refers. However, the relatively low correlations suggest that only a small amount of the variance in persuasibility is accounted for by individual differences in the basic cognitive skills which make for a good recall score (e.g. abilities to attend to, comprehend, and retain verbal material). Moreover, such abilities appear to be quite unrelated to any of the personality factors which were found to be predictive of persuasibility. The two recall tests yielded correlation coefficients that were close to zero for each of the following factors: (1) overt antisocial behavior, (2) paranoid symptoms, (3) depressive symptoms, (4) social passivity, (5) self-ratings on self-esteem, (6) self-ratings on fantasy constriction, (7) self-ratings on hyperaggressiveness, (8) self-ratings on suspiciousness, (9) self-ratings on argumentativeness, and (10) self-ratings on emotionality.

Thus it seems improbable that any of the personality correlates of persuasibility found in the present investigation will prove to be attributable to individual differences in ability to attend, comprehend, or retain. In this connection it is noteworthy that, for our sample of 56 patients, the correlation between IQ (as measured by the Wechsler-Bellevue intelligence test) and persuasibility scores proved to be almost zero: Pearson $r = .08$; $p > .40$. This negative finding, like the ones reported earlier (pp. 59–60), carries the same general implication as the recall test findings: namely, that differences in general intellectual ability make no apparent difference in the degree to which people are predisposed to accept or reject persuasive pressures—provided, of course, that they have the minimum degree of intelligence necessary to be able to read and understand the usual types of persuasive communications that are encountered in daily life. However, the findings based on the IQ test and the recall tests do not preclude the possibility that the complex cognitive functions in fantasy activity may be an important source of individual differences in persuasibility.

Comparison of the abnormal group with a normal group. The sample of 56 male patients was compared with the normal sample of 86 male high school students in the study reported by Janis and Field in Chapter 3. The persuasibility scores from the two samples gave similar distribution curves, both being somewhat skewed with a slight preponderance at the low persuasibility end. There was only a small, nonsignificant difference in the variances; the standard deviations were 4.8 and 4.5 for the abnormal and normal samples, respectively. However, a substantial difference was found in the means. For the abnormal group, the mean persuasibility score was 12.2; for the normal group, the mean was 10.7. The difference approaches significance at beyond the 10 per cent confidence level ($t = 1.81$; $p < .08$, two-tail). This finding suggests that, on the average, institutionalized patients suffering from emotional disorders are more persuasible than normals.

Additional evidence was examined in order to evaluate the following explanation of the observed difference between the abnormal and normal samples: After living in the institutional environment for a period of time, many mental patients may become docile and unaccustomed to relying upon their own judgment, thus tending to conform with any impressive persuasive communication. The plausibility of an acculturation process of this kind is lessened by the fact that patients who had been in the institution for only a short time were found to be slightly more persuasible than those who had been there for a longer time: the Pearson r between length of time in the institution and persuasibility was —.18, which approaches significance at slightly beyond the 10 per cent level.[3]

Another possible explanation we investigated was that the differences in persuasibility scores of the normal and abnormal groups might reflect differences in educational level or age. However, the average schooling of both groups was at the high school level. Moreover, both samples consisted mainly of male adolescents, and the fact that there were a few older males in the abnormal sample would tend to make for a lower rather than a higher average persuasibility score. The correlation between age and persuasibility in the total sample of 56 male patients was found to be —.18, which approaches statistical significance at slightly beyond the 10 per cent level. It should be noted that this finding is consistent with the following general proposition, often assumed to hold true but not yet adequately tested in the normal population: After adolescence a man's opinions gradually become more fixed as he grows older, and he becomes cor-

3. A final exploratory inspection was made of the case study records to see if any new leads might be discovered concerning personality factors that would help to differentiate the high, medium, and low persuasibility groups. This analysis revealed only one difference between the high and low groups and it is in line with the inverse relationship between length of institutionalization and persuasibility: Patients with *acute* disturbances were found to be more persuasible than those with *chronic* symptoms, as judged by the examining psychiatrists. Of the 12 patients diagnosed as acute cases, 58 per cent had high persuasibility scores (i.e. were in the upper third of the total distribution); whereas, of the remaining 44 patients, all of whom were diagnosed as chronic cases, only 30 per cent had high persuasibility scores. (The 28 per cent difference is significant at beyond the 5 per cent level.) This finding cannot be assumed to imply that the patients who receive the most serious diagnostic labels (and hence are kept in the hospital longer) are less persuasible than others. No relationship was found between psychiatric diagnosis and persuasibility scores. Thus, for example, the patients classified as schizophrenics were just as persuasible as those classified a having nonschizophrenic character disorders or as neurotics.

respondingly less responsive to communications which attempt to influence him to adopt a new point of view.

The difference in mean persuasibility scores between normal and abnormal groups, if confirmed by subsequent research, will require careful investigation of a number of additional explanations which cannot be adequately evaluated from the data currently at hand. The results from the present study show rather clearly, however, that irrespective of the difference in mean score, the personality correlates of the persuasibility scores are essentially the same in the abnormal group as in the normal group. We have seen that the findings from the present study of mental patients closely parallel those reported in Chapter 3 from the study of normal high school students. Both studies indicate that males with low self-esteem tend to be highly persuasible and that males with a high degree of fantasy constriction tend to be relatively unpersuasible. It remains to be seen, of course, whether subsequent studies of normal males will also repeat the new findings from the present study, notably those showing an inverse relationship between persuasibility and (1) age, (2) emotionality, as assessed by self-ratings on negative affects, and (3) antisocial hostile tendencies, as assessed by direct behavioral observations of overt aggressive behavior.

For the present, the available evidence suggests that the determinants of persuasibility are essentially the same in neurotics, psychotics, and psychopaths as in the normal male population and that the role of some of the predispositional factors in the population at large may be accentuated in the abnormal group.

PART TWO

Developmental Aspects of Persuasibility

CHAPTER 7

The Measurement of Persuasibility
in Children

ROBERT P. ABELSON AND GERALD S. LESSER

THIS CHAPTER and the two that follow present a body of research and theory on persuasibility in young children. The use of children as subjects for persuasibility studies serves to extend the range of knowledge about persuasibility and the persuasion process. If persuasibility can be fruitfully regarded as a meaningful and unitary variable in children (our evidence leads us to believe that it can be), then many hypothesized correlations between personality variables and persuasibility in adults discussed in preceding chapters may be examined at the child level. In addition, one may explore the child-training antecedents of persuasibility and the trend of its development. The material to be presented begins these several explorations. The main focus is developmental, with persuasibility viewed as a dependent variable. This tends to emphasize somewhat different theoretical factors than those considered in previous chapters.

It is well to state at the outset, however, that our ultimate

This research was supported by a grant (No. M-1020) from the National Institute of Mental Health of the National Institutes of Health, Public Health Service, administered through Adelphi College.

interest in persuasibility in children is as a variable which mediates the transmission of attitudes from parents to children. We hypothesize that, for persuasible children, there is a strong positive association between parent and child attitudes, whereas for unpersuasible children there is a tendency to defect from parental views, often even in early grade school (Berenda, 1950; Duncker, 1938; Marinho, 1942; Trager and Radke-Yarrow, 1947). Thus a heterogeneous group of persuasible and unpersuasible children would yield the low positive correlations commonly found between parent and child attitudes (Berelson, Lazarsfeld, and McPhee, 1954; Bird, Monachesi, and Burdick, 1952; Hartshorne, May, and Shuttleworth, 1930; Helfant, 1952; Hirschberg and Gilliland, 1942; Maccoby, Matthews, and Morton, 1954). An empirical verification of this hypothesis, with persuasibility measured independently of the agreement between parent and child attitudes, is presented below.

The present chapter is concerned with the definition and measurement of persuasibility in children. Chapter 8 presents a developmental theory of persuasibility, and Chapter 9 relates persuasibility to other personality tendencies in children.

Persuasibility Distinguished from Other Conformity Tendencies

We begin with a working statement of persuasibility similar to the statement of Chapter 1. In the next chapter a more formal definition is presented. A "generally persuasible" individual is one who, under a wide variety of conditions, readily repeats with conviction a wide variety of opinion statements of others, or whose actions imply such conviction.

The word "opinion" is crucial to this statement. Persuasibility should be distinguished from "conformity" in situations where there exists a reality basis for making judgments, and also from "suggestibility." When an individual is confronted with a false group consensus in well-structured psychophysical or problem-solving situations (Asch, 1952; Berenda, 1950; Crutchfield, 1955; Hoffman, 1953; Weiner, Carpenter, and Carpenter, 1956) or with "prestige suggestion" in ambiguous tasks (Eysenck and Furneaux, 1945; Furneaux, 1946), he knows at least that a correct judgment exists, although it may be difficult to ascertain. Thus, not only is some social conformity motive involved, but also the motive *to be right,* i.e. to be in agreement with the demands of objective reality. Individual differences in the strength of the latter motive may well confound the interpretation of individual differences in the former motive.[1] We are concerned with individual differences in the general tendency to conform to opinions rather than to purported facts.

The motive to be right is an example of a class of "extraneous" motives and factors—extraneous in the sense of introducing specific variance that may conceal the properties of an underlying general persuasibility factor. In Chapter 1 it was pointed out that there are many other specific factors which operate in social influence processes and that conceptualization of general persuasibility can be purified by sifting out some of these specific persuasibilities.

Of three available schema (Jahoda, 1956; Kelman, 1959; Sarnoff and Katz, 1954) for distinguishing among different forms of susceptibility to social influence, that of Kelman is most helpful for present purposes. He has postulated three distinct types of conformity processes: "internalization"— integration of new opinions into an established value frame-

1. A distinction has been drawn by Thibaut and Strickland (1956) between "task set" and "group set." They treat the "sets" by experimental manipulation rather than by consideration of individual predispositions, but the distinction parallels ours. Orientation toward the task works in the opposite direction from orientation toward the group in determining conformity behavior.

work; "compliance"—overt but not necessarily covert conformity to an authority who manipulates conditions of reward and punishment; and "identification"—the individual's continual attempt to maintain opinions concordant with those of some model, whether an individual or a group.

A host of antecedent variables are involved in Kelman's three conformity types:

1. *Internalization.* The communication uses rational appeals, the communicator is in some measure an "expert," and the extent of opinion change is determined primarily by the communicatee's prior knowledge of the issue, by his ability to understand and integrate the arguments of the communicator, and also by the communicatee's value system which serves to anchor the rational considerations.

2. *Compliance.* The communication specifies rewards for compliance or punishments for noncompliance, the communicator is in a position to carry out these sanctions, and the extent of opinion change is determined primarily by the strength of these incentives for the communicatee.

3. *Identification.* The extent of the change is primarily dependent upon the symbolic identity of the communicator. The communicator may represent, psychologically, an embodiment of the peer group, of "father," of "other people," etc. Presumably, the effect of the communication is enhanced by implicit references on the part of the communicator to this symbolic relationship. The content of the communication itself is not of consequence. *The individual conforms in order to establish and maintain a satisfying self-defining relationship with respect to the communicator.*

Of these types of opinion-change mechanisms, the first depends mainly upon the arguments in the communication, and the second mainly upon temporary situational factors. The third type, identification, is general with respect to content and context, depending only upon individual predisposition toward a particular communicator or class of communicators. When the class of communicators is very broad, this type is close to what we mean by general persuasibility. An individual who has a strong need to identify (in the above sense) with *all* communicators would be the most generally persuasible individual imaginable.

Conformity irrespective of the topic is designated as "topic-free"; when communication or situational appeals are irrelevant, conformity is "appeal-free"; and when the identity of the communicator is of no consequence, it is "communicator-free" (see above, pp. 6–16). General persuasibility is topic-free, appeal-free, and communicator-free—it is opinion conformity in its barest psychological essence, i.e. the tendency to conform not because of who the communicator is, what he says, or how he says it, but because conformity itself brings satisfaction.

Measurement Methodology

How to evaluate an individual's persuasibility is a central research task. Some of the considerations involved in measurement of persuasibility in adults have been discussed in earlier chapters (pp. 16–21). The problem is even more complex in the case of children, where only very simple communications are feasible. As a consequence, the authors review measurement methods with an eye to their possible utilization in child development research but recognize that many of the considerations apply with equal force at older age levels.

Measurement techniques for persuasibility may be categorized as either "behavioral" or "judgmental." The behavioral techniques employ an actual persuasion situation and assign scores on the basis of the observed behavior of the subjects. The judgmental techniques—reports, self-ratings, and the like—assign scores on the basis of a judge's perception of the typical behavior of the subject.

Behavioral techniques for measuring persuasibility present several problems which merit detailed discussion. One set of problems involves the control of specific factors, as discussed in the previous section—the motive to be right, specialized communication appeals, topics, rewards and punishments, and the identity of the communicator. In addition, there is the further problem of how to handle the subjects' initial opinions on the communication topics. A choice must be made between the before-and-after design, using opinion change as a persuasibility measure, and the after-only design, using final opinion as the measure.

Earlier studies suggest a variety of methods for coping with these problems. Our review is limited to those techniques which involve the manipulation of opinions (rather than judgments) by one or more specified communicators, ruling out communicator-less presentations of opinion statements, as in the Social Acquiescence Scale (Bass, 1956). Ferguson (1944) used "communications" without verbal content. They were simply check marks indicating (bogus) average peer-group opinion along a graphic rating scale. This controlled for specialized appeal variables, though of course it did not eliminate the specific variables of topic and communicator. Ferguson attempted to control for initial opinions by placing the peer-group check marks a distance away from each subject's own check marks, wherever they happened to be. King (Chapter 10) and Hovland and Pritzker (1957) also used the check-mark method.

This method involves the assumption that an opinion change of a given amount along a rating scale has a constant meaning regardless of direction and starting point. Consider what might happen if initial opinions on a number of issues were not independent. In the extreme case, for example, the several issues might form one opinion cluster, with some individuals originally assuming positions favorable to the cluster, while others were unfavorable. Furthermore, change away from one pole of the cluster might be more easily produced than change away from the other pole. Also change away from neutrality may be easier than change away from extremity. In these cases, the "total change" score serving as the measure of persuasibility could be more readily interpreted in terms of initial position. This "initial opinion artifact" is particularly bothersome in factor-analytic studies of the generality of individual differences.

Helson, Blake, Mouton, and Olmstead (1956) described another procedure using "stripped-down" communications. They used tape-recorded statements as a means of persuasion. Since the tapes were standardized beforehand, the discrepancy between a single "group" opinion and the subject's initial opinion could not be constant for all subjects. Instead, the "group" took several positions on the same issue on different occasions. No matter what the subject's initial position, it was inevitable that the "group" sometimes agreed and sometimes disagreed with him. Amount of change toward the "group" was the persuasibility measure. This device suffers even more from the "initial opinion artifact" than does the check-list procedure, since only one issue is used. In addition, some subjects may puzzle over the chameleon-like behavior of the "group," thereby obscuring the pure operation of peer-group persuasion (Beloff, 1958, p. 99). On the other hand, prepared tape recordings are a flexible research device; we have modified the technique and used it on children (p. 151).

In Crutchfield's (1955) research also, the communications were minimal; the opinions of the subjects' peers were simply (falsely) indicated in multiple-choice fashion on a lighted panel. Crutchfield sought to control for initial opinion by using a wide assortment of issues, although he does not report the relationships among initial opinions on the issues. "Before" measures were not obtained.

A different approach toward the control of extraneous factors was employed by Janis (1954, 1955) and Janis and Field (Chapters 2 and 3). Control over specialized appeal factors was exercised by systematic variation; the identity of the communicators was also systematically varied. One method of controlling variations in initial opinions was to choose issues which were so unfamiliar that initial opinions were very weak.

Our Persuasibility Booklet measure, described in detail in the next section, also uses unfamiliar issues. When initial opinions do not exist, when it is known that they are homogeneous, or when a large number of independent issues are used, then a "before" measure of opinion is unnecessary. However, it is imperative that at some point a control group which has not received the communications be run. "Persuasibility" scores for the control group can be computed as though the group had received the communications. If the reliability of these scores is significantly greater than zero, then there is opinion clustering unrelated to persuasibility, and the measurement procedure should be changed.

A technique mentioned in passing by Bass (1956, p. 296) carries the unfamiliar-issue approach to its extreme. The experimenter tells the subjects that he has some (unknown) statement in mind, and asks them whether they agree or disagree. This is repeated for a series of "items." In spite of the seeming frivolity of this technique, Bass reports (1956, p. 297) that the total agreement score possesses some reliability.

Properties of these several techniques are summarized in Table 16. Attention is focused on the means of control of specific factors in the persuasion situation.

TABLE 16. *Methods for the Behavioral Measurement of Persuasibility*

Author	Method	Design *	Communicator	Special appeal	Topic	Initial opinion	Position of communication
Ferguson (1944) King (1955) Hovland and Pritzker (1957)	Check marks on rating scale attributed to a source	BA	Peers Peers, parents, teachers Experts	Absent	Varied	Present (independent?)	At given distance from subject's initial opinion
Helson et al. (1956)	Tape-recorded bogus opinions	BA	Peers	Absent	Constant	Present (dependent)	Varied
Crutchfield (1955)	Panel light falsely indicating peers' choice	AO	Peers	Absent	Varied	Present (independent?)	Extreme
Janis (1954, 1955) Janis and Field (Chapters 2 and 3)	Persuasive essays read by subjects	BA	Anonymous, experts	Varied	Varied	Weak or absent	Extreme
Bass (1956, p. 296)	"Telepathic" communication	AO	Experimenter	Absent	Absent	Absent	None
Abelson and Lesser (p. 150)	Stated preferences of communicator	AO	Teacher, experimenter	Absent	Varied	Weak or absent	Varied
Abelson and Lesser (p. 151)	Tape-recorded bogus opinions	AO	Peers, adults	Absent	Varied	Weak or absent	Varied

* BA denotes before-and-after; AO denotes after-only.

Measures of Persuasibility in Children

Our measures of persuasibility in children are: (1) the Persuasibility Booklet, (2) Incomplete Stories, (3) Recorded Opinions, and (4) the Parental Questionnaire. The first and third are behavioral, the second and fourth judgmental.

The Persuasibility Booklet may be administered either in group session by the class teacher or in individual session by an experimenter. The adult serves as a communicator of opinions on unfamiliar issues, using a minimal persuasive appeal. The communicator presents pictures of a pair of unfamiliar objects to the children, saying, "I like this one" (indicating one or the other object predetermined by the experimenter). "Now tell me which one you like. Circle the one you like." Each child marks his own opinion in the booklet, in which the objects are reproduced. The communicator is nondirective in eliciting choices from the children. No hint of rewarding or punishing consequences is given. Persuasibility is scored as the number of agreements between child and communicator over a varied series of pairs of objects. Variants of the basic procedure are possible and are referred to below. When the booklet is administered by the class teacher, the subject's score is called the "Teacher Persuasibility" score; when the booklet is administered by the experimenter, the "Experimenter Persuasibility" score. (A list of the object pairs is presented in Appendix B, p. 306.)

The Incomplete Stories measure is intended to yield indirectly a self-report from each child of his own persuasibility toward his parents. The measure is administered individually by an experimenter. Each of the stories describes a situation in which a mother (or father) states a novel opinion or fact, or makes an unusual or ambiguous request of a child. The subject is asked what the child in the story (named "Johnny" for boy subjects and "Susie" for girl subjects)

would think or do as a result of the mother's (father's) statements. For example: "One day Johnny's mother said to
Johnny, 'Johnny, stay away from simians.' Did Johnny go
near simians?"

The score is the number of persuasible responses (e.g.
"Johnny stayed away from simians") that the subject attributes to the child. When the mother is the parental figure in
the stories, the subject's score is referred to as the "Mother
Persuasibility" score. (The entire set of stories is presented
in Appendix B, p. 306f.)

The Recorded Opinions measure uses the technique of
Helson, Blake, et al. (1956) but has the rationale of our booklet measure. It is administered in an individual session represented to the subject as an opinion poll. Various unusual
questions (e.g. "Which would you rather watch, a sunrise or
a sunset?") are posed. Before the subject gives his answer, he
listens to a tape recording of what "some other people
thought about this question." The tape recording has been
prepared so that on the key items there is unanimity in favor
of a particular answer. Several dummy items on which there
is disagreement are interspersed to allay suspicion. The
voices on the tape may be either adult voices (one male, one
female) or peer voices. The score is the number of times the
subject agrees with the unanimous recorded opinion on the
key items. The score is referred to as the "Adult Persuasibility" score or the "Peer Persuasibility" score. (Two Adult
Persuasibility scripts and two Peer Persuasibility scripts are
presented in Appendix B, pp. 309ff.)

The Parental Questionnaire is an instrument to be administered to parents. Various scales may be included in the
questionnaire, but the one of principal interest is an eight-
item Likert-type scale on which the parent indicates his
judgment of the child's persuasibility. (The items are given
in Appendix B, p. 318.)

Reliability of Persuasibility Measures

The reliabilities of the measures outlined above should be regarded as first approximations to the true reliabilities of the measures. Ideally one would need larger samples than we used in certain studies in order to establish stable values for reliability coefficients. Furthermore, in some instances large variations in reliability occurred when the measures were administered by different people or when the Parental Questionnaire was answered by parents in different neighborhoods.

All reliability coefficients are given as corrected split-half (odd-even) coefficients, except in the one case in which test-retest reliabilities were available. Coefficients are given separately for each school class, and over-all values are computed by pooling within-class sums of squares and cross-products. For this pooling method, total degrees of freedom equal the total number of subjects minus the number of classes minus one. Data for boys and girls are given separately, inasmuch as the question of sex differences arises in many of our studies.

Table 17 presents the mean, standard deviation, and reliability in twelve first-grade classes for the Teacher Persua-

TABLE 17. *Teacher Persuasibility Data*

Class *	N	Mean	S.D.	Reliability	Test-retest reliability †	Control group reliability
1 Boys	13	6.92	3.49	.63	na ‡	
Girls	9	6.11	3.14	.76	na	
2 Boys	15	5.67	1.92	—.04	na	
Girls	10	5.90	1.79	—.11	na	
3 Boys	11	8.27	3.52	.73	na	
Girls	14	7.57	3.81	.76	na	
4 Boys	11	7.64	2.67	.31	na	
Girls	14	6.93	2.94	.52	na	

Class *	N	Mean	S.D.	Reliability	Test-retest reliability †	Control group reliability
5 Boys	7	7.29	1.03	—.61	na	
Girls	17	7.41	3.20	.70	na	
6 Boys	10	7.60	3.17	.80	na	
Girls	17	6.94	3.69	.82	na	
7 Boys	14	8.29	4.22	.91	na	
Girls	14	6.64	4.11	.86	na	
8 Boys	17	9.18	3.99	.79	.58	
Girls	10	10.00	4.00	.98	.61	
9 Boys	15	6.53	2.51	.71	.16	
Girls	13	6.77	2.22	.00	.50	
10 Boys	12	5.33	3.33	.83	na	
Girls	15	5.27	3.61	.93	na	
11 Boys	13	5.27	2.33	.08	.72	
Girls	12	5.83	2.68	.80	.72	
12 Boys	13	6.38	2.76	.80	.52	
Girls	11	6.45	2.57	.79	.52	
35 Boys	15	6.53	2.03			.06
Girls	13	6.92	1.98			—.15
36 Boys	12	7.50	2.09			—.09
Girls	13	7.08	2.01			.21
Over-all						
Boys	151	7.06	3.41	.73		
Girls	156	6.82	3.43	.79		
Boys	58				.41	
Girls	46				.61	
Boys	27					—.02
Girls	26					.04
p value for significance of sex difference				ns	ns	ns

* Classes 1–5 are from schools in New Haven; Classes 6–12, 35, and 36 are from schools in Uniondale, New York.

† The following intervals elapsed between the initial Teacher Persuasibility test and the retest: Classes 8 and 9, 5 months; Class 11, 2 months; Class 12, 3 weeks.

‡ na = not available.

sibility measure (the Persuasibility Booklet administered by the teacher). At the time these data were gathered, the booklet contained 14 picture-pairs (the first 14 listed in Appendix B). Five picture-pairs were added later to increase the reliability. In Table 17, the means and standard deviations refer to a scale of scores from 0 (agreement with none of the teacher's opinions) to 14 (agreement with all the teacher's opinions). Since we have employed the Teacher Persuasibility measure more frequently than any other measure of persuasibility, the means and standard deviations are included in Table 17, whereas only the reliability information is presented for the other measures in the tables that follow.

The over-all reliability of the Teacher Persuasibility measure is reasonably good, considering that initial preferences by each child for particular pictures in the booklet necessarily contribute error variance. However, an occasional single administration of the booklet exhibits extremely low reliability (as in Class 2 in Table 17). This we tentatively attribute to peculiarities in the style of administration by individual teachers. The teacher must be carefully instructed to be clear but not prepossessing in indicating her own picture preferences and to be nondirective in requesting the children's preferences.

The reliabilities of scores for control groups, which did not receive the communications, are negligible, as desired.

An important datum in Table 17 is the lack of significant difference between the mean Teacher Persuasibility scores for boys and for girls. This finding is in contrast to results on high school students, discussed in Chapter 3, and on adults (Crutchfield, 1955). Nor are there significant sex differences in standard deviations or reliabilities of Teacher Persuasibility scores.

As Table 18 suggests, the reliability of the booklet measure tends to be higher when administered in individual session by an experimenter. This is probably attributable to the better control of extraneous influences in the individual administration.

The over-all reliability of the Incomplete Stories (Mother

TABLE 18. *Reliabilities of Experimenter Persuasibility Measure*

Class *	N	Reliability
13 Boys	9	.95
Girls	13	.91
14 Boys	9	.91
Girls	10	.88
15 Boys	12	.60
Girls	11	.96
16 Boys	8	.50
Girls	11	.94
Over-all		
Boys	38	.71
Girls	45	.92
p value for significance of sex difference		<.01

* Classes 13–16 are from two schools in New Haven. In Classes 13 and 14 the experimenter was male, in Classes 15 and 16, female.

Persuasibility) measure is above .85 for both girls and boys. These data are presented in Table 19. The Mother Persuasibility measure is, like the Experimenter Persuasibility measure, individually administered. Data on the Father Persuasibility measure (Incomplete Stories using the father as the parental figure) are fragmentary, but the indications are that it is as reliable as the Mother Persuasibility measure.

The Recorded Opinions measures of Adult Persuasibility and Peer Persuasibility were also individually administered. Scores were obtained for groups of boys aged 6–7, 8–9, 10–11, 12–13. (The measure has not been applied to girls.)

Both experimental and control groups were used. "Persuasibility" scores for the control groups were computed as though the subjects had heard the recorded opinions. It will be re-

TABLE 19. *Reliabilities of Incomplete Stories Measure of Mother Persuasibility*

Class		N	Reliability
1	Boys	13	.91
	Girls	9	.92
2	Boys	15	.89
	Girls	10	.80
3	Boys	11	.95
	Girls	14	.82
4	Boys	11	.81
	Girls	14	.85
5	Boys	7	.70
	Girls	17	.84
6	Boys	10	.88
	Girls	17	.96
7	Boys	14	.95
	Girls	14	.87
8	Boys	17	.92
	Girls	10	.97
9	Boys	15	.92
	Girls	13	.94
11	Boys	13	.78
	Girls	11	.92
	Over-all		
	Boys	126	.86
	Girls	129	.89
	p value for significance of sex difference		ns

called from the discussion on page 148 that it is desirable for control group reliability to be zero. Table 20 presents the reliabilities of the Recorded Opinions measures.

The reliabilities for the experimental groups in the original experiment are minimally acceptable, with the exceptions of the Peer Persuasibility reliability of —.40 for Class 19 and the Adult Persuasibility reliability of .20 for Class 20. For the

TABLE 20. *Reliabilities of Recorded Opinions Measures*

ORIGINAL EXPERIMENT

Class *	Age	Treatment	N	Adult Persuasibility	Peer Persuasibility
17	7	Experimental	18	.67	.48
18	9	Experimental	18	.58	.59
19	11	Experimental	18	.53	—.40
20	13	Experimental	18	.20	.52
21	7	Control	18	—.54	—.37
22	11	Control	12	.18	.29

REPLICATION

Class *	Age	Treatment	N	Adult Persuasibility	Peer Persuasibility
23	7	Experimental	13	.69	.74
24	11	Experimental	12	.70	.62
25	7	Control	13	.28	.29
26	11	Control	12	.39	.06

* Classes 17–22 are from summer schools in East Williston, New York; Classes 23–26 are from a school in New York City.

control groups, in the original experiment, none of the positive reliability coefficients significantly exceed zero. Because of spotty reliability for the experimental groups in the original experiment, a replication study used somewhat modified Recorded Opinions topics. The reliabilities for the experimental groups in the replication are improved while the reliabilities for the control groups in the replication do not significantly exceed zero.

The Parental Questionnaire measure of persuasibility possesses slightly erratic reliability. Mothers in two of the school classes received an earlier form of the questionnaire, somewhat different from the form in Appendix B. The reliabilities for both forms of the questionnaire are given in Table 21.

Significant sex differences were found for the reliabilities of certain persuasibility measures. Tables 17–21 indicate that, in two out of the six comparisons, the reliability for girls significantly exceeds the corresponding reliability for boys.

TABLE 21. *Reliabilities of Parental Questionnaire*

Class	N *	Reliability
OLD FORM		
6 Boys	7	.63
Girls	10	.59
7 Boys	10	.55
Girls	10	.50
Over-all		
Boys	17	.57
Girls	20	.53
p value for significance of sex difference		ns
NEW FORM		
1 Boys	9	—.83
Girls	6	.97
4 Boys	9	.65
Girls	8	.88
8 Boys	12	.65
Girls	10	.55
9 Boys	13	.58
Girls	9	.60
10 Boys	12	.62
Girls	9	.55
Over-all		
Boys	55	.41
Girls	42	.70
p value for significance of sex difference		$< .05$

* Some loss of cases is due to nonreturn of questionnaires. With the old form, there was a 67% return; 93% of the new form were returned.

Validity of Persuasibility Measures

We have accumulated many data bearing upon the validity of the various measures, particularly the Teacher Persuasibility measure. The "construct validity" (Cronbach and Meehl, 1955) of the persuasibility measures may be examined in terms of their intercorrelations with each other. Relationships between the measures and personality and developmental variables are presented in Chapters 8 and 9. If persuasibility is indeed a fairly general predisposition in six-year-old children and, in particular, is communicator-free, then we would expect to find consistently high positive intercorrelations among Teacher, Mother, and Experimenter Persuasibility measures and also between all these and the Parental Questionnaire measure and teachers' ratings of persuasibility. (No data are available on the relationship between the Recorded Opinions measure and the other measures.)

We must require that the network of relationships among persuasibility measures be unexplainable by some simple irrelevant factor. Thus, if intelligence correlated strongly with all the measures, we might find ourselves with a series of intelligence tests instead of persuasibility tests. Relationships between "persuasibility" and other variables might then be explained in terms of relationships between intelligence and the other variables.[2] Similarly, should what we measure and label as persuasibility turn out to be something specific to behavior in school (e.g. awe of teacher, obedience in school because of specific training toward that end), we would not be dealing with the variable we thought. Measurements made

2. Crutchfield's (1955) measure is subject to this difficulty. He reports negative correlations exceeding .50 between his measure of conformity and general intelligence. The explanation for this may lie in his experimental situation, which includes various psychophysical judgments wherein the false group concensus distorts objective reality. Subjects high in intelligence are probably more motivated to conform to the demands of objective reality, and thereby would oppose the group judgment. This well illustrates the theoretical complexity of situations involving the "motive to be right."

outside the school context thereby assume special importance.

Table 22 presents the product-moment correlations between Teacher Persuasibility and Mother Persuasibility, and
between Teacher Persuasibility and Teacher Ratings of

TABLE 22. *Correlations of Teacher Persuasibility with*
Other Variables

Class	N	Mother Persuasibility	Teacher Ratings of Persuasibility	IQ
1 Boys	13	.76	na	—.09
Girls	9	.36	na	—.63
2 Boys	15	.20	na	—.15
Girls	10	.78	na	.62
3 Boys	11	.91	na	—.59
Girls	14	.72	na	.05
4 Boys	11	.67	na	.04
Girls	14	.61	na	—.22
5 Boys	7	.71	na	na
Girls	17	.10	na	na
6 Boys	10	.66	na	.42
Girls	17	.10	na	.00
7 Boys	14	.54	na	.14
Girls	14	.11	na	—.01
8 Boys	17	.77	.59	—.63
Girls	10	—.13	.17	—.10
9 Boys	15	.35	.67	—.40
Girls	13	.03	.39	—.24
10 Boys	12	na	.74	.21
Girls	15	na	.09	—.10
11 Boys	13	.53	.72	.38
Girls	12	.04	.57	—.05
12 Boys	13	na	.54	.44
Girls	11	na	.57	—.24
Over-all				
Boys	126	.55 *		
Girls	130	.29 *		

Over-all	N	Mother Persuasibility	Teacher Ratings of Persuasibility	IQ
Boys	70		.63 *	
Girls	61		.29 †	
Boys	125			.02
Girls	131			—.07
p value for significance of sex difference		<.02	<.02	ns

* Significant at the 1% level.
† Significant at the 5% level.

Persuasibility. To obtain teachers' ratings, the teacher was asked to place each child in her class in one of five simply worded persuasibility categories. The two extreme categories were: (1) Very responsive to suggestions, as compared to other children in the class. Extremely willing to listen to and accept what you say; and (5) Very resistant to suggestions, as compared to other children in the class. Extremely unwilling to listen to and accept what you say.

The over-all correlation coefficients in Table 22 are quite satisfactory for samples of boys. For samples of girls the correlations, although significantly different from zero, are also significantly worse than those for the boys.

The product-moment correlations between Teacher Persuasibility and parental reports of persuasibility (see Table 23) are statistically significant but not robust. The low reliability of the Parental Questionnaire may be in part responsible. The fact that the correlations are significantly positive, however, provides validation for the Teacher Persuasibility measure from a source external to the school situation.

In order to rule out the possibility that correlations between Teacher Persuasibility and other measures might be attributable to covariation with intelligence, measures of intelligence were obtained for the boys and girls of eleven

TABLE 23. *Correlations between Teacher Persuasibility and the Parental Questionnaire*

Class	N	Correlation
OLD FORM		
6 Boys	7	.89
Girls	10	—.18
7 Boys	10	.68
Girls	10	.55
Over-all		
Boys	17	.72 *
Girls	20	.26
p value for significance of sex difference		ns
NEW FORM		
1 Boys	9	—.26
Girls	6	—.22
4 Boys	9	—.16
Girls	8	.54
8 Boys	12	.35
Girls	10	.00
9 Boys	13	.54
Girls	9	.47
10 Boys	12	.61
Girls	9	.47
Over-all		
Boys	55	.32 †
Girls	42	.33 †
p value for significance of sex difference		ns

* Significant at the 1% level.
† Significant at the 5% level.

first-grade classes. In four classes (Classes 1–4) the Kuhlmann-Anderson group-administered test (1952), Form B, was given; in seven classes (Classes 6–12) the Pintner-Cunningham Primary Test (1946) was used.

The product-moment correlations between IQ and Teacher Persuasibility in Table 22 display no consistencies. The overall correlations are neither significant nor substantial. Nor is there significant heterogeneity among the individual class coefficients (for boys, $\chi^2 = 15.88$, $p > .10$; for girls, $\chi^2 = 8.11$, $p > .50$).

The possibility of some nonlinear relationship between intelligence and Teacher Persuasibility was explored. The only discernible nonlinear relationship occurred in Class 1, where both the brightest and dullest children tended to have high Teacher Persuasibility scores. This result, however, was unique to this class.

The relationship between the Experimenter Persuasibility measure and other persuasibility measures has been explored in a number of small studies, which have yielded similar results. In one study, a variant of the Experimenter Persuasibility (Booklet) measure was related to the Mother Persuasibility (Incomplete Stories) measure. A female experimenter went through the booklet page by page, asking the subject to circle in black the pictured object he preferred in each pair. Then the experimenter went through the booklet again indicating to the subject which objects she, the experimenter, preferred. These objects the subject circled in red. The experimenter disagreed with the subject's choices on a prearranged set of 12 of the 19 pairs. Finally, the third time through the booklet the subject was reminded of the meanings of the black and red circles and instructed: "Mark the one you like now." His persuasibility score was the number of times out of a possible 12 that he changed his choice to agree with that of the experimenter. This score we refer to as

"Experimenter Persuasibility-Immediate" to distinguish it from the score derived in a second testing session a week later.

In the second testing session, the subject was presented with an unmarked booklet and asked to indicate his present preference on each picture pair. He was not reminded of the experimenter's choices or of his previous two choices, nor was there any implication in the instructions that he try to remember the previous conditions. The "Experimenter Persuasibility-Delayed" score was the number of times the subject now chose objects which the experimenter had endorsed the week before in opposition to the subject's initial choice. Table 24 presents the product-moment correlations among the three measures for three first-grade classes: E.P.-Immediate, E.P.-Delayed, and Mother Persuasibility. The Incomplete Stories measure of Mother Persuasibility had been administered in a separate session preceding the two booklet sessions.

The correlations between Mother and Experimenter Per-

TABLE 24. *Intercorrelations with Variants of Experimenter Persuasibility (E.P.) Measure*

Class *	N	Mother Persuasibility vs. E.P.-Immediate	Mother Persuasibility vs. E.P.-Delayed	E.P.-Immediate vs. E.P.-Delayed
27 Boys	16	.45	.52	.90
Girls	5	—.13	.50	.51
28 Boys	14	.59	.39	.21
Girls	8	.37	.66	.17
29 Boys	14	.90	.93	.85
Girls	11	.85	.93	.89
Over-all				
Boys	44	.64 †	.61 †	.80 †
Girls	24	.68 †	.85 †	.72 †
p value for significance of sex difference		ns	<.05	ns

* Classes 27–29 are from schools in New Haven.
† Significant at the 1% level.

suasibility are uniformly positive, with one exception, and often are extremely high. Rather extraordinarily, the correlation of Mother Persuasibility with E.P.-Delayed is significantly greater than with E.P.-Immediate, according to a significance test suggested by Quenouille (1952, p. 70). Highly persuasible subjects (as measured by the Incomplete Stories) still hold to the experimenter's opinions after a lapse of a week, while highly unpersuasible subjects still resist the experimenter's opinions.

Analysis of the data from this study indicates that the reliability of the E.P.-Delayed measure is significantly greater than that of the E.P.-Immediate measure. The reliability of the latter measure is quite low (.64) in comparison to the reliability of the straightforward variation of the Experimenter Persuasibility measure (see Table 18). Perhaps the confrontation of the subject with the red and black circles imposes momentary confusion upon him which disappears when the the booklet is unmarked. At any rate, the differential reliabilities of the Immediate and Delayed measures are sufficient to account for the significantly superior correlation of the Delayed measure with the measure of Mother Persuasibility.

One of the most important validity checks of our measures is the test of the hypothesis (p. 142) that the degree of similarity of opinions between parent and child over a wide variety of topics is positively correlated with the degree of the child's persuasibility. The degree of similarity was measured by comparing the opinions of the mother, father, and child on a wide variety of items. A 50-item opinion questionnaire was sent to mothers and fathers (see Appendix B, p. 319). The same 50 items were administered to first-grade children in school by a male examiner. Three scores of parent-child opinion similarity were obtained: (1) the number of times the child's opinion agreed with the mother's opinion (Mother Agreement), (2) the number of times the child's opinion agreed with the father's opinion (Father Agreement), and (3) a percentage score representing the proportion of times the child agreed with both parents on those items where the mother and father agreed (Both-Parent Agreement).

The product-moment correlations between the booklet measure of Teacher Persuasibility and these three scores of parent-child attitude similarity are presented in Table 25. Significant positive correlations are found for both boys and girls between Teacher Persuasibility and Mother Agreement and Both-Parent Agreement. Sex differences are nonsignificant.

TABLE 25. *Correlations of Teacher Persuasibility with Parental Agreement Scores*

Class *	N †	Mother Agreement	Father Agreement	Both-Parent Agreement
30 Boys	8	.51	.36	.35
Girls	9	.59	.41	.70
31 Boys	8	.89	.25	.54
Girls	7	—.19	—.23	—.22
32 Boys	8	.52	.38	.56
Girls	9	.62	.49	.63
33 Boys	11	—.46	—.20	—.27
Girls	8	.55	—.16	.30
34 Boys	11	.34	.13	.68
Girls	7	.73	.51	.82
Over-all				
Boys	46	.35 ‡	.18	.38 ‡
Girls	40	.43 **	.20	.45 **
p value for significance of sex difference		ns	ns	ns

* Classes 30–34 are from schools in Uniondale, New York.
† Some loss of cases is due to nonreturn of questionnaires; 70% of the questionnaires from both parents were returned.
‡ Significant at the 5% level.
** Significant at the 1% level.

CHAPTER 8

A Developmental Theory
of Persuasibility

ROBERT P. ABELSON AND GERALD S. LESSER

IN THIS CHAPTER we propose a theory concerning the manner in which persuasibility, or its obverse, unpersuasibility, develops in the child as a function of the history of interactive experiences between the child and his parents. This theory generates testable predictions concerning the relationships between persuasibility and certain gross characteristics of parental attitudes and practices. These predictions are checked against various sources of research evidence, including our own research on persuasibility in children.

General Theory

In Chapter 7, persuasibility was defined as opinion conformity in its barest psychological essence—conformity which brings satisfaction per se. The presumed motive force toward such conformity is the need to establish and maintain a satisfying self-defining relationship with the communicator. The particular nature of self-defining relationships with communicators may be of many kinds, but there exists a clear dichotomy within the set of potential relationships: *similarity to, or agreement with, the communicator* vs. *discrepancy from, or disagreement with, the communicator.* An individual who is persuasible to a given communicator strives to relate himself to that communicator in such a way that their opinions agree or are consonant; an individual at the opposite extreme of unpersuasibility strives to relate himself to the communicator in such a way that their opinions disagree or are dissonant. Newcomb (1953) postulates a general motivation producing a "strain toward symmetry" in the attitudes of two people, A and B, toward an object, X. We postulate that in some persons there is also the converse "strain toward asymmetry." Whether A strives for symmetry or asymmetry with B in relation to X would, in our terms, depend upon whether A were a persuasible or an unpersuasible individual.

The present view thus identifies persuasibility with agreement-seeking. The persuasible individual makes a series of explicit or implicit "comparisons" (Festinger, 1954) between his own opinions and the opinions of others, seeking to produce and maintain agreement and reduce disagreement. Thus viewed, *persuasibility is more than a conformity tendency.* It is "conformity-plus," for there are other ways to produce perceived agreement between the self and the other besides conforming to the other. For example, one may lack information about the other's opinion but imagine it to be in agreement with one's own.

This amplified conception of persuasibility leads directly to the statement of a theoretical position on the developmental antecedents of persuasibility.

Definition. The degree of persuasibility of an individual is the probability, defined on a population of possible communication situations varying in topic and communicator, that the individual will respond so as to attempt to produce agreement between himself and the communicator.

Proposition 1. The degree of persuasibility of an individual is the resultant of a series of implicit comparisons between his own opinions and the opinions of others. The outcome of each comparison may be categorized either as agreement or as disagreement.

Proposition 2. The circumstances surrounding the incidence of agreement or disagreement may be either positively reinforcing or negatively reinforcing.

Proposition 3. Positively reinforced instances of agreement or negatively reinforced instances of disagreement tend to increase persuasibility; positively reinforced instances of disagreement or negatively reinforced instances of agreement tend to decrease persuasibility.

This set of statements constitutes the general theory. Persuasibility is conceptualized probabilistically in order to introduce a continuum of variation rather than a simple trait dichotomy. This definition is consistent with our behavioral methods of obtaining persuasibility scores (see Chapters 1 and 7).

We assume that to produce persuasibility in an individual, a tendency to seek agreement or disagreement with others must be learned. Propositions 2 and 3 specify the conditions for the differential strengthening of either the one tendency or the other. The propositions, to be useful, require that positively reinforcing circumstances be reliably distinguished from negatively reinforcing ones. Although this may be impossible of perfect achievement in nomothetic analysis of complex interpersonal situations, it is still possible to realize useful generalizations.

Development of Persuasibility

We seek now to implement the general theory with a set of more detailed statements concerning the circumstances of parent-child interaction which produce persuasibility or unpersuasibility. The general theory postulates that positively reinforcing instances of opinion agreement or negatively reinforcing instances of opinion disagreement between parents and child tend to increase persuasibility. Accordingly, we must specify the circumstances in which *opinion agreement is at issue* between parents and child. We ignore instances wherein potential disagreement is not a likely possibility and agreement would not be psychologically salient for either child or parents, as in mutual participation in habitual commonplace activities, and examine instead those situations in which there is uncertainty as to whether agreement or disagreement will be the outcome. Two broad categories of such situations may be distinguished: control situations and acceptance situations.

Control situations are typified by the initiation by one or both parents of a demand upon the child requiring that he do something different from what he would have done had the demand not been made. A potential change in the status quo is implied. Consider the alternatives available to the child in this situation: he may either do or attempt not to do what is demanded. Similarly, and more germane to the analysis of "opinions," he may either *agree* (internally) that the demand is right, reasonable, and proper, or he may *disagree*. Although only his action is observable, our theory proceeds in terms of his belief. We assume that in normal psychological functioning under free choice, action and belief will be consistent or "consonant" (Festinger, 1957), although perhaps not without some internal struggle. Consider further what alternatives are available to the parent if the child disagrees overtly with the demand. The parent may reinstate the demand or let the child have his way and abandon the request.

Definition. The degree of firmness of parental control is the conditional probability, defined over a population of control situations, that the parent will reinstate a demand once the child has expressed disagreement with it. This definition leads us to Proposition 4a.

Proposition 4a. Low firmness of parental control operates

to decrease persuasibility. It is presumed that a child who disagrees initially with a demand does so because he finds disagreement more satisfying than agreement; lack of reinstatement of the demand will terminate the situation in a disagreement which is presumably rewarding for the child. Therefore disagreement is reinforced and the probability of disagreement in future situations will increase.

It is not so simple to derive the consequences at the other pole—high firmness of parental control—since even if we assume that very firm control produces eventual agreement through conformity, it is not clear whether such agreement will be reinforcing in the absence of knowledge of other factors. In spite of this indeterminacy for the case of firm parental control, we can nevertheless make the following gross prediction, primarily on the basis of Proposition 4a:

Proposition 4b. Firmness of parental control correlates positively with persuasibility. There is a danger that this proposition will be seen as tautological, since under a colloquial interpretation of firmness of parental control, viz. "parental behavior such that child conformity is produced," the proposition reduces to: Parental behavior producing conformity in children is associated with the possession of conforming children. However, we have defined firmness of control in a way which avoids the circularity.

Another control variable which has received considerable attention in the literature is the *amount of control,* that is, the frequency with which control attempts are initiated by the parents. In the present theory, amount of control determines the frequency of reinforcement, whether positive or negative, for the predominant outcome, either agreement or disagreement. Whatever predisposition toward persuasibility is generated by a few control attempts will be generated in greater degree by many control attempts. The variable of amount of control thus plays an interactive role.

Proposition 5. The greater the frequency of control at-

tempts by parents, the higher will be the relationship between firmness of control and persuasibility.

Returning to the second broad category of parent-child interactive situations we define *acceptance situations* as episodes in which the child initiates a suggestion or request that the parent do something other than what would have been done had the suggestion not been made. Again a potential change in the status quo is implied. The parent's choice is either to agree or to disagree with the suggestion. If the parent initially agrees with the child's suggestion, such agreement is presumably positively reinforcing.

Definition. The degree of acceptance of the child by the parent is the probability, defined over a population of acceptance situations, that the parent will agree to a request initiated by the child, provided that the child's request is not one that challenges prior control attempts.

Proposition 6a. Parental acceptance operates to increase persuasibility. This proposition suggests the correlational proposition:

Proposition 6b. Parental acceptance correlates positively with child persuasibility.

To clarify the relative status of Propositions 4 and 6, the definitions of acceptance and control situations should be interpreted as follows: Acceptance situations involve requests by the child which do not challenge prior controls (if they do, the situation becomes a control situation). Control situations involve demands by the parents which do not countermand prior acceptances (otherwise the situation becomes an acceptance situation).

Thus far the theory deals only with the parent-child unit and does not explicitly extend to cases of interaction of the child with siblings, peers, or other adults. The question of the generality of persuasibility tendencies toward other figures than the parents is the complicated question of communicator-freeness of persuasibility. A careful theoretical analysis based upon Propositions 1 through 3 and principles of stimulus and response generalization has not yet been performed. Nevertheless, the following proposition is offered as a probable finding of such an analysis.

Proposition 7. In young children, persuasibility tendencies toward the parents generalize widely to other communicators; the older the child, however, the greater the differentiation between communicators.

Research Evidence

Persuasibility as agreement-seeking. In support of our contention that persuasibility should be conceptualized as agreement-seeking in general rather than solely as a conformity tendency, we present the details of a study on first-grade children. Two classes—47 children in all—from a public school in New Haven were the subjects of the experiment.

A female experimenter saw each child individually two days after the preliminary administration of the Mother Persuasibility measure (see pp. 150–1). The subject was presented with the Persuasibility Booklet (p. 150) containing 19 picture pairs (see Appendix B) and asked to circle in red the one in each pair that he liked better. When all the pages had been marked, he was asked to go through the booklet again and indicate which picture on each page he thought the experimenter preferred. The Attribution of Agreement score was the number of picture pairs for which there was agreement between the child's choice and his guess of the experimenter's preference.

Product-moment correlation coefficients between the Attribution of Agreement score and the Mother Persuasibility score were .60 in one class (22 subjects) and .84 in the other class (25 subjects). These extremely high values approach the magnitude of the reliabilities of the measures. This is especially noteworthy in view of the disparate form and content of the two measures. On the Mother Persuasibility measure, the child is essentially being asked, "Would you agree with Mother?" On the Attribution of Agreement measure, the child is asked, "Will I [the experimenter] agree with you?" The persuasible child projects agreement into this ambiguous guessing situation; the unpersuasible child, disagreement. This supports the view that the motive of the persuasible child is not so much to be persuaded as it is to see that agreement is produced.

Further evidence may be found in Cattell's (1957, p. 245) factor analysis studies. One of his many personality factors, labeled "comention," is very much akin to persuasibility. From an inspection of the tests with high loadings on this factor, one may infer that persuasible individuals tend to have better recall for paired opinion statements which agree with one another, while unpersuasible individuals tend to have better recall for paired opinion statements which disagree with one another.

Experimental effect of reinforcement on persuasibility. One of our studies, intended primarily for another purpose (see pp. 191–2), provides some incidental support for Proposition 3. One portion of that proposition states that positively reinforced instances of opinion agreement tend to increase persuasibility, while positively reinforced instances of opinion disagreement tend to decrease persuasibility. In this particular study, the child's experience of agreement or disagreement with an adult (the experimenter) was experimentally manipulated during a relaxed, gamelike individual session immediately preceding attempts at persuasion by the adult.

The *agreement condition* was established by having the child express his own preferences for members of seven picture pairs (not those in Appendix B), following which the experimenter expressed agreement with a prearranged six of the seven choices. The contrary *disagreement condition* saw the experimenter disagree with a prearranged six choices of the child's initial seven. The experimenter's manner in both conditions was attentive, reassuring, and friendly. The intention was to achieve a mild degree of positive reinforcement for the condition at hand. This could not be done by explicit rewards to the child, since it was the experimenter's behavior and not the child's which brought about the agreement or disagreement.

Both conditions were followed by a standard administration of the Experimenter Persuasibility measure (p. 150). First the experimenter expressed a choice on each picture pair, and then the child was asked to give his choice. (The first 14 pairs of the measure in Appendix B, p. 306, were used.)

Two groups of subjects were used. One group of 24, 12 for each condition, was drawn from a first-grade class in New Haven. A replication group of 32, with 16 for each condition, came from a public summer school class in a suburban community outside New York City. The children in this group had just completed, or were about to enter, first grade. The groups contained an equal number of boys and girls.

The difference between the mean Experimenter Persuasibility scores in agreement and disagreement conditions is significant at well beyond the .001 level in both replications. The details are presented in Table 32 (p. 193), which also presents a cross break of the experimental groups on a personality variable.

In interpreting this result, it must be noted that the experimental manipulation did not involve the reinforcement of a conformity or a nonconformity response; what was reinforced was the state of agreement or disagreement between experimenter and child (or, more technically, the internal responses of the child concurrent with the state of agreement or disagreement). The result thus supports Proposition 3 and also the conception of persuasibility as agreement-seeking.

Parental control. For information relevant to the relationship between parental control and child persuasibility, we turn first to the literature on parental practices and attitudes. The literature is difficult to integrate because of the wide variety of parental and child variables involved and the diversity of measurements employed. There is a tendency for variables to be defined colloquially rather than operationally and to pertain to gross, manifest, observable behavior. Almost no objective studies are concerned with the tendency to adopt the communicated opinions of others or to seek opinion agreement with others. Therefore, we must rely on studies of child variables labeled "imitation," "submission," "obedience," "nonrivalrousness," "cooperation," "nonaggressiveness," and "compliance," in the hope that consistency can be observed and that the results are pertinent to persuasibility. The generic term "conformity" will be used to refer to the set of terms just mentioned.

In reviewing the literature, we must keep in mind the distinction (pp. 170–1) between firmness of parental control when it is attempted and the frequency with which control is exercised. We must also be alert to the possibility that the relationships between the two aspects of parental control and child conformity may well change drastically as the child reaches adolescence, and change differentially for boys and for girls.

At the nursery and early grade-school level, firm parental control has been found associated with child conformity and weak control with nonconformity (Meyers, 1944; Roberts, 1934; Symonds, 1939). There is suggestive evidence (Baldwin, 1948, 1949; Radke, 1946) that when control is firm and frequent, child conformity is even greater; however, when weak control is frequent, conformity tendencies are low (Bishop, 1951). Probably frequency of control interacts with firmness of control in determining the conformity of the preadolescent child, as suggested by Proposition 5. However, the story may be different for adolescents and postadolescents. Frequency of parental control has been found strongly associated with political rebellion (Maccoby, Matthews, and Morton, 1954) and with low persuasibility in high school boys (Chapter 10). Firmness of control is not dealt with in these studies.

The above citations of measurements of child conformity should not be taken to imply that conformity was always measured in the same way or that these measurements were all germane to persuasibility. We have tried to integrate parental control variables into our own studies to overcome the ambiguities that arise in attempting to reinterpret previous work. There is difficulty, however, in obtaining a useful measure of firmness of control directly from the parents themselves. On questionnaires, there is very little spread of answers to the question (with suitable wording), "If your child is disobedient, are you firm?" Virtually all parents report that they are indeed quite firm. In an open-ended interview situation with the interviewer free to probe, the parent is usually not able to describe the firmness of his or her *own* behavior, falling back instead on a description of the way in which the child responds to attempts at control. Firmness of control then becomes circularly defined. Faced with these difficulties, we have measured firmness of control by questions put to the child. Direct observations of parent-child interactions would, of course, have been superior, but were not feasible.

The measure of firmness of parental control was designed to accord with our definition of firmness as the conditional probability, over a population of control situations, that the

parent will reinstate a demand when the child has expressed
disagreement with it. Six incomplete stories [1] were read to the
subject, describing a situation in which a parent had stated a
demand and the child had demurred. The subject was then
asked, in effect, "What did the parent do then? Did he repeat
the demand or did he not?" If the subject gave the former
response, he was then asked, in effect, "What did the child do
then? Did he still refuse, or did he do what was demanded of
him?" If the subject gave the former response, the experimenter then asked what the parent did. As with the Incomplete Stories measure of Mother Persuasibility (pp. 150–1),
the assumption is made that the child's responses are representative of actual parental behavior.

In all, there were four possible outcomes to each story. The
Firmness of Control scoring scheme follows the simple rule:
if the parent gives up at any point in the sequence, score 0;
if the parent never gives up, score 1.

The Firmness of Control measure was administered in
individual session to 83 first-grade children in four classes
from New Haven schools after the Experimenter Persuasibility measure (see p. 150) had been administered. Two
experimenters were used, one male and one female, each for

1. The following is a representative Firmness of Control story:
One day, Willie and his father were listening to Willie's favorite program
on the radio when the telephone rang. Willie's father got up to answer the
telephone and told Willie to turn the radio off so he could hear the person
on the telephone. But Willie didn't pay any attention and went right on listening to the radio.
What do you think Willie's father did? Did he say, "Willie, turn the radio
off so I can hear the person on the telephone," or did he just stick his finger
in his ear and try real hard to hear what the person was saying?
[If "Willie, turn the radio off":]
Well, what do you think Willie did then? Did he finally turn the radio
off, or did he pay no attention to what his father said?
[If he paid no attention:]
Well, what happened now? Did Willie's father stop asking him to turn
the radio off, or did he say, "Willie, if you don't turn that radio off this
minute, I'll . . ."

two classes. The male experimenter, in the Firmness of Control measure, used "Father" as the parental figure while the female experimenter used "Mother."

Table 26 presents the product-moment correlations between the Firmness of Parental Control measure and the Experimenter Persuasibility measure. Correlations are given class by class, separately for boys and for girls. Over-all correlations are computed by pooling within-class sums of squares and cross-products, in accordance with the procedure followed in Chapter 7.

TABLE 26. *Correlations between Experimenter Persuasibility and Firmness of Parental Control*

Class	N	Correlation
13 Boys	9	.58
Girls	13	.24
14 Boys	9	.11
Girls	10	—.19
15 Boys	12	.42
Girls	11	.44
16 Boys	7	.80
Girls	12	—.44
Over-all		
Boys	37	.38 *
Girls	46	—.01
p value for significance of sex difference		ns

* Significant at the 5% level.

It is seen that Proposition 4b, predicting a positive correlation between firmness of parental control and persuasibility, is supported for boys, but not for girls. The question of sex differences, pervasive in our results, is discussed in Chapter 9, pp. 204ff.

Granting the inconclusive nature of research to date and the desirability of further persuasibility studies in which firmness of control is measured by observations of interactions between parent and child instead of by children's reports, we nevertheless find in present and past research some concurrence for Propositions 4b and 5.

Parental acceptance. One of the studies most directly relevant to the relationship between acceptance and persuasibility is that of Ausubel et al. (1954). These authors found that fourth- and fifth-grade children who perceived themselves as rejected by their parents tended to perceive themselves in more disagreement with a variety of parental opinions than did other children. Payne and Mussen (1956) found that boys who perceive their fathers as warm and approving tended to respond similarly to the way their fathers did on behavioral inventory scales. Ausubel gave the following rationale for this kind of result: "By parental acceptance children are provided with intrinsic feelings of security and adequacy. . . . They accordingly become disposed to accept parental values implicitly and unconditionally out of loyalty to the individuals to whom they owe their status and self-esteem" (1955, p. 380).

Bishop (1951), in direct observation of mother-child interactions, found that maternal "nonacceptance" of the child correlated positively with the frequency of "aggressive refusals" by the child. Bishop emphasized the circular causation involved in maternal nonacceptance of a noncooperative child. Lesser (1952) found inventory scores of maternal rejection or neglect of boys aged 10 to 13 markedly related to overt aggression in these boys, as judged by their classmates. Other authors (Hattwick, 1936; Meyers, 1944; Newell, 1936) have found an association between parental rejection and child nonconformity or disobedience, using a variety of measures.

In all the studies cited, the direction of the relationship is

the same, namely that parental acceptance is positively correlated with child conformity. No empirical study known to
the authors yields the opposite relationship. The doubt at-
taching to this body of evidence in the present context is
whether such measures of child behavior as noncompliance,
"aggressive refusal," and the like are entirely relevant to
persuasibility as here defined.

The results of our own study on the relationship between
parental acceptance and child persuasibility showed a positive relationship, as predicted by Proposition 6b. The subjects were 59 boys and 67 girls from five first-grade classes in
schools in Uniondale, N.Y., and New Haven. Each child
was given the Teacher Persuasibility measure (see p. 150).
Then a female experimenter administered the Mother Persuasibility (see pp. 150–1) and Favorable Image of Mother
measures in individual sessions.

The Favorable Image measure attempts to assess the child's
perception of the mother as accepting, rewarding, and approving or as rejecting, punishing, and disapproving. The
measure is composed of 16 incomplete stories, each describing
a child seeking the approval or support of his mother or
coming into casual contact with her during some activity.
After each story was read, the child completed it in his own
words. Two categories of completion were distinguished:
those in which the subject attributed approval or support to
the mother, and those in which the subject attributed rejection, disapproval, or avoidance to the mother. One of the
stories was: "Johnny was playing with his toys. He was having
lots of fun building bridges and houses. Johnny's mother
came into the room to see Johnny. And then what happened?"

Two warm-up stories were read and completed for the subject in order to suggest the two alternative types of com-
pletions. The Favorable Image score was the number of sup-

porting or approving responses (e.g. "Johnny's mother said, 'That's a nice bridge, Johnny.'") attributed to the mother.

Table 27 presents the product-moment correlations between the two Persuasibility scores and the Favorable Image

TABLE 27. *Correlations between Favorable Image of Mother Score and Persuasibility Scores*

Class	N	Teacher Persuasibility	Mother Persuasibility
1 Boys	13	.74	.79
Girls	9	.30	.70
2 Boys	15	.30	.01
Girls	10	.27	.48
3 Boys	7	.55	.84
Girls	17	.63	.60
6 Boys	10	.64	.71
Girls	17	.37	.31
7 Boys	14	.44	.52
Girls	14	.11	—.19
Over-all			
Boys	59	.47 *	.56 *
Girls	67	.37 *	.38 *
p value for significance of sex difference	ns		ns

* Significant at the 1% level.

of Mother score. The over-all correlations between Teacher Persuasibility and Favorable Image and between Mother Persuasibility and Favorable Image are significant at the .01 level for both sexes. There is a tendency—nonsignificant—toward higher correlation of Favorable Image with Mother Persuasibility than with Teacher Persuasibility. One would expect such a tendency.

The evidence from this study is consistent with the prior literature and solidifies the conclusion that parental acceptance is positively related to persuasibility.

Persuasibility to nonparental figures. Thus far we have dealt only with factors in parent-child interaction which pre-dispose the child toward persuasibility to parents. Proposi-tion 7 claims that persuasibility to parents generalizes widely to other communicators. The evidence assembled in Chapter 7 indicates that persuasibility in first-grade children may be regarded as communicator-free to a considerable extent, so long as the range of communicators is confined to certain adult figures (parents, teachers, experimenters). We now ask what happens if the range of communicators is extended to include peers, and address ourselves to two questions: the relationship between persuasibility to adults and persuasi-bility to peers, and the change, if any, in this relationship with age.

The experimental subjects in one run were 72 boys at-tending summer play session at a school in East Williston, New York. Four age levels were studied: 7, 9, 11, and 13 years. In a replication, 25 experimental subjects aged 7 or 11 were drawn from an elementary school for gifted children in New York City. All experimental subjects were given the Recorded Opinions measure (see p. 151), which yields an Adult Per-suasibility score and a Peer Persuasibility score. Control sub-jects were asked the opinion questions, but did not hear the persuasive tape recordings. There were 31 seven-year-old and 24 eleven-year-old control subjects in all.

Before proceeding to the question of the intercorrelation of the Peer and Adult Persuasibility scores at the different age levels, we shall examine whether the recorded opinions were effective in persuasion. Table 28 compares the experimental and control groups at the two age levels, 7 and 11, for which control data were available. For both ages, for both replica-tions, for both Peer and Adult Persuasibility scores, the mean differences between experimental and control groups are in the expected direction. Statistical significance is achieved uniformly in the original run but not in the replication. Difference between experimental and control groups indicates that exposure to the recordings increases the likelihood of concurrence with the recorded majority opinions. This is a group

TABLE 28. *Mean Persuasibility Scores for Recorded Opinions Measure*

ORIGINAL EXPERIMENT Class	Age	Treatment	N	Peer Persuasibility	S.D.	t	p	Adult Persuasibility	S.D.	t	p
17	7	Experimental	18	5.17	1.74	4.20	<.01	4.77	1.51	2.82	<.01
21	7	Control	18	3.00	1.18			3.56	.88		
19	11	Experimental	18	5.06	1.03	2.12	<.05	4.67	1.45	3.29	<.01
22	11	Control	12	4.18	1.14			3.00	1.08		
REPLICATION											
23	7	Experimental	13	5.54	1.98	1.52	ns	6.15	2.03	0.76	ns
25	7	Control	13	4.46	1.45			5.46	2.44		
24	11	Experimental	12	6.75	1.74	1.81	ns	5.08	1.12	0.35	ns
26	11	Control	12	5.42	1.71			4.83	2.08		

result, however, which still leaves room for individual differences within the experimental group. In particular, we expect that some individuals (the unpersuasible ones) are *less* prone to acceptance after exposure.

Table 29 gives the correlations between the Peer and Adult

TABLE 29. *Correlations for Boys of Peer Persuasibility with Adult Persuasibility and Social Isolation*

ORIGINAL EXPERIMENT Class	Age	N	Adult Persuasibility	Social Isolation
17	7	18	.42	.48 *
18	9	18	.54 *	.62 †
19	11	18	.16	.17
20	13	18	—.18	.05
REPLICATION				
23	7	13	.40	.31
24	11	12	—.47	—.33

* Significant at the 5% level.
† Significant at the 1% level.

Persuasibility scores for each of the four age groups in the original run and the two age groups in the replication. On the original run, one notes a tendency for the correlations to decrease with increasing age. The "linear trend comparison" of the z-transformed correlation coefficient [2] is in fact significant at the 5 per cent level; that is, the tendency for the coefficients to decrease with age is not reasonably attributable to sampling fluctuations in the correlations. Conceivably the trend might be attributable to the poorer reliability of the measures for the older groups (Table 20). However, an age trend significant at the 5 per cent level is also manifested in the replication, which is not subject to variable reliabilities.

The results indicate that for boys in early grade school the communicator-freeness of persuasibility may obtain to the same extent between an adult and a peer communicator as between one adult communicator and another. The correlations of .40 and .54 that we find here between Adult Persuasibility and Peer Persuasibility for the 7- and 9-year-old boys are of the same order of magnitude as the correlations among Mother, Teacher, and Experimenter Persuasibility for the 6- and 7-year-old boys in other studies (Chapter 7). However, the falling away of the positive relationship between Peer and Adult Persuasibility for the 11- and 13-year-old groups suggests that there is some age at which children begin to differentiate the peer group from adults as a significant anchoring point for opinions. One speculates that 9 to 11 is the age range in which children begin to consider seriously the possibility

2. Fisher's z-transformation applied to correlation coefficients on N cases yields approximately a normally distributed statistic with variance $1/(N-3)$. If several z are available (in the present case, there is one z for each age group), the weighted linear combination $\sum w_i z_i \Big/ \sqrt{\sum \dfrac{w_i^2}{N_i - 3}}$ is distributed as a critical ratio under the null hypothesis of equal z_i and provided $\Sigma w_i = 0$. Weights sensitive to testing trend are such that they themselves reflect a trend (Abelson and Morrisett, 1959). For the present case, weights (-3, -1, 1, 3) were applied to the four age groups, yielding a critical ratio of 2.02.

that the general peer group can be an authoritative source of beliefs differentiated from the parents. This is consistent with Criswell's (1937, 1939) sociometric findings, among others. She found in her study that 9 to 11 was the age range of first occurrence of sociometric group cleavages along racial lines, presumably supported by normative peer group beliefs.

CHAPTER 9

Personality Correlates
of Persuasibility in Children

GERALD S. LESSER AND ROBERT P. ABELSON

A THEORY of the developmental conditions which influence the learning of persuasibility or unpersuasibility has been presented in Chapter 8. This developmental theory implies a variety of relationships between persuasibility and other personality characteristics of children. These relationships and the empirical evidence bearing upon them are discussed in the present chapter.

The personality variables investigated were self-esteem, overt aggressiveness, social isolation, and interpersonal attractiveness. In addition, we considered the relationship between persuasibility and intelligence and the question of sex differences.

Self-Esteem and Persuasibility

We have presented evidence above (pp. 173–4) to support the contention that the motive of the persuasible child is to seek agreement with others and to avoid disagreement. We now consider personality variables which operate to accentuate the motive to seek agreement and to avoid disagreement. One such personality variable is self-esteem, which has been found to be related to persuasibility among adults and young adults (Chapters 3, 4, and 5). In this chapter we shall examine evidence to see whether the same relationship holds among young children.

It is proposed that a child with low self-esteem has had a history of particularly negatively reinforcing circumstances accompanying disagreement (and also, perhaps, positively reinforcing circumstances following agreement). It appears likely that the most common developmental antecedents to feelings of low self-esteem are negatively reinforced, recurrent invidious comparisons between the self and some "other." As noted in Proposition 3 (p. 169), conditions of negatively reinforced disagreement tend to increase persuasibility.

Thus, we assume that low self-esteem and high persuasibility are produced by recurrent, negatively reinforced "disagreements" (presentations of discrepancy) between the self and some actual person, a class of actual persons, or some hypothetical standard. The agent which forces such comparisons on young children may be one or both parents, siblings, or, possibly, actual competitive experience. Discrepancy alone is not necessarily an invidious state of affairs; continual experiences of opinion disagreement may sometimes produce a stable and positively reinforcing psychological state. But where the opinions and acts of the self are made to seem not only different from, but also not as worthy as, the opinions and acts of the other, then we assume that the experience is negatively reinforcing and that the individual will attempt to compensate for the feeling of inferiority so created. Compensation may take the form of a continuing attempt to be the same as or similar to other people or to hold opinions which are in agreement with the opinions of others.

Janis has argued in a similar vein: "Excessive compliance might therefore be a compensatory mechanism which leads to chameleon-like changes in response to any new source of persuasive influence. Thus, the compliance manifested by people with low self-esteem might be a defensive form of behavior that permits the individual to agree with everyone in an attempt to guarantee that nobody will be displeased by him" (1954, pp. 515–16).

Proposition 8. Self-esteem correlates negatively with persuasibility. Much evidence for this relationship exists in the literature. Janis (1954, 1955, Chapter 3), using adolescent and adult subjects, thrice found low self-esteem associated with high persuasibility. "Low self-esteem" refers to "feelings of shyness, personal inadequacy, and social inhibitions in coping with everyday situations" (Hovland, Janis, and Kelley, 1953, p. 187). Crutchfield (1955) described the adults who conform highly in his group-pressure situation as lacking in "ego strength." Cattell (1957, p. 245), in factor analyses on adult populations, found tests of "ego weakness" to have positive loading on a personality factor which closely resembles persuasibility. Hovland, Janis, and Kelley (1953, p. 190) review additional studies which are consistent with the proposition that, in adults, low self-esteem is associated with high persuasibility. There has been little documentation of this relationship in children aside from McKinnon's (1942) early contention that conforming children are especially lacking in self-confidence.

We have performed a series of studies to test Proposition 8 in children. The variable of self-esteem was measured through sociometric self-ratings and relational analyses (Lindzey and Borgatta, 1954).

Each child in the class was photographed, and the pictures were mounted on a large card in such a way that the experimenter could change the position of the pictures at will. The subject was treated individually by the experimenter and was asked first to name each child depicted. When a subject did not know the name of a classmate, he was helped by the experimenter to recall it.

The first measure of self-esteem (SE1) was derived by asking each child to compare himself with the other children in the class for certain favorable but ambiguous characteristics. For example, each subject was asked to "show me some of the children in your class that you think are nicer than you are." The experimenter asked the child to make a judgment of "nicer" or "not nicer" for every child in the class. Five such items were employed: "nicer," "better helper," "smarter," "more polite," and "plays nicer." The subject's SE1 score was the total number of children that he did not judge as superior to himself on these particular characteristics.

The second self-esteem measure (SE2) was obtained by asking the subject which children liked him or would, if allowed, choose to sit next to him. The experimenter asked the subject to make a judgment of "likes me" or "does not like me" for each child in the class. The subject's SE2 score was the total number of children that "like" him and "would like to sit next to" him.

The third self-esteem measure (SE3) was the discrepancy between the subject's self-estimate (SE2) and a measure of his actual sociometric position. In deriving the Social Isolation measure (see below), a measure of each child's popularity was obtained. To compute the SE3 score, each subject's ranked position on the popularity measure was subtracted from his ranked position on the SE2 score. Thus, a child who reported that everyone in his class "liked" him but who was actually "liked" by none of his classmates would obtain the highest rank-discrepancy self-esteem score (SE3), whereas a child who reported that none of his classmates "liked" him but who was actually "liked" by all the children would obtain the lowest rank-discrepancy self-esteem score.

Table 30 presents the product-moment correlation co-efficients between the Teacher Persuasibility measure (see p. 150) and the three self-esteem measures for the boys of six first-grade classes and the girls of five first-grade classes. Although the correlations are all in the predicted direction,

TABLE 30. *Correlations between Teacher Persuasibility and Self-Esteem Scores*

Class	N	SE_1	SE_2	SE_3
7 Boys	13	—.38	—.21	—.14
Girls	11	—.08	.27	.31
8 Boys	15	.20	—.23	—.70
Girls	10	.03	—.43	—.37
9 Boys	15	—.17	—.31	—.54
Girls	13	na	na	na
10 Boys	12	.16	—.19	—.27
Girls	15	—.22	—.49	—.44
11 Boys	13	—.08	.15	.36
Girls	10	—.08	.01	.51
12 Boys	13	—.18	—.07	—.34
Girls	11	—.21	.06	.28
Over-all				
Boys	81	—.01	—.18	—.29 *
Girls	57	—.09	—.23	—.10
p value for significance of sex difference		ns	ns	ns

* Significant at the 5% level.

only the correlation for boys between Teacher Persuasibility and SE_3 is statistically significant.

In a second study, also investigating self-esteem and persuasibility, a female experimenter attempted to induce temporary persuasibility or unpersuasibility tendencies in children encountered for the first time in individual experimental session. Children high and low in self-esteem (selected through a combined measure based upon SE1 and SE2) had been randomly assigned in equal numbers to the two experimental groups. The experimenter first elicited initial preferences from the children with a modified Persuasibility Booklet. With one group of subjects, she agreed with a preponderance of their choices; with the second group, she disagreed. Next, the experimenter attempted to influence each child's selections in 14 new pairs of pictured objects. An Experimenter Persuasibility score, ranging from 0 through 14, represents the frequency of successful persuasion by the experimenter.

Experimenter Persuasibility scores are arrayed in a 2 by 2 factorial design, children of high and low self-esteem encountering an agreeing or disagreeing experimenter. Subjects numbered 24 in the original experiment and 32 in the replication.

Table 31 indicates that, in both the original experiment and the replication, children low in self-esteem are more persuasible in this situation than children high in self-esteem.

TABLE 31. *Mean Experimenter Persuasibility Scores for Experimental Groups*

| | ORIGINAL EXPERIMENT $(N = 24)$ | | REPLICATION $(N = 32)$ | |
	Agreement	Disagreement	Agreement	Disagreement
High self-esteem	8.00	5.33	8.00	4.50
Low self-esteem	12.83	5.50	12.00	5.50

Note: Equal numbers of boys and girls were included in each cell. Sex differences did not appear in the results; the sex variable is omitted for compactness of presentation.

The F obtained for the self-esteem effect is significant beyond the .05 level in both the original experiment and the replication, as indicated in Table 32.

However, a qualifying condition is apparent in the significant interaction effect in the analysis of variance, indicating that the position taken by the communicator (i.e. preliminary agreement or disagreement with the subject) makes a greater

TABLE 32. *Analysis of Variance of Experimenter Persuasibility Scores*

ORIGINAL EXPERIMENT ($N = 24$)

Source	df	Mean square	F
Agreement-disagreement	1	150.00	28.96 †
Self-esteem	1	37.50	7.24 *
Agreement-disagreement X self-esteem	1	32.58	6.29 *
Residual	20	5.18	

REPLICATION ($N = 32$)

Agreement-disagreement	1	200.00	34.54 †
Self-esteem	1	50.00	8.64 †
Agreement-disagreement X self-esteem	1	18.00	3.11 *
Residual	28	5.79	

* Significant at the 5% level.
† Significant at the 1% level.

difference for children of low self-esteem than for those of high self-esteem. When the experimenter disagrees with his initial choices, a child with low self-esteem is subsequently no more persuaded than is a child with high self-esteem. When the experimeter agrees with his initial choices, however, a child of low self-esteem is subsequently much more persuaded than is a child of high self-esteem. Apparently a child with low self-esteem reacts sensitively to the approval he seeks. Thus, low self-esteem appears to predispose the child toward high persuasibility, provided that the communicator indicates to him that agreement between them is a likely state of affairs.

Overt Aggressiveness and Persuasibility

The prediction of a relationship between overt aggressiveness and persuasibility is derived by extending Propositions 4b (Firmness of parental control correlates positively with child persuasibility) and 6b (Parental acceptance correlates positively with child persuasibility). We have already presented some evidence (pp. 176–80) that low firmness of parental control is associated with low persuasibility. There is also much support (Baldwin, 1948; Hollenberg and Sperry, 1951; Meyers, 1944; Radke, 1946; Symonds, 1939) for a relationship between high aggressiveness and parental variables which closely resemble low firmness of control. Thus, one theoretical basis for predicting an association between high overt aggressiveness and low persuasibility is that these variables are both associated with the developmental variable contained in Proposition 4b, i.e. low firmness of parental control.

In Chapter 8 (see pp. 180–2) evidence is presented, in support of Proposition 6b, that rejection is associated with low persuasibility. Many studies offer substantiation of the relationship between rejection and high overt aggressiveness. Radke (1946) has summarized the early evidence for the relationship, and other studies (Bishop, 1951; Lesser, 1952; Meyers, 1944; Wittenborn, 1956) have added confirmation to this result. Thus, the second theoretical basis for predicting an association between high overt aggressiveness and low persuasibility is that these variables are both associated with the developmental condition stipulated in Proposition 6b, i.e. parental rejection.

Thus, following the evidence that both high overt aggressiveness and low persuasibility are produced by conditions of low firmness of parental control and/or parental rejection, we state:

Proposition 9. Overt aggressiveness correlates negatively with persuasibility. Overt aggressiveness is found consistently to be negatively related to persuasibility in adult subjects. Janis (1954) found this relationship and considerable additional evidence exists (Hovland, Janis, and Kelley, 1953, pp. 192–5; and above, pp. 128–32). Our studies examine the relationship with children as subjects, especially important in this instance because the prediction is based upon developmental propositions.

The overt aggressiveness of first-grade children was measured through another variation of sociometric procedures. A "Guess Who" method was adapted, again using photographs of the children. Each child, tested individually, was asked the following warm-up question in order to acquaint him with the nature of the task: "There is a child in the class who is taller than most of the other children. Show me the tallest child in the class." The subject was encouraged to offer at least two names.

The subject was then asked the 16 "Guess Who" questions, which describe various forms of aggressive behavior. For example, an item depicting verbal aggressiveness was: "Show me some children who say mean things to other children." Items involved uncontrolled or explosive forms of aggressiveness, unprovoked physical aggressiveness, provoked physical aggressiveness, verbal aggressiveness, and indirect or covert aggressiveness. The subject's total aggressiveness score was the sum of the number of mentions he received from his classmates on the 16 aggressiveness items. In addition, 4 submissiveness items were included, and a separate overt submissiveness score was calculated for each subject. The reliabilities and validity of this technique are described elsewhere (Lesser, 1952, 1957).

Table 33 gives the product-moment correlations between the Teacher Persuasibility measure and the measures of aggressiveness and submissiveness for boys and girls in six first-grade classes. For boys, support is indicated for the predicted negative relationship between persuasibility and aggressive-

TABLE 33. *Correlations of Teacher Persuasibility with Other Variables*

Class	N	Aggressiveness	Submissiveness	Popularity	Unpopularity	Social Isolation
6 Boys	10	—.36	.25			
Girls	17	—.39	.11			
7 Boys	13			—.23	.11	.41
Girls	11			—.10	—.06	.16
8 Boys	15	—.48	.54	.03	—.61	.42
Girls	10	—.13	.23	.20	—.17	.02
9 Boys	15	—.37	.37	—.06	—.32	.49
Girls	13	.00	—.01	—.46	—.16	.26
10 Boys	12	—.43	.29	.00	—.58	.69
Girls	15	—.23	—.07	—.01	—.09	.07
11 Boys	13	—.14	.18	—.23	.00	.43
Girls	10	.02	.07	—.25	.03	.36
12 Boys	13	—.26	.46	.44	—.40	.14
Girls	11	.42	—.23	—.22	.49	—.07
Over-all						
Boys	78	—.36 *	.33 *			
Girls	76	—.22	—.01			
Boys	81			—.02	—.28 †	.43 *
Girls	70			—.11	—.03	.09
p value for significance of sex difference		ns	<.05	ns	ns	<.05

* Significant at the 1% level.
† Significant at the 5% level.

ness and for the corollary relationship between persuasibility and submissiveness. For girls, no consistency is apparent in these results.

To control for the possible artifact of the differential frequency with which children's names are mentioned, regardless of the content of the sociometric question, a "Prominence" score was derived from spontaneous answers to the experimenter's request to "name some children in your class." Correlations between persuasibility and aggressiveness or submissiveness are negligibly (no more than .03 correlation points) altered when Prominence is partialled out.

Up to this point our analysis has considered manifest aggressiveness. Since resistance to persuasion involves the ability to express disagreement, over and beyond the need to disagree, one wonders whether the relationship would still exist were "need for aggression'" substituted for manifest aggressiveness. Conceivably, high persuasibles might have as strong a need to disagree as low persuasibles, but could not countenance overt expressions of disagreement as readily. Crutchfield (1955), for example, observed that high conformers are unable to "tolerate their own impulses." Differential willingness to express aggression, then, would tend to inflate the association between high aggressiveness and low persuasibility.

A preliminary investigation of this qualification has been carried out by obtaining a measure of need for aggression from the fantasy productions of first-grade children. An adaptation of the standard TAT procedure (Murray, 1943) was used; a complete description of the stimulus pictures and scoring system is presented elsewhere (Lesser, 1957). The product-moment correlation between the Mother Persuasibility measure and need for aggression for 14 first-grade boys was —.58. Despite the extremely small sample employed, the correlation is significantly different from zero (p < .05). Thus, not only is manifest aggressiveness negatively related to persuasibility in boys, but preliminary evidence suggests that a measure of need to express aggression is also significantly negatively related to persuasibility in boys.

Social Isolation and Persuasibility

In Chapter 8 we presented evidence for the view that agreement-seeking is a crucial acquired motive in the highly persuasible child. We now propose that the condition of social isolation from the peer group tends to accentuate the agreement-seeking process, and that this variable will therefore be positively related to persuasibility. By a "socially isolated child" we mean one who is ignored by the peer group, being neither actively accepted nor actively rejected.

We assume that the child who has been socially isolated learns to anticipate, perhaps without awareness of this expectation, that a possible reward for agreement with the members of the group will be a degree of establishment or integration within the group. If membership in the group is to some extent valued by the child, this condition of anticipated reward for agreement should be associated with high persuasibility in the child.

Proposition 10. Social isolation correlates positively with persuasibility. Newcomb presents (1950) a similar position, stating that one would expect that a person who fails to become closely affiliated with primary and secondary groups in the community would have relatively "unanchored" attitudes and hence would be indiscriminately amenable to sources of pressure. Dittes and Kelley (1956, p. 100) state, "Assuming valuation constant, information communicated from fellow members that a person is little accepted by them increases his sense of insecurity, activating various acquired motives (to avoid criticism, etc.) to which conformity behavior has been learned."

However, Hovland, Janis, and Kelley (1953, pp. 195–6) review evidence for adult subjects indicating that high "social withdrawal" is associated with low persuasibility. They conclude that there is systematic information that adults who display withdrawal tendencies are less likely to be influenced by persuasive communications.

An extension of the typical sociometric procedure was employed to measure the variable of social isolation. The assumption underlying the measure of social isolation is that a child who is mentioned neither favorably nor unfavorably by his classmates is a socially isolated individual.

Each child was shown the class photographs described earlier and asked to name (1) the children he would like to have for his best friends, (2) the children he would if allowed, select to sit next to in class, (3) the children he wished were not in the class at all, and (4) the children he would prefer not to sit next to in class. The sum of mentions the subject received from his classmates on the four items was computed. This scale was then inverted to yield a social isolation score. Thus, a child receiving no popularity and no unpopularity nominations was scored as most socially isolated, whereas the child mentioned most often on both popularity and unpopularity items was scored as least socially isolated.

Table 33 presents the Pearson product-moment correlations between the Teacher Persuasibility measure and the measures of popularity, unpopularity, and social isolation for the boys and girls of six first-grade classes. For boys, a significant positive correlation exists between Teacher Persuasibility and social isolation. No significant relationships are found for girls.

The social isolation measure is composed of both popularity and unpopularity items. For boys, there is a small but statistically significant negative correlation between Teacher Persuasibility and unpopularity. Thus, according to this result, highly persuasible boys are less unpopular than boys of low persuasibility. However, the insignificant correlations between Teacher Persuasibility and popularity do not provide evidence that highly persuasible children are more popular than relatively unpersuasible children. Rather, the popularity score serves as a "suppressor variable" in contributing to the social isolation-persuasibility relationship. The significant over-all correlation between Teacher Persuasibility and social isolation suggests that boys who are usually uninvolved in the group by virtue of being neither popular nor unpopular tend to be more highly persuasible.

Thus, it appears that a boy who is, voluntarily or involuntarily, detached from classroom group affiliations is more persuasible to, at least, teacher communications. As noted earlier, Hovland, Janis, and Kelley (1953) have reviewed the documentation for the opposite direction of relationship for adults. If both the findings of the present study and the studies with adults prove to be replicable, we might infer a developmental change in the nature of this relationship. We speculate that, longitudinally, if conditions of social isolation persist throughout childhood and into adulthood, the social isolate who originally displays persuasible behavior may later manifest greater and greater resistance to the communications of others. We have found indirect support for the longitudinal trend by examing the relationship between persuasibility and social isolation for a series of cross-sectional samples of boys.

In conjunction with the studies reported in Chapter 8 (see pp. 183–6), the correlations (Table 29) between the Recorded Opinions measure of Peer Persuasibility and the measure of social isolation for four age groups, 7, 9, 11, and 13, provide additional evidence of the positive relationship between these measures for boys in the younger age groups. The "linear trend comparison" of these correlation coefficients, transformed by Fisher's z, is significant at the .05 level (one-tail test). Although the correlations are not negative for the older age groups, a decreasing positive relationship with age between persuasibility and social isolation is suggested.

The number of subjects available for the replication of this study was too small to produce clear results, but the findings of the replication, shown in Table 29, are in the direction of a positive relationship between persuasibility and social isolation in young children and a decrease in this relationship with age.

An important qualification for the conclusion that persuasibility and social isolation are positively related in young children is that, if the child places no value upon group membership and group approval, our theory is inapplicable. In fact, Hovland, Janis, and Kelley have proposed a negative relationship between persuasibility and social isolation by including in the definition of social isolation "generalized attitudes of indifference toward others" (1953, p. 195). It is perhaps a difference in this variable of group valuation which produces the differential results for different age groups. It is reasonable to suppose that most children ignored by their peers in early experience initially place high valuation upon entry into the group, but if they remain isolated, they come in time to lower their valuation of the group, with an attendant change in persuasibility. This is a promising avenue for further investigation.

Friendship Selection and Persuasibility

The conceptualization of persuasibility as agreement-seeking also leads to a prediction concerning the relationship between persuasibility and friendship selection among children. A highly persuasible child seeking opinion agreement is more likely to find agreement positively reinforced and disagreement negatively reinforced in the presence of another highly persuasible child with a reciprocal need. Conversely, a highly unpersuasible child seeking opinion disagreement is more likely to find disagreement positively reinforced and agreement negatively reinforced in the presence of another highly unpersuasible child with a reciprocal need. These statements are consonant with Propositions 3 and 7. Thus, the opportunities for the appropriate "reciprocal rewards" (Newcomb, 1956) for agreement or disagreement are maximized when two highly persuasible (or two highly unpersuasible) children interact.

Proposition 11. Persuasibility of children correlates positively with the persuasibility of their friends. In measuring social isolation sociometrically, information was obtained concerning each child's friendship choices and rejections. The mean Teacher Persuasibility scores of each child's friends and of those children toward whom he was unfriendly were correlated with the child's own Teacher Persuasibility score. These correlations were computed for the boys and girls of six first-grade classes and are presented in Table 34.

Because of constraints on each set of scores, there is a bias in the correlations tending to make them negative. If each child in a class of size n were to pick k friends (or enemies) at random, the expected correlation between "own score" and "average of friends' scores" would be $-\sqrt{\dfrac{k}{(n-1)(n-k)}}$. Computed in this manner, the average bias introduced in each class is approximately $-.25$. This substantial bias makes significant positive correlations even more convincing, but makes it difficult to assign meaning to the negative correlations.

The data reported in Table 34 suggest that first-grade boys tend to select friends who are co-oriented with regard to their degree of persuasibility. The results for the samples of boys support Proposition 11. For the samples of girls, no support for this proposition is evident.

Additional evidence for boys concerning the relationship between persuasibility and friendship choices is derived from the study (see pp. 183–6) in which the Recorded Opinions measure of Peer Persuasibility was obtained. The boys were

TABLE 34. *Correlations of Teacher Persuasibility with Mean Teacher Persuasibility of Friends and of Disliked Children*

Class	N	Friends	N *	Disliked children
7 Boys	13	+.18	10	—.39
Girls	11	—.80	5	+.51
8 Boys	15	+.55	13	—.64
Girls	9	—.44	9	—.63
9 Boys	13	+.48	13	—.40
Girls	13	+.14	10	—.47
10 Boys	11	+.19	9	—.55
Girls	15	—.62	9	+.44
11 Boys	12	—.16	11	—.37
Girls	10	—.48	7	—.12
12 Boys	12	+.08	12	—.20
Girls	10	—.58	5	—.35
Over-all				
Boys	76	+.30 †	68	—.47
Girls	68	—.42	45	—.15
p value for significance of sex difference		<.01		ns

* Loss of cases is due to unwillingness of some children to select children they dislike.
† Significant at the 5% level.

asked to select the children they liked and those they disliked. The mean Peer Persuasibility scores of each child's friends and of those children toward whom he was unfriendly were correlated with the child's own Peer Persuasibility score. These correlations are presented in Table 35.

For the two youngest age groups (Classes 17 and 23), the combined correlation coefficient between Peer Persuasibility and mean Peer Persuasibility of friends was $+.44$ ($p < .05$), and the combined correlation coefficient between Peer Persuasi-

TABLE 35. *Correlations for Boys of Peer Persuasibility with Mean Peer Persuasibilities of Friends and of Disliked Children*

ORIGINAL EXPERIMENT

Class	Age	N	Friends	N *	Disliked children
17	7	18	+.37	10	—.66
18	9	18	+.08	11	—.12
19	11	18	—.12	11	—.16
20	13	18	+.17	10	+.08

REPLICATION

23	7	13	+.53	12	—.54
24	11	12	—.14	11	+.34

* Loss of cases is due to unwillingness of some children to select children they dislike.

bility and mean Peer Persuasibility of disliked children was —.60. Despite the small samples, these results suggest confirmation of the relationship for young boys in Table 34. No consistency is apparent in the results for older groups.

Sex Differences and Persuasibility

The relationships between persuasibility and developmental and personality variables are almost invariably stronger in the predicted direction for boys than for girls. Of ten pairs of correlations between persuasibility measures and developmental or personality measures, nine are greater for boys in the predicted direction, and in three cases the difference is statistically significant.

This result of stronger relationships for boys between persuasibility and other variables is in accord with other studies of persuasibility. Studies by Janis and Field (Chapter 3), King (Chapter 10), Macfarlane, Allen, and Honzik (1954), and Beloff (1958) indicate that relationships between persuasibility and personality variables are almost uniformly stronger in male samples than in female samples.

These authors account for differential results in terms of the powerful social influence of sex role typing. King, for example, hypothesizes that in adolescent girls the sex role requires a high degree of persuasibility as part of a generally docile, dependent orientation toward others. Individual differences in persuasibility among girls are said to stem from differences in the pressures toward the social role and the degree of acceptance of the role, rather than from personality differences. For adolescent boys, there is no unambiguous role requirement as far as general persuasibility is concerned. King's sample of adolescent boys possesses high peer persuasibility, low parent persuasibility, and moderate teacher persuasibility. In the absence of a general role requirement for boys, one might expect that personality variables would be more clearly related to persuasibility.

Sex differences in our studies of first-rate children may also be related to differences in sex role training, operative by age six or earlier, but such a conclusion is highly tentative. In our data, there are sex differences not only in the correlations of personality variables with persuasibility, but also in the correlations of the personality variables with each other. The correlations among measures of self-esteem, aggressiveness, submissiveness, social isolation, and intelligence are presented in Table 36. They indicate that these personality measures may possess very different psychological meanings for boys and for girls.

The Teacher Persuasibility measure has been extensively applied in these studies in assessing the relationships between persuasibility and personality variables. Some evidence

(Tables 22 and 23) suggests that this particular measure of persuasibility is more valid for boys than for girls. However, other validation information concerning the Teacher Persuasibility measure (Table 25) indicates no difference. Nor is

TABLE 36. *Over-All Correlations among Personality Variables for Boys and Girls* *

	Rank-Discrepancy Self-Esteem	Aggressiveness	Submissiveness	Social Isolation	IQ
Rank-Discrepancy Self-Esteem		.37	—.62 †	.37 ‡	—.37
Aggressiveness	.40		—.34	—.31 †	—.16
Submissiveness	—.29 †	—.23		—.59 ‡	.36
Social Isolation	—.32 ‡	—.62 †	.20 ‡		.27
IQ	—.37	—.22	.17	.01	

* Correlations for boys ($N = 67$) are below the diagonal; correlations for girls ($N = 49$), above the diagonal.
† Sex differences are significant at the 5% level.
‡ Sex differences are significant at the 1% level.

there good evidence that the persuasibility measures are more reliable for boys than for girls. If anything, the reverse is true.

The sex difference in strength of relationships between personality variables and persuasibility remains essentially unexplained. It appears likely that a separate theoretical formulation is needed to understand persuasibility differences in girls; the theoretical framework provided here has had utility only for boys. This situation represents an important challenge to future theory and research.

Relationships between Susceptibility to Opinion Change and Child-Rearing Practices

BERT T. KING

THE PRESENT STUDY provides further information concerning the generality of persuasibility as inferred from consistency of individual differences in the tendency to exhibit changes of opinion in the direction of communications indicating the position of a group majority on a wide variety of issues. In the studies of Janis and Field, Linton and Graham, and Janis and Rife which are reported in Chapters 2, 3, 4, and 6, the communications used were complete with arguments, appeals, and conclusions. The method utilized in the latter studies is the method of systematic variation that was discussed in Chapter 1. In the present study the method of "exclusion" is employed, in which arguments and appeals are eliminated and a communication on a particular topic is restricted to the mere opinion position of the source. Under

This study represents part of the material from a dissertation submitted to Yale University in partial fulfillment of the requirements for the degree of Doctor of Philosophy.

these conditions, generality of content is achieved by employing a large variety of topics, a procedure much more feasible here than with full-fledged communications. The device of attributing opinions to different sources by previously marking one of the multiple-choice answer categories for each opinion item on a questionnaire was used in earlier studies by Arnett, Davidson, and Lewis (1931), Marple (1933), Kulp (1934), Burtt and Falkenberg (1941), and Hovland and Pritzker (1957).

The results of the present study also provide additional data on the problems raised in Chapters 7, 8, and 9 by Abelson and Lesser concerning relationships between parental control and persuasibility. Earlier observations supporting the hypothesis that susceptibility to opinion change is a function of attempts at domination are provided by clinical studies (cf. Anna Freud's concept, 1946, of "identification with the aggressor") and by anecdotal reports that concentration camp prisoners identified with their highly dominating and punitive guards to the extent of finally accepting some of the latter's values which had been strongly rejected at the outset (Bettelheim, 1943). In addition, studies which involved observations and behavioral ratings of parent-child interaction provide evidence of submissive behavior in the children of dominating parents (Baldwin, 1949; Mueller, 1945). Finally, Hoffman (1953) reported that subjects whose Thematic Apperception Test stories involved parental domination themes showed greater changes in their estimates of line distances after exposure to information on group norms than did other subjects. The present study was designed so that the degree of susceptibility to majority influence in the area of opinion could be studied as a function of the child-rearing practices to which subjects reported having been exposed.

Further data are also provided on the topic of sex differences in persuasibility which was discussed in Chapter 3 by Janis and Field and by Abelson and Lesser in Chapter 9. In addition to the direct effects of this variable, it seems likely that sex differences may interact with certain home background variables in determining the subject's degree of susceptibility to communications. Parental domination, for example, might differ in its effects on males and females in view of their different constitutions and social roles. It might be predicted that parental domination of girls would produce a submissive child susceptible to mass communications, whereas parental domination of boys would produce a personality resistant to persuasion and social influence. Such a notion suggests the importance of studying not only parental domination but also the subjects' reaction to such domination.

Method

The over-all design of the experiment adheres to the model designated by Hovland, Janis, and Kelley (1953) as the "controlled exposure design." Opinion measures were obtained before and after communications were administered to the experimental groups (N = 254). A control group (N = 44) was treated in the same way except that no communications were given. In addition to opinion items, items designed to measure personality and home background variables were included in the questionnaires. A more comprehensive description of the design follows.

The "Before" questionnaire. The subjects indicated their opinions on 45 opinion items by checking one of the seven answer categories ("Agree strongly" through "Disagree strongly") for each item. The opinion items were heterogenous and covered the areas of political issues, aesthetic preferences, economic policies, academic affairs, scientific progress, and parent-child relationships.[1] At this time the

1. These opinion items as well as items on subjects' home backgrounds are listed in King (1955).

Bell Adjustment Inventory (1934) was also administered to the subjects.

The "After" questionnaire. Twenty-one days after the Before test, the After test was administered. Besides the same opinion items that were used in the Before test, the After questionnaire included a section consisting of questions concerning the subjects' home life and their attitudes toward their parents.

The experimental treatment. The communications were part of the After questionnaire, and consisted of a check mark placed next to one of the seven answer categories for each opinion item, accompanied by a label identifying the source (parents, teachers, and peers) whose opinion the given check mark represented. The check mark for each item was placed in the same position for all the experimental groups, whereas the label varied for each group.

On all the opinion items in the analysis the check mark was placed at an extreme of the answer scale (i.e. either "Agree strongly" or "Disagree strongly"). The communication was placed at the "Agree strongly" position if the median original opinion of the group had been on the "Agree" side of the scale. In order to prevent arousing the subjects' suspicions, seven opinion items were checked at points other than the extremes. These seven items were not used in the analysis, leaving 38 items for the measurement of opinion change. The order in which the three sources were combined with the opinion items was varied systematically so as to balance source across items.

Written explanations of the labels and check marks were provided in the questionnaire administered to the experimental subjects. The explanation was as follows for the parent source: "One of the answers for each of the following questions has an X beside it and in the margin the words 'Parents' Opinion' and an arrow pointing to the X. In each case this shows the answer that was checked by the majority of a group of about *400 parents of high school students.*" The same explanation was provided for the Teacher and Student communications except that the suitable substitutions were made for each.

Personality and home background variables. The Bell Adjustment Inventory was administered immediately after the Before questionnaire. In addition, a number of specially selected questions bearing on the subjects' perceptions of their parents' behavior and attitudes were answered by all groups immediately after the After questionnaire. These additional home items were selected or adapted from several published lists of inventories (Anderson, 1940; Hayward, 1935; Myers, 1935). Thirty-five items from the Bell scale and 34 supplementary items pertaining to parental behavior were given to six judges who were instructed to select from them three non-overlapping sets of items: (1) a set measuring "parental domination"; (2) a set measuring "parental rejection"; and (3) a set measuring "parental aggression."

1. *Parental Domination scale.* Ten items were categorized as measuring parental domination, each of them by four or more of the judges. An internal consistency analysis of the ten items revealed that each was significantly consistent with the total score for all ten (no correction was made for the self-correlation involved), which was arrived at by scoring each item 0 or 1. The split-half reliability (corrected for length) of the resulting scale is .74. For subsequent analyses, the distribution of Parental Domination scores was divided into low (0–3 dominating responses) and high (4–10 dominating responses) domination categories.

2. *Parental Aggression scale.* The judges agreed in selecting nine items tapping parental aggression toward the child. These items made reference to parental scolding, criticism, and punishment of the child. A total score for the nine items

was derived by dichotomizing responses and scoring each item
0 or 1. The resulting scale has a reliability coefficient of .66
as estimated from Kuder-Richardson (1937) formula 20.

3. *Parental Rejection scale.* Seven items were agreed upon
by the raters as measuring parental rejection. The manifest content of these items involves parental lack of interest
and attention and the child's feeling of a lack, or deficiency,
of parental love. Each item was scored 0 or 1, and the total
score yielded a reliability coefficient of .72 as estimated from
Kuder-Richardson formula 20.

Subjects. The subjects were 298 students in the senior high
school in a medium-sized Connecticut town. They are presumed to be a representative sample of the student body in
the school since they were drawn from English classes, which
all students attend. For analyses of home background variables, only the 229 subjects who were currently living with
both parents were used.

Results

Effect of the communications. For each subject the difference between his Before and After responses to a given item
was his change score for that item. Changes in the direction
of the communication are designated positive changes; those
in the opposite direction, negative changes. The possible
range of change is from +6 steps to —6 steps on each item.
For example, a subject who changes his opinion from answer
7 to 2 on an item whose communication is at answer 1 is
scored +5.

A subject's total Opinion Change score consisted of the al-
gebraic sum of his changes on the 38 opinion items. The resulting mean total Opinion Change score was 37.5 for the
experimental group and 4.4 for the control group. The difference of 33.1 units is statistically reliable at less than the
.001 level (t = 9.14 with 296 df) and indicates that the ex-

perimental procedures were effective in changing opinions in the predicted direction.

Consistency of susceptibility to majority communication. The 38 items were divided into odd and even halves in order to derive a measure of the consistency of the item changes for a given individual. The resulting split-half reliability (corrected for length) was found to be .67, which is significant at well beyond the .01 level. Thus the data support the hypothesis of a trait of susceptibility to majority opinion communications.

Refinement of the Opinion Change score. The Change scores were analyzed item by item with respect to two criteria: (1) internal consistency and (2) size of experimental effect (that is, the experimental mean change minus the control mean change). Application of these criteria resulted in selecting 20 from the original 38 items. Each of the 20 items yielded an experimental effect significant at the .01 level or better, and each was significantly consistent with the original total Change score. The 20-item scale yielded a split-half reliability coefficient of .70 (corrected for length). While this scale is not appreciably more reliable than the original scale, the fact that it approximates the same reliability with about half the original number of items indicates a considerable gain in homogeneity as a result of the item analysis. It is accordingly used in the subsequent analyses and is referred to as the "Susceptibility to Majority Opinion" scale.[2]

Sex and susceptibility. A sizable difference was found between the mean Susceptibility scores of boys and girls. Table 37 shows that the difference of 5.2 steps between the boys' and girls' mean Susceptibility scores is reliable at better than

2. Methodological checks indicate that initial position (distance from the stand advocated by the communications) of the subject does not account for any large part of the variance in the Change scores and also that initial distance is not related to any of the sorting variables used in this study.

the .01 level.[3] These data support the hypothesis of greater susceptibility to majority communications among girls than among boys. Consequently, in making further analyses of relationships between susceptibility and personality variables, sex was used as a sorting variable.

TABLE 37. *Relationship between Sex and Opinion Change*

	EXPERIMENTAL GROUP	
	Boys ($N = 118$)	*Girls* ($N = 136$)
Mean score *	17.8	23.0
t		2.81
p		$<.01$

* Score of 20-item Susceptibility to Majority Opinion scale.

Opinion change in relation to parental aggression and parental rejection. Analyses made separately for boys and for girls revealed that neither the Parental Aggression score nor the Parental Rejection score was significantly related to degree of opinion change. Item-by-item analyses of each of the scales also failed to reveal any consistent relationships with degree of opinion change (although several of the individual items yielded interesting findings which are covered below).

In order to evaluate the relevance of general home back-ground factors, the Bell Home Adjustment scale was also analyzed in relation to degree of opinion change for boys and for girls. These data provide no evidence of a significant relationship between Home Adjustment scores and opinion change. Thus, it is apparent that susceptibility to opinion change is not related to general home adjustment, nor to perception of parental aggression or parental rejection, insofar as these variables are measured by the present scales.

Susceptibility and parental domination. Table 38 shows the relationship between Susceptibility to Majority Opinion

3. This and all subsequent p values are two-tail.

and reports of parental domination.[4] It is apparent that there is not a simple relationship, but an interaction of parental domination, susceptibility, and sex. For the boys in the experimental group, perception of parental domination is not related to susceptibility. For girls in the experimental group, however, high Parental Domination scores are associated with

TABLE 38. *Relationship between Parental Domination and Opinion Change*

	PROPORTION OF EXPERIMENTAL GROUP WITH LARGE OPINION CHANGES *		
	High † parental domination	*Low † parental domination*	*p ‡ for low vs. high comparison*
Boys	.43 (N = 30)	.43 (N = 58)	
Girls	.79 (N = 42)	.48 (N = 56)	<.01
Both sexes	.64 (N = 72)	.46 (N = 114)	<.02

* Changes of 21 or more steps on the 20-item Susceptibility scale; the cutting point near the median makes all control subjects' scores come below it.

† Low scores defined as 0–3 dominating responses; high scores as 4–10 dominating responses.

‡ Two-tailed p values.

a significantly greater degree of susceptibility: 79 per cent of the "high domination" girls, compared with 48 per cent of the "low domination" girls, earned high Susceptibility scores (p < .01). The second-order difference between the zero difference for the boys and the 31 per cent difference for the girls is significant (p < .05), indicating a significant interaction of the sex, parental domination, and susceptibility variables.

Inspection of the third row of Table 38 reveals that, when the experimental boys and girls are pooled, a significant dif-

4. In Table 38 and in subsequent analyses a cutting point near the median Susceptibility score was used. This gives zero as the proportion showing "large" changes in the control group. Of the 192 experimental subjects who were living with both parents 186 have Parental Domination scores (the other six subjects omitted responses to one or more of the domination items).

ference (p < .02) is found between the high and low domination subgroups. As can be seen from the breakdown by sex, however, this difference is entirely attributable to the "effect" within the female group. That is, all the "effect" occurs within the female group.

In addition to using the total Parental Domination scale score, each item in the scale was individually analyzed using dichotomized Susceptibility scores as the criterion. For the girls, those giving the high domination response had higher rates of opinion change than the other girls on nine of the ten items. Four of these differences were significant at the .05 level. For boys, those giving the high domination response had a higher rate of opinion change on only six of the ten items, and none of the differences reached the .05 level of significance. Thus, it is apparent that, for the Parental Domination scale taken as a whole, there is a relationship between high parental domination and high susceptibility to opinion change for girls but not for boys.

For the two following items, however, there is a sizable positive relationship between opinion change and domination for boys as well as for girls: (1) "My father expects me to obey him without questioning why" and (2) "My mother expects me to obey her without questioning why." For these two items the subjects were dichotomized into high obedience ("Agree" and "Undecided") and low obedience ("Disagree") groups. For the first item (father) 70 per cent of the high obedience girls and 50 per cent of the low obedience girls had high opinion changes (p value of .04); 46 per cent of the high obedience boys and 33 per cent of the low obedience boys had large opinion changes (p = .14). For the second item (mother) large opinion changes were shown by 75 per cent of the high obedience and 50 per cent of the low obedience girls (p value of .01) and by 48 per cent of the high obedience compared with 30 per cent of the low obedience boys (p =

.12). It will be noticed that, although the *direction* of the relationship is the same for both boys and girls, the relationship is statistically significant only for girls. However, the fact that for boys the relationship is consistent for both items makes the finding somewhat more impressive than the individual significance levels might indicate and suggests that for boys as well as girls there may be a positive relationship between susceptibility to opinion change and parental demands for obedience.

While no over-all or consistent relationship was found between opinion change and the Parental Aggression scale or items, an interesting result was furnished by the item: "Did your parents frequently punish you when you were between 10 and 15 years of age?" Seventy-six per cent of those who answered "Yes" (N = 29) and 49 per cent of those who answered "No" (N = 152) had high opinion changes. (Eleven of the 192 experimental subjects living with both parents did not answer this item.) The 27 per cent difference is statistically significant at the .02 level. This association between frequent parental punishment and high opinion change was also found when males and females were examined separately (although the latter results were not as significant as the data for the combined group).

Rebelliousness and susceptibility. A single questionnaire item measuring feelings of rebelliousness toward parents was available: "I feel rebellious around my family: Very often; Often; Occasionally; Seldom or never." Seventy-one per cent of the subjects responded "Seldom or never," which was coded as the low rebellion response; the other three responses to the item were pooled into the high rebellion category. Then, for experimental subjects sorted simultaneously on sex and parental domination, comparisons were made between the percentages of low and high rebellion subgroups who showed large Susceptibility scores. A significant difference in susceptibility was found only among high domination boys. Here 67 per cent of those in the low rebellion category ($N = 15$) and 17 per cent of those in the high rebellion category ($N = 12$) earned large Susceptibility scores. (Three of the 30 high domination boys did not answer this item.) The 50 per cent difference is significant at the .01 level, and indicates that, for boys who report high parental domination, susceptibility to majority communications is a function of the degree of rebelliousness experienced.

Discussion

These results demonstrate, first of all, the feasibility of the use of the present check-mark technique of changing opinions in the study of personality and other variables related to susceptibility to communications of majority opinion. Since this technique demonstrably taps consistent individual differences and easily covers a wide range of opinion content, its use should lead to results that can be generalized beyond one, two, or a few opinion topics, unlike most studies of propaganda and opinion change. It will be noted that the technique could be used to investigate many of the variables which have been studied by using actual persuasive communications replete with data, arguments, and appeals relevant to a single issue. For example, this technique could be used to study "credibility" of the communication source, fear-arousing appeals, group membership factors and resistance to change, retention of opinion changes, and personality factors related to opinion changes. In passing, it should also be noted that the technique is admirably suited to large-scale survey investigations of the relationship of demographic variables to susceptibility to opinion change.

In making comparisons between the present measures of susceptibility to communications of majority opinion and other measures of social influencibility, it is interesting to note that several of the present findings are paralleled by analogous results in the other areas mentioned. First, the present finding that females are more susceptible to communications of majority opinion corresponds to findings by conventional suggestibility tests that females are more suggestible than males (Coffin, 1941; Grimes, 1948).

A second instance of congruence between the present findings and those of investigators who used a different measure of social responsiveness is the relationship between parental domination and responsiveness to majority influence on perceptions. Hoffman (1953) found that subjects who showed the largest changes in their line judgments after exposure to group norms had larger frequencies of parental domination themes in their Thematic Apperception stories.

In addition, it should be noted that there is considerable correspondence between these findings and those of investigations of the authoritarian personality. Authoritarian individuals have been described as coming from homes characterized by relatively harsh and threatening discipline in which interpersonal relationships were based on clearly defined roles of dominance and submission. As a result, these individuals tend to develop submission to parental authority and conformity to conventional values (Adorno et al., 1950, pp. 384 ff.). Systematic exploration of this relationship will be found in the study by Linton and Graham reported in Chapter 4.

Taken altogether, the similarity of these findings from the areas of classical suggestion tests, majority influence on perception, the authoritarian personality, and communications of majority opinion suggests that factor analysis would, indeed, yield evidence of common elements.

Quite unclear from the data available at present is the reason for the correlation between parental domination and opinion change in the case of girls and the lack of it for boys. One might hypothesize that dominated girls become more socially submissive or more emotionally unstable than nondominated girls. Either generalized social submissiveness or emotional instability could then account for the enhanced susceptibility to opinion change of the dominated girls. To check on these possibilities, supplementary analyses were conducted using the Bell Social Adjustment Scale as a measure of social aggressiveness-submissiveness and the Bell Emotional Adjustment Scale as a measure of emotional instability. These analyses indicated that neither social submissiveness nor emotional instability account for the demonstrated relationship between parental domination and opinion change in girls.

Consideration of feelings of rebelliousness gives rise to another possible explanation of the interaction. Responses to the rebelliousness item cited above indicate a significant tendency for high domination boys and girls to *feel* more rebellious around the home than low domination boys and girls. It is possible that the dominated boys who feel rebellious act out some of their rebelliousness while the dominated girls do not. If rejection of reasonable-appearing communications of majority opinion is considered to be a form of negativism or rebelliousness, this reasoning would lead to a prediction of lowered opinion change among dominated boys. Actually, of course, this just pushes the inquiry one step further, to the question why dominated boys would tend to act out their rebellious feelings more than would girls. Here we might speculate that girls may be subject to stronger feelings of weakness in relation to other people than boys, or that they may experience a greater need to preserve frictionless social relationships than boys. In this event, the dominated girls might be motivated to engage in less acting out of their rebellious impulses and, hence, be more susceptible to influence than the dominated boys.

It will be remembered that while the Parental Aggression

scale as a whole was not related to opinion change, one of its component items, referring to frequent punishment, was related to opinion change for both sexes. The item in question is the only one of the Aggression scale items referring to punishment per se; all the other items on the Parental Aggression scale refer to verbal scolding and criticism. This suggests that a critical element may be actual (physical?) punishment and/or deprivation of privileges. Such methods of manipulating the environment of the child may be effective in producing personalities susceptible to communication influence, whereas mere verbal scolding may not be effective in this respect. The association of frequent parental punishment with enhanced susceptibility to social influence seems relevant to the psychoanalytic notion of "identification with the aggressor" and suggests that frequently punished children may internalize some of the standards and directives of the punitive parents. Since these standards would presumably include unquestioning obedience to authority, the punished children might develop tendencies to avoid displeasing authority figures by conforming and could eventually generalize such conforming tendencies even to "sources" of the type utilized in this study, in spite of the fact that such sources have no power to reward or punish the subjects.

PART THREE

Conclusions and Integration

CHAPTER 11

Summary and Implications for Future Research

CARL I. HOVLAND AND IRVING L. JANIS

THIS VOLUME has presented a series of studies dealing with the individual trait of persuasibility and the factors which influence its occurrence. As pointed out in Chapter 1, general persuasibility is a predispositional factor reflecting an individual's susceptibility to influence from many different sources, on a wide variety of topics, and irrespective of the media employed. In its widest sense, general persuasibility should be free of influences emanating from any particular or specific aspect of the persuasion situation. The question to be answered is: To what extent is the trait of persuasibility actually found experimentally and what degree of generality does it exhibit?

Consistency of Individual Differences

The present series of studies indicates that there is such a factor as general persuasibility, although there are certain limitations to its generality imposed by the experimental procedures employed. There is evidence that persuasibility exists as a "content-free" factor; that is, it exists independently of the subject matter or appeals presented in any particular persuasive communication.

General persuasibility is demonstrated in the studies of Janis and Field which are described in Chapter 2. The procedure devised by these experimenters to assess general persuasibility consisted of (1) an Initial Questionnaire measuring opinion on 15 items, (2) a booklet (I) containing five persuasive communications on widely varying topics, each followed by three questions identical with the questions included in the Initial Questionnaire, and (3) another booklet (II) presenting a second series of five persuasive communications on exactly the same topics as the first series but taking diametrically opposite positions. After each communication in Booklet II, the subjects were asked the same opinion questions as in the Initial Questionnaire and Booklet I.

The communications were intentionally varied with respect to type of appeal and arguments. They were all attributed to an identical type of source—reporters writing on "Opinions in the News." The existence of widespread diversity of opinion on the topics was stressed for the subjects, and they were encouraged to express their own views. A general Persuasibility score was assigned to each subject on the basis of his opinion changes in response to both booklets. In order for an opinion change to be counted as such, the subject who had changed his Initial opinion in one direction in response to the communication in Booklet I must change following the Booklet II communication all the way back to his original position or beyond on the provided scale.

The results from this procedure showed consistent individual differences in persuasibility, some subjects shifting first in one and then in the other direction following receipt of the conflicting communications in Booklets I and II. A factor analysis was computed from the intercorrelations between persuasibility subscores on each communication. The results support the hypothesis of a general factor in persuasibility and indicate that the predisposition to change opinions is not wholly specific to the topic or subject matter of the communications.

An investigation of the consistency of individual differences in susceptibility to persuasion by majority opinion was reported by King in Chapter 10. His procedure for measuring persuasibility used first a Before questionnaire consisting of 45 opinion items on which subjects checked their scale position from "Agree strongly" to "Disagree strongly." The After questionnaire was identical to the Before questionnaire except that, as a persuasive "communication," each item was checked at a prearranged scale position by the experimenter. The check marks were attributed to one of three sources: a majority of 400 parents of high school students, a majority of 400 high school teachers, and a majority of 400 high school students.

Results from this procedure provide evidence of consistent susceptibility to majority communications over different sources and different content areas. This was demonstrated by the significantly high positive correlation between opinion changes on odd and even items for each subject (split-half reliability score).

A different type of measure of persuasibility was employed by Abelson and Lesser, using first-grade children for subjects (cf. Chapter 7). Defining persuasibility as the tendency to seek a state of agreement on matters of opinion, these authors devised three tests of general persuasibility:

1. The Persuasibility Booklet, consisting of pairs of unfamiliar objects, was administered either in group form by the teacher (Teacher Persuasibility measure) or in individual session by the experimenter (Experimenter Persuasibility measure). The communicator showed each pair of pictures to the subjects, first indicating her own preference for one of

the objects and then asking the subjects to state their preferences.

2. The Incomplete Stories test was administered individually by the experimenter. Each story described a situation involving a mother (or father) and child, in which the parent figure stated a novel opinion, fact, or bit of advice. The subject was asked to tell what the child in the story would think or do in response.

3. The Recorded Opinions measure, also administered in individual session, was represented as an opinion poll. Unusual opinion questions were posed to the subjects. Before giving their views, the subjects heard a tape recording on which either two adult voices (one male and one female) or peer voices expressed unanimity of opinion in favor of one choice. Subjects were then asked to state their own preferences.

Two additional measures were obtained, one a Parent Rating of the subjects on persuasibility and the other a Teacher Rating of the same trait.

The results of these procedures yielded statistically significant intercorrelations among the various measures, showing a tendency toward persuasibility, or lack of it, over various topics and in relation to various sources (parents, teachers, experimenters, peers). Significant correlations were obtained for both boys and girls between the Teacher Persuasibility measure and (1) the Teacher Ratings of persuasibility and (2) the Mother Persuasibility measure. The Parent Rating of persuasibility yielded low reliability; nevertheless, there was a significant positive correlation between Parent Ratings and the Teacher Persuasibility measure for the boys in the sample, although not for the girls.

In the Experimenter Persuasibility test subjects were presented with an actual disagreement between their preferences and those of the experimenter and then asked to give

their choices again. The results were significantly correlated
with the Mother Persuasibility test. The pupils were tested
not only immediately but also after a week's delay. At the
later session, no effort was made to reinstate the experimenter's preferences or the subject's previous choices; the
subject was simply asked to give his present preferences. The
correlations between Mother Persuasibility and Experimenter Persuasibility were almost the same for the Immediate and Delayed measures among the boys in the sample,
but among the girls there was a significantly higher correlation for the Delayed measure than for the Immediate one.

Additional data concerning the positive relationships
among various measures of persuasibility are provided in
Chapter 4, by Linton and Graham.

Personality Correlates of Persuasibility

As a further analysis of individual differences in persuasibility, the studies in this volume have attempted to determine what other personality variables are concomitant with
high and low responsiveness to verbal communications. Certain variables, such as self-esteem, hostility or aggressiveness,
and intelligence, have been investigated by several methods
and replicated in more than one study. Other personality
correlates are suggested by the evidence from single studies.

SELF-ESTEEM

Janis and Field (Chapter 3) investigated the hypothesis
that high persuasibility is related to low self-esteem. Using a
self-rating personality inventory, these authors measured
three types of inferiority feelings: feelings of inadequacy,
social inhibitions, and test anxiety. Their results showed significant correlations between high persuasibility and the
measures of inadequacy feelings and social inhibitions; the
correlation between persuasibility and test anxiety was in the

expected direction but not significant. These results were obtained from the male subjects in the sample; with the female sample the self-esteem hypothesis was not supported.

The same hypothesis was investigated by Janis and Rife (Chapter 6) with institutionalized male mental patients, employing the identical personality inventory and persuasibility measure as in the previous study. The correlation between persuasibility and the scores on feelings of inadequacy and guilt proved to be significantly higher than the correlation for the normal sample. This finding, together with the fact that personality scores of the patients showed greater variance than those of the normals, lends some weight to the authors' assumption that the personality predispositions underlying persuasibility in the population at large may be more pronounced in emotionally disturbed persons and therefore more readily observable.

In view of the importance of the self-esteem variable as a concomitant of persuasibility, Cohen (Chapter 5) performed a study analyzing some of the components of self-esteem as well as its effect on the social influence process. Self-esteem was defined in terms of the value an individual places upon himself, which is assumed to be a function of past success and failure experiences. For experimental purposes, self-esteem was measured by the correspondence or discrepancy between a subject's ideals and his achievement of them, the subjects being sorted into high and low self-esteem groups on this basis.

The effect of level of self-esteem on social influence was measured in a set of interpersonal rather than mass-media persuasion situations. Results showed persons of high self-esteem to be less susceptible to influence from persons of low self-esteem than vice versa and also to be more active in attempting to exert influence. Individuals of high self-esteem were better able in general to protect themselves against unfavorable reactions from their social group and reacted less to any specific group expectations communicated to them.

An investigation of the relation of self-esteem to persuasibility in children made by Lesser and Abelson is reported in Chapter 9. In view of their definition of persuasibility as the desire to seek agreement with others they hypothesize that low self-esteem and high persuasibility stem from the same type of previous experience, viz. negatively reinforced instances of disagreement or discrepancy. (A related view is expressed by Cohen in Chapter 5.)

In one experiment, three measures of self-esteem were taken, based on sociometric techniques: (1) Each child was asked to name those classmates he regarded as "nicer," "smarter," etc. than he. (2) Each was asked to judge which classmates liked him or would choose to sit next to him. (3) A measure was taken of the direction and extent of discrepancy between the subject's judgment on the second measure and his actual position of popularity in the class.

Correlations between the three measures of self-esteem and the Teacher Persuasibility measure were in the predicted direction. However, only the correlation between the rank-discrepancy self-esteem score (measure 3) and Teacher Persuasibility was statistically significant, and that only for the boys in the sample.

A second experiment related subjects high and low in self-esteem, divided on the basis of measures 1 and 2 above, to an Experimenter Persuasibility measure. The latter was based on a test in which the experimenter stated her preferences for certain objects after the subject had stated his. The experimenter contradicted the majority of the choices of some subjects; with others the experimenter agreed. The child was then asked to state his preferences for new objects after hearing the experimenter's preferences. Results from this experiment showed that children below the median in self-esteem were significantly more persuasible than those above the median. A qualifying condition was evident from the interaction effect with the variable of preliminary agreement or disagreement between the subject's choices and those of the experimenter. Low self-esteem children were more persuasible than high self-esteem children when the experimenter had agreed with their choices; under conditions of previous disagreement, however, those low in self-esteem were not significantly more persuasible than the highs. The authors interpret these results in terms of the sensitivity of the low self-esteem child to both approval and rebuff.

HOSTILITY AND AGGRESSIVENESS

The hypothesis that hostile personalities tend to be relatively less persuasible than nonhostile ones was tested by Janis and Field (Chapter 3). Three measures of aggressiveness were taken from the self-rating questionnaire: items relating to hyperaggressiveness, argumentativeness, and suspiciousness. A fourth measure was based on a projective Judgment of Motives test, in which the subject could attribute hostile motives or motives of manipulative intent to persons in ambiguous situations.

Results showed no significant correlations between Persuasibility scores and scores on the four measures of aggressiveness for either male or female subjects. In fact, two correlations, Persuasibility with Hyperaggressiveness and with Argumentativeness, approached significance in the opposite direction for the male subjects. The authors suggest the following interpretation for this finding: Many subjects who rate themselves low on self-esteem may have a general tendency toward self-derogation and therefore also rate themselves high on aggressiveness. There was, in fact, an unexpected significant positive correlation between scores on feelings of inadequacy (low self-esteem) and argumentativeness for both males and females.

Janis and Rife (Chapter 6) studied the same relationship among male mental patients. Using the identical self-rating questionnaire measures of aggressiveness, no significant correlations with persuasibility were found. The authors suggest, however, that these self-rating items may involve a mixture of opposing personality tendencies, because many of the aggressiveness items refer to strong negative emotions that are likely to be regarded as socially undesirable. An investigation of the relation between strong negative emotions and persuasibility revealed a significant correlation: Persons who more readily admitted having unpleasant emotional reactions, such as episodes of intense anger, irritability, and worry, also proved to be more persuasible. This relationship would obscure the hypothesized negative relation between persuasibility and aggressiveness. The most crucial evidence came from clinical records bearing on the subjects' paranoid symptoms and antisocial aggressive behavior. Large and statistically significant differences were found in the incidence of antisocial behavior among high, medium, and low persuasibility groups: the antisocial patients fell predominantly in the low persuasibility category. Thus the expected inverse relationship with persuasibility emerged when aggressiveness was assessed from observations of overt behavior rather than from self-appraisals.

Further support for the hypothesized relation between aggressiveness and low persuasibility is offered by Linton and Graham (Chapter 4). They report that subjects who did not change their views in response to mass-media communications scored significantly higher on a questionnaire scale of self-assertive aggression than subjects who changed their opinions.

In investigating correlates of persuasibility among adolescents, King (Chapter 10) included a questionnaire item on feelings of rebelliousness which might be relevant to the findings on aggressiveness. King sorted his subjects by both sex and parental domination variables and then made comparisons between the percentages of the low and high rebellion subgroups who showed large Susceptibility scores. He found a significant difference only for boys who perceived a high degree of parental domination; among them, those in the low rebellion category were significantly more susceptible to persuasion than those who were highly rebellious.

Evidence concerning the relationship between aggressiveness and persuasibility in children is given by Lesser and Abelson in Chapter 9. These authors advance the theoretical proposition that aggressiveness is related to low persuasibility by virtue of their both stemming from the same antecedent factors: parental rejection and/or low firmness of parental control.

An aggressiveness score and a submissiveness score was assigned to each child on the basis of the number of times he was mentioned by his classmates on a "Guess Who" test. Children were asked to mention those classmates who say "mean things" and act aggressively, both verbally and physically, as well as those who exhibit submissive behavior. The correlation between the Teacher Persuasibility measure and the measure of aggressiveness was significantly negative for the boys in the sample, whereas the correlation between submissiveness and Teacher Persuasibility was significantly positive. Neither correlation was significant for the girls.

OTHER PERSONALITY CORRELATES

Neurotic defensiveness. The evidence from the Janis and Field study (Chapter 3) failed to support the hypothesis that neurotic defensiveness is related to low persuasibility. Two earlier studies (Janis, 1954, 1955) had yielded contradictory results with respect to this hypothesis. The present study, attempting a more precise assessment of the neurotic-defensiveness hypothesis, included self-rating measures of (1) obsessive-compulsive symptoms and (2) symptoms of acute neurotic anxiety. These measures showed no relationship to scores on the Persuasibility test.

Perceptual dependence. The relation between persuasibility and perceptual-field dependency was investigated by Linton and Graham (Chapter 4). *Field dependency,* as measured by Witkin's tilting-room–tilting-chair test, is defined as the extent to which an individual's perceptions are affected by the surrounding field. These authors found that persuasibility correlated with field dependency. The subjects whose opinions were changed by the communication were more affected by the interfering aspects of the stimulus field than nonchangers.

Authoritarianism. No over-all relationship was found between scores on the Authoritarian Personality questionnaire and persuasibility in the study by Linton and Graham (Chapter 4). They found, however, a significant correlation between persuasibility and questionnaire responses on all the subscales the authors of *The Authoritarian Personality* (Adorno et al., 1950) consider as reflecting personality patterns predisposing the individual toward authoritarianism. In contrast, the two subscales that directly reflect social attitudes (Politico-Economic Conservatism and Ethnocentrism) did not correlate with opinion change measures.

Inner- and other-directed attitudes. Persuasibility in relation to inner- or other-directed orientation, in Riesman's terms, was also investigated by Linton and Graham (Chapter 4). *Inner-direction* was defined as a value system stressing personal goals and standards as against *other-direction,* which places more emphasis on group conformity and adaptation.

The two value orientations were measured in a questionnaire presenting hypothetical dilemmas for which the subject could choose an inner-directed or an other-directed solution. A significant positive correlation was found between
degree of other-direction and degree of persuasibility, as
measured by the Opinion Change test.

Social isolation. From their work with children, Lesser and
Abelson (Chapter 9) advance the hypothesis that social isolation will correlate positively with persuasibility. They base
this expectation on the assumption that social isolation of a
child from his peers will accentuate an agreement-seeking
process, and hence lead to greater persuasibility. In their research on this problem, they measured social isolation by an
extension of the sociometric technique used to assess other
personality variables, and they assumed that a child who is
mentioned neither favorably nor unfavorably by his classmates is a socially isolated individual. Results indicated a
significant positive correlation between the Teacher Persuasibility measure and the measure of social isolation for the
boys in the sample. Among the girls, no significant relationship was found.

The results with children differ from the findings with
adults, who appear to be relatively less persuasible when socially isolated (cf. Hovland, Janis, and Kelley, 1953, pp.
195–6). Abelson and Lesser suggest that the relationship may
vary at different ages. Children ignored by their peers in
early grade school may initially place high valuation upon
entry into the group, but those who remain isolated may
come in time to lower their valuation of all groups, with an
attendant change in persuasibility.

Interpersonal attractiveness. Among the boys in their sample, Lesser and Abelson (Chapter 9) found a tendency for
children to select as their friends other children who had

similar ratings on the persuasibility dimension. Thus relatively persuasible children preferred other persuasible children, while unpersuasible ones selected friends low on the persuasibility dimension. These results found support both on the Teacher Persuasibility and Peer Persuasibility measures for boys but not for girls.

Richness of fantasy. Janis and Field (Chapter 3) postulated a relation between richness of fantasy and persuasibility on the theory that a major mediating mechanism in attitude change is the anticipation of rewards and punishments explicitly or implicitly conveyed by the communicator. Individuals with a rich fantasy life would presumably have greater facility than others in imagining these anticipated results. As a measure of richness of fantasy, eleven questionnaire items were devised concerning vividness of daydreams, ease of imagining future events, etc. Results showed a significant positive correlation between the fantasy score and persuasibility for male subjects but not for females.

The same relationship was tested on a male hospital population by Janis and Rife (Chapter 6). This study yielded a correlation approaching significance ($p = .07$), thus partially supporting the Janis and Field findings.

INTELLIGENCE

None of the studies presented has found a relationship between persuasibility and level of general intelligence either with normal subjects or with mental patients (cf. Chapters 3, 4, 6, and 9). These negative findings are consistent with the results from earlier studies of the relationship between responsiveness to persuasibility and general intelligence (Murphy, Murphy, and Newcomb, 1937, p. 930; Hovland, Janis, and Kelley, 1953, pp. 181-4). There is some reason to expect, however, that differentiated measures of

various types of intellectual ability may yield significant relationships (see the discussion of ability factors below, pp. 257–
64).

Sex Differences

Two of the three studies in this volume which used both
male and female subjects found significant differences in general persuasibility related to sex. Janis and Field (Chapter
3), working with high school students, found the mean persuasibility of female subjects to be significantly higher (at
the .01 level of confidence) than that of male subjects. King
(Chapter 10), also using high school students, found a greater
over-all susceptibility to influence on the part of girls than
of boys (difference at the .02 level of confidence).

Abelson and Lesser, on the other hand, with first-grade
children as subjects (Chapter 7), found no significant differences between boys and girls with respect to general level of
persuasibility on any of their persuasibility measures.

The fact that sex differences in degree of persuasibility do
not emerge in young children is not necessarily incompatible
with the finding that there are clear-cut differences between
older males and females. A developmental factor may account for both sets of findings: During early childhood the
social norms and verbal training which influence responsiveness to communications may be essentially the same for both
sexes; but then, at a later phase of development (perhaps
during puberty), there may be powerful social pressures, associated with sex-typing and differentiated sex roles, which
could give rise to somewhat different predispositions in
young men and women.

The relation of sex to persuasibility is most clearly evidenced in assessing personality correlates of general persuasibility. Here marked differences between male and female
subjects appear at all the age levels studied.

Janis and Field (Chapter 3) report that although there were significant relationships between personality factors and persuasibility for the males in their sample of adolescents, there were no significant relationships for the female subjects. For two personality correlates (fantasy and social inhibitions), the sizable differences between the male and female correlations approached significance. The authors suggest that if these results are supported by future research evidence, it may be necessary to postulate two classes of predispositional variables affecting persuasibility: one based on personality factors and the other on cultural sex-typing influences.

King (Chapter 10), in his study of high school adolescents, found that the relationship between parental domination and general persuasibility varied according to the sex of the subject. For boys, scores indicating perception of low or high parental domination were not related to susceptibility. For girls, however, high parental domination scores were associated with a significantly greater degree of susceptibility.

With first-grade children, Abelson and Lesser (Chapters 8 and 9) also found marked differences between boys and girls on their measures of the personality correlates of persuasibility. The correlation between the measure of firmness of parental control and the Experimenter Persuasibility measure, which is important to their developmental theory of persuasibility discussed below, was significant for the boys in their sample but nonexistent for the girls. Similarly, the correlations between the Teacher Persuasibility measure and the personality variables of self-esteem, aggressiveness, social isolation, and friendship orientation were all significant for the boys in the sample but were nonsignificant for the girls. Of ten pairs of independent correlations between persuasibility measures and developmental or personality measures, nine were greater for boys in the expected direction, and for three correlations the differences were statistically significant.

The disparity between male and female subjects in the personality correlates of persuasibility is interpreted by the authors of all three studies (Janis and Field, King, Abelson and Lesser) as indicating the influence of culturally sex-typed roles which outweigh personality differences in relation to persuasibility. It has been suggested that personality differences may serve as indicators of level of persuasibility in boys since the cultural sex role for boys is less definitive in prescribing how to react to persuasive influences. However, the culture seems to demand of girls greater acquiescence in relation to prestigeful sources of information and a pattern of frictionless social relationships, with the result that girls on the whole are more susceptible to influence regardless of their personality traits. Especially under conditions of high parental domination, girls may feel less able to act out their rebellious feelings than boys, a difference which carries over into the communication situation, where rejection of suggestions from high-prestige sources would constitute a form of rebellion (see Chapter 10).

Developmental Factors

In Chapter 8, Abelson and Lesser propose a developmental theory of persuasibility in terms of reinforcement and learning principles. Defining persuasibility as the probability of obtaining a response from the subject which will produce agreement between himself and the communicator, these authors point out that such instances of agreement or disagreement may be either positively or negatively reinforcing for the subject. As a primary antecedent to persuasibility, they postulate that positively reinforced instances of agreement or negatively reinforced instances of disagreement will tend to increase general persuasibility, whereas the reverse conditions will tend to decrease it.

In fitting these general propositions into a developmental framework, the authors first examine those parent-child interactions in which opinion agreement is at issue. These fall into two broad categories: control situations and acceptance situations. In control situations the child is required to do something he did not intend to do and, in meeting this requirement, he may either agree with the demand or disagree with it. The following relationships are postulated between degree of parental control and level of persuasibility in the child:

1. Low firmness of parental control (where firm control is defined as the reinstatement of a parental demand once the child has expressed disagreement) tends to decrease persuasibility. Firmness of control, therefore, should correlate positively with persuasibility.

2. The greater the frequency of parental control attempts, the higher the relationship between firmness of control and persuasibility.

These postulated relationships are derived from the negative or positive reinforcement which is assumed to accrue to instances of agreement or disagreement between child and parent.

In acceptance situations, the second broad category of parent-child interaction, the child initiates a request or demand on the parent. For these situations it is postulated that parental acceptance correlates positively with child persuasibility.

Research evidence is presented in support of these propositions. To substantiate the view that persuasibility may profitably be considered as agreement-seeking, Abelson and Lesser found a remarkably high correlation between scores

on the Mother Persuasibility measure and scores on an Attribution of Agreement test, in which the subjects were first
asked to indicate their own preferences and then to pick the
objects they thought the experimenter would prefer. A significant relationship was shown between the subjects' attitude of agreement toward the mother and their assumption
of agreement between themselves and the experimenter.

Research evidence also supports the proposition that previously reinforced agreement tends to produce persuasibility.
In this procedure a female experimenter varied the extent of
her agreement with the subjects' choices, following which the
subjects were tested for persuasibility. The difference between the agreement and disagreement conditions in mean
persuasibility scores was again highly significant.

Firmness of control proved a difficult variable to measure.
Parental responses to questionnaire items were not discriminating, and the authors had recourse to a Firmness of Control test administered to the children. This again made use
of incomplete stories, and the subjects were given a choice
of parental behavior sequences in situations of conflict between the wishes of parent and child. In these fixed choices
the parent either reinstated his demand or let his request
drop after disagreement from the child. Partial support for
the proposed positive correlation between firmness of parental control and persuasibility was evidenced by the correlation between scores on this test and on the Experimenter
Persuasibility measure. The correlation was significantly positive for the boys in the sample but not for the girls.

A test of the relation between parental acceptance and
persuasibility was also made. Subjects were given the Teacher
Persuasibility and Mother Persuasibility measures and also
a Favorable Image of Mother test, which consisted of another
set of incomplete stories, this time giving the child an opportunity to attribute either supporting or rejecting responses

to the mother figure. The correlations between both persuasibility measures and the Favorable Image of Mother scores were significant for both boys and girls in the sample.

The above findings provide tentative support for the theoretical assumptions put forth by Abelson and Lesser concerning the way in which individual differences in persuasibility arise from parent-child interactions.

OPPORTUNITIES FOR FURTHER RESEARCH

The present volume is no exception to the rule that research on a new set of problems typically generates more questions than it answers. Some of these were hinted at in the summaries of the individual studies; now we shall reexamine briefly several key problems, this time focusing on opportunities for obtaining additional information needed to settle some of the unsolved issues.

Consistency of Individual Differences

From our present findings on persuasibility, we have concluded that it is possible to isolate and measure one or more general predispositional factors which are not bound to content, source, medium, or situation. What additional research data would help to test the validity and degree of generality of such factors?

Considerable variation in content has been achieved in the present investigations. The type of persuasibility investigated has been shown to be free of content characteristics such as topics, appeals, types of arguments, and stylistic features. This has been done by the two methods discussed in Chapter 1, "systematic variation" and "exclusion" (see pp. 17–19).

But variation in source was probably less broadly achieved, partly because it is much more difficult to specify the range of sources necessary to achieve generality. For example, the persuasibility test developed by Janis and Field (Chapter 2) attributes the communications to unknown newspaper reporters, whose trustworthiness and credibility were intended to be quite variable. The opinion change measures showed high intercorrelations, but it is likely that many subjects regarded all the sources as highly prestigeful and that therefore they do not represent a very extensive range. The study by King used sources who were highly respected by the recipients, e.g. teachers, historians, parents. Similarly, teachers, parents, experimenters, and peers were employed as sources by Lesser and Abelson, and positive intercorrelations were obtained among them.

Perhaps it is unreasonable to expect a trait of persuasibility with such a high degree of generality that the individual would respond with agreement to any statement on any topic emanating from any source. At present, however, we can say that it has been demonstrated that there is a trait of persuasibility which has sufficient generality to be applicable to a wide range of respected and prestigeful sources.

Relatively little systematic variation in communication media has so far been achieved. Within any study, the same medium has been used for all the various communications, with the possible exception of the Linton and Graham research (Chapter 4). In the Janis and Field studies, printed communications were used throughout; this was also the case with the King study. Several different methods of measurement were employed by Abelson and Lesser, but it cannot be claimed that the medium was systematically varied and the trait of persuasibility found to be medium-free. The same remarks apply to a considerable extent to generality of situation.

Is persuasibility to mass-media communications the same as susceptibility to interpersonal influence? This question naturally arises from the foregoing discussion. The present results do not give a clear-cut answer. Some of the studies utilized communications which can be subsumed under a mass-medium rubric, such as printed articles and statements about majority opinion; others investigated persuasibility in situations of direct interpersonal communication. The study reported in Chapter 5, by Cohen, suggests that high persuasibility in a face-to-face situation is determined by some of the same personality predispositions as high persuasibility in response to mass-media communications, as reported by Janis and Field (Chapter 3) and King (Chapter 10). More directly related to the problem at hand is the study by Linton and Graham (Chapter 4). These authors compared susceptibility to influence by printed communications with persuasibility in a face-to-face situation where a confederate attempted to influence perceptual judgments of autokinetic movements. A significant degree of relationship was obtained. From the limited data available, however, the degree of relationship cannot be fixed with sufficient precision to know accurately the extent to which persuasibility in face-to-face situations can be predicted from tests of responsiveness to mass-media communications. Correlations between the persuasibility tests reported in this volume and measures of influence of the type used by Asch (1952), Crutchfield (1955), and others would be of great interest in pursuing this problem.

Another question concerning generality arises from the relatively narrow range of social, educational, and demographic composition of the samples in the various studies. By and large, the research reported in this volume comes from observations of young middle-class Americans. In most studies, educational level was held fairly constant by restricting the sample to students in the same classroom. The samples were drawn from urban educational institutions and probably involve a restricted range of social class and other social background factors. The generality of the findings

might therefore prove to be applicable only to those limited
sections of the population from which the samples were
drawn. The studies obviously need replication with samples
representing diverse nationalities, ethnic subcultural backgrounds, social classes, and other such attributes. In carrying
out such replications, the investigators will also have the
opportunity to observe the way social status and various social background factors are related to degree of persuasibility.

Sex Differences

Differences between males and females in responsiveness
to psychological stimuli continue to intrigue researchers. In
the present studies sex differences interact with the factor
of persuasibility in an interesting manner. Girls on the whole
appear more persuasible, but correlations between various
personality factors and persuasibility scores are higher in
general for boys, perhaps because there is a greater spread
of persuasibility scores among boys.

A great deal more information is required to understand
the factors responsible for the pronounced sex differences.
All the authors who compared males and females suggest
that the differences are due to cultural sex roles which require a greater degree of submissiveness on the part of girls.
But within our own society there is considerable variation
in this emphasis, particularly from one social class to another.
Here would seem to be a good opportunity to test the "sex-
role" hypothesis by investigating differences among social
classes. Moreover, the hypothesis may involve a type of phenomenon which can be best understood through investigation of other cultures. Thus, for example, research workers
using the Human Relations Area Files may be able to make
cross-cultural comparisons which would show how persua-

sibility is related to the type of role assigned to females in different cultures.

Again, cross-national and cross-cultural studies on a problem of this kind would have the desirable indirect effect of extending the scope of communication research, which, like so many phases of systematic research in social psychology, is based primarily on studies in the United States, and is often restricted further to high school and college students.

Developmental Factors

Another set of problems requiring several kinds of additional research pertains to the developmental aspects of persuasibility. Even at the purely descriptive level, we have only a fragmentary picture of how persuasibility changes with chronological age. One of the studies by Abelson and Lesser (Chapter 9) provides data suggesting that by the age of seven children have acquired a fairly marked tendency to respond consistently to social influence from adults and peers; but, as the child grows older, a process of differentiation takes place so that by the age of 13 responsiveness to communication from peers is unrelated to responsiveness to communications from adults. There are no data available at present to show whether this trend continues during the late teens or whether the highly differentiated development during the early teens is merely an age-specific characteristic of early adolescence. Nor have studies of normal adults provided any systematic data on the relationship between persuasibility and chronological age. Janis and Rife (Chapter 6) report a near-significant negative correlation between age and persuasibility for their sample of adolescents and young adults, all of whom were institutionalized because of emotional disorders. It remains to be seen whether there is a significant relationship that holds for samples of normal subjects.

In addition to the purely descriptive information necessary to fill in the gaps in our knowledge about developmental sequences, several types of comparative studies are needed for clarification of theoretical issues. Of special interest are the variations in (1) the social norms concerning independence training and (2) the modes of discipline actually used in child-rearing. Here again it should be possible to extract important information from comparative studies of different national, religious, and cultural groups. Such information might prove to be valuable for testing a number of hypotheses, such as those formulated by Abelson and Lesser (Chapter 8) concerning parent-child interactions and the "reinforcing conditions" which foster high and low persuasibility tendencies. Detailed longitudinal studies within a single subculture might also contribute to knowledge about the ways in which parent-child relationships give rise to low and high persuasibility.

Determinants of Persuasibility

Another major question which arises from the present series of studies is: How important are personality factors as sources of individual differences in persuasibility? If we attempt to answer this question from the correlational data already at hand, it must be said that personality factors appear to play only a very minor role as determinants of persuasibility. Almost all the correlations obtained so far are relatively low, and even those that are statistically significant can account for only a small proportion of the variance.

It is probably premature, however, to draw any definitive conclusions about the relative importance of personality factors. In any new field of research, we cannot hope to obtain large correlations until the crude measuring instruments used in the initial studies are gradually replaced by measures of greater precision. Low correlations, of course, do not necessarily imply a low degree of relationship, since they may reflect low reliability or low validity of the measures employed. As the measures are improved, an apparently low correlation between two variables may turn out to be quite substantial.

The tests of persuasibility used in the various studies reported in this volume have generally been found to have fairly high reliability coefficients, but some improvements in this respect can probably be brought about by using larger numbers of topics and opinion items selected according to the criterion of internal consistency. The main difficulty with the tests used so far, however, is probably in the sphere of validity. A great deal of technical research is needed to develop more valid measures. For instance, in order to improve the measures based on the method of systematic variation (see pp. 17f.), it would probably be worth while to set up a long-range panel study in which a large number of opinion changes would be investigated following exposure to hundreds of different communications transmitted by all available media by a representative sample of sources. From a factor analysis of the opinion-change scores, it should be possible to select the communications with the highest loadings so as to develop more adequate measures of persuasibility than the ones available so far. Similarly, more refined techniques of test construction might be applied to those persuasibility measures based on the method of exclusion (see pp. 18f.) to develop measuring instruments with higher potential validity.

Perhaps the validity of all the measures used so far is detrimentally affected by the fact that only *verbal reports* have been obtained. It is undoubtedly economical to restrict the measures of persuasibility to observed changes in verbalized opinions, but it might prove to be much more valid to include observations of other types of behavior, such as changes in affective responses, overt actions, and other components of "attitude change" (see Chapter 1, pp. 2–5). Attempts to improve validity by including a variety of nonverbal indicators of social influence might have the added advantage of leading to better understanding of the relationship between changes in privately expressed verbal responses and changes in overt social behavior.

It is not only the measures of persuasibility that require improvement, but also the measures of the personality correlates. Most studies so far have used questionnaires requiring the subjects to give self-ratings on rather complex personality attributes. This inexpensive way of assessing personality factors has occasionally been strikingly successful in yielding statistically significant relationships between certain personality attributes and persuasibility; but it may, nevertheless, be such a crude method that it makes for a relatively high error variance, which may markedly reduce the size of the correlations. That self-ratings may sometimes be grossly inadequate for testing such relationships is strongly suggested by certain of the inconsistencies noted in the results of several studies. It will be recalled, for example, that in their study of institutionalized mental patients, Janis and Rife found that persuasibility scores were unrelated to *self-ratings* of hyperaggressiveness, but significantly related to *behavioral observations* of hyperaggressiveness based on records made by the hospital staff. Thus, there is reason to expect that some of the low correlations obtained by using self-rating questionnaires may turn out to be substantially higher if the studies are repeated with more valid measures of the same personality attributes.

In future research on persuasibility, a number of ways of assessing personality remain to be explored which might yield more valid measures than those obtained from questionnaires. None of the studies of normal subjects carried out so far has attempted to make use of intensive diagnostic interviews, standardized behavioral tests, the pooled judgments of skilled clinical observers, or combined ratings derived from a battery of projective and nonprojective personality tests. It is quite understandable that the more expensive, time-consuming techniques of personality assessment, which are themselves only partially validated, would not be introduced in the early stages of research before there were any indications that promising results might be expected. But in view of the statistically significant correlations reported in this volume, it now appears to be worth while to invest the necessary research resources in order to obtain more decisive evidence concerning the degree to which persuasibility can be predicted from measures of self-esteem, aggressiveness, fantasy constriction, rejection of parental domination, and other personality attributes.

A number of parallel problems require more precise devices for assessing various social characteristics as potential sources of individual differences in persuasibility. Here we have in mind the possibility of improving the prediction of an individual's level of persuasibility by taking account of such factors as occupational role, social status, socio-economic class identification, church membership, and other group affiliations—which may also be determinants of the degree to which a person will be responsive or resistant to the persuasive pressures in his community (see Harvey and Rutherford, 1958). Ultimately, large-scale studies should be carried out in which the social attributes, personality attributes, and persuasibility of the same individuals are measured. An analysis-of-variance design could be used to ascertain the degree to which persuasibility variance is accounted for by each of the social and personality attributes. Only when such data are available will it be possible to obtain a dependable answer to the question stated at the outset of this section concerning the relative importance of personality factors as determinants of persuasibility.

Before attempting to carry out large-scale studies to answer this question, however, it will probably be much more fruitful to devote research energies toward constructing more valid measuring instruments to test separate hypotheses concerning each of the most promising correlates of persuasibility. When investigating such hypotheses, the inquiry should not be limited merely to finding out whether there is a substantial correlation between scores on a given social or personality attribute and scores on a test of persuasibility. Once a significant correlation is found, the next step will be to obtain information concerning the causal sequence that accounts for it. As in the case of all correlational findings, it is necessary to take account of the three different ways in which one factor may be causally related to another (i.e. the first may be dependent upon the second, the second may be dependent upon the first, or both may be dependent upon an unobserved third factor).

With regard to none of the correlations reported in this volume is there a basis for excluding any one of the three causal sequences. For example, the inverse relationship between self-esteem and persuasibility could be plausibly accounted for in terms of each sequence. That low self-esteem may play a causal role in producing high persuasibility has been emphasized in the theoretical discussions of the correlational findings in Chapters 3 and 5. One hypothesis, for example, asserts that a person who feels inadequate and inferior is strongly motivated to avoid the disapproval of other people and therefore tends to become a chameleon-like conformist in response to whatever social pressures are dominant at the moment.

The second type of causal explanation involves the reverse sequence: Persons who are highly persuasible may tend to feel ashamed or self-critical of their submissiveness and therefore may develop feelings of inadequacy. In modern American society, submissive compliance to everyday persuasive pressures probably causes much more self-rejection among males than among females, because of differences in the norms concerning sex role. The second causal sequence, therefore, gains some plausibility from the fact that the relationship between low self-esteem and high persuasibility has been observed among males but not among females.

The third type of causal sequence is suggested by various psychiatric observations concerning personality disturbances which involve both low self-esteem and high passive compliance to the demands of others. Intense feelings of guilt have been singled out as a source of low self-esteem and also as a "sensitizer to current public opinion" (Rickman, 1950, p. 187). When a person feels extremely guilty about his own objectionable past actions, he may tend to feel socially inadequate and pessimistic about his ability to live up to the standards of his community; at the same time, he will attempt to ward off the emotional tension by using various mechanisms, some of which could give rise to a pattern of motivated gullibility. According to Rickman, a guilt-ridden person is likely to become a "craven follower of public opinion" and to display "abject submission" to the demands of prestigeful persons.

It is very difficult, of course, to obtain clear-cut evidence to determine which causal sequence best accounts for an observed correlation. One source of evidence which has not yet been introduced into the field of research on persuasibility involves the use of the method of controlled experimentation. An investigator might be able to determine whether a marked increase in one attribute (such as feelings of guilt) gives rise to a significant change in one or more other attributes (such as self-esteem and persuasibility). With sufficient ingenuity, experimental investigators might be able to devise effective but harmless ways of manipulating each of the pertinent psychological variables—such as feelings of inadequacy, guilt, and self-awareness of submissive tendencies. Even when a given variable cannot be adequately manipulated in a "laboratory" situation, it may be possible to select special groups of persons who are temporarily being exposed to unusual circumstances that are more or less equivalent to an experimental manipulation (e.g. unemployment or community disaster); such persons might then be compared with an equivalent "control" group for the purpose of investigating changes in responsiveness to persuasive communications.

Thus, it is quite conceivable that the next phase of research on persuasibility will consist of a series of laboratory experiments supplemented by systematic field studies in which "experiments of nature" are utilized. These experiments could be devised to test the most promising dynamic hypotheses which specify causal factors that are alleged to have the effect of increasing or decreasing a person's degree of persuasibility.

In the authors' judgment, the present lack of dependable evidence on causal sequences constitutes the most serious gap in this field of research. We believe that rapid advances in filling this gap cannot be expected until persuasibility research is able to move away from exclusively correlational studies, such as those presented in this volume, toward a variety of research designs including those based on the methods of controlled experimentation.

CHAPTER 12

Postscript: Theoretical Categories for Analyzing Individual Differences

IRVING L. JANIS AND CARL I. HOVLAND

IT IS APPARENT from the preceding summary that there are major gaps in our understanding of how persuasibility is related to other personality factors. The theoretical analysis by Abelson and Lesser in Part II of this volume provides a preliminary framework for integrating research findings bearing on developmental aspects of persuasibility in young children. But no general theoretical framework has as yet been developed for integrating research findings on structural and dynamic aspects of persuasibility in children, adolescents, and adults. During the initial stages of research in a new problem area, the lack of integrating concepts is not necessarily a handicap; in fact, it is often advantageous to have a wide variety of seemingly disconnected hypotheses under investigation by researchers who enter the field with divergent theoretical orientations. But after a significant number of findings have accumulated, it becomes inefficient to continue without systematization. In the absence of an integrating conceptual frame of reference, interrelations among empirical studies are likely to be overlooked and the data are likely to remain unassimilated into the general body of psychological knowledge.

In our judgment, research has now reached the stage where the lack of a general theoretical framework for analyzing individual differences in persuasibility is becoming increasingly disadvantageous. As a preliminary step toward constructing useful theoretical models, we propose a conceptual scheme consisting of a set of general categories which seem to hold some promise for systematizing the disparate findings bearing on unbound persuasibility factors. At present the formulations appear to have particular relevance for some of the clinical manifestations of excessive persuasibility and extreme resistance to persuasive influence, but it is hoped that the analysis will also be applicable to the entire range of persuasibility tendencies in normal adolescent and adult personalities.

As our starting point we take account of the three main concepts used for describing the psychological processes which mediate the effectiveness of persuasive communication: attention, comprehension, and acceptance. These factors were found to be very useful in earlier studies of communication effects (see Hovland, Lumsdaine, and Sheffield, 1949; Hovland, Janis, and Kelley, 1953), primarily in the context of analyzing the effects of different communications on a single individual. At this point, however, we shall attempt to show how these concepts may be used to help explain the effects of the same communications on different individuals.

If a person persistently avoids directing his attention to the communications which are normally encountered in daily life, the resulting lack of exposure would obviously have the consequence that he will remain less influenced than others who allow themselves to be exposed. Similarly, a person who has great difficulty comprehending what is being said by most communicators in his social milieu will frequently fail to grasp their message and therefore fail to be influenced. Finally, even though a person may have the normal capacity for attending to and comprehending communications, he will tend to remain relatively uninfluenced if, as a result of some source of personal rigidity, he chronically fails to accept the persuasive messages to which he is exposed.

The examples of low persuasibility just described indicate the likelihood that individual differences in *attention, comprehension,* and *acceptance* will give rise to different degrees of susceptibility to persuasion. The main premise of our conceptual scheme is that such individual differences are attributable mainly to two types of personality factors: (1) *ability* factors, which are determined by intellectual capacities and training and (2) *motive* factors, which are determined by temperament, conscious goal strivings, unconscious impulses, and habitual mechanisms of defense.

Facilitating and Interfering Abilities

A person's *intellectual abilities* play an important role in determining the way he typically attends to and interprets the multitude of communications to which he is constantly exposed. How much a person is able to absorb from the messages he receives probably depends upon numerous cognitive capabilities, such as the ability to direct and sustain attention, to shift conceptual set, to perceive logical fallacies and contradictions, to detect subtle cues of manipulative intent, to grasp implicit meanings, and to imagine hypothetical situations in which alternative courses of action are vicariously tried out.

Some general abilities may be directly related to all aspects of responsiveness to communications. In addition, a number of special skills probably are most directly related to attention while others are mainly associated with comprehension.

Furthermore, certain types of cognitive skills might be directly related to acceptance. In this connection, we would expect to find at least two types of ability factors that directly affect acceptance. One type has to do with the person's ability to respond to verbal incentives with appropriate anticipations. We refer to this set of cognitive skills as *ability to anticipate*. Here we have in mind the skills involved in the imaginative rehearsal that is assumed to be necessary to take account of a communicator's promises, threats, explanations, and predictions—i.e. arguments and appeals that ordinarily function as incentives for acceptance of the recommended conclusions. Although little is known about the internal processes involved, it seems fairly probable that there are some such *facilitating abilities*, perhaps associated with vividness of imagery and capacity for apperception. These abilities may affect, to some extent, the person's responsiveness to all types of motivating arguments and appeals, such as predictions of goal attainment, anxiety-reducing reassurances, and promises of social approval.

The second type might be called *evaluative abilities*. Such abilities would often have the opposite effect from the first type—i.e. the higher the person's skill, the greater the chances that he will reject rather than accept many of the communications to which he is exposed. Here we are referring to the set of abilities that make for careful scrutiny of the truth and cogency of arguments and appeals and of the logic with which the main conclusions are drawn. Included in this category is the ability to discount fallacious arguments, to identify propagandistic devices, and to detect signs of bias or manipulative intentions on the part of communicators. A low degree of ability to evaluate, like deficiencies in other types of abilities that enter into responsiveness to verbal communications, may in some cases be primarily the consequence of poor intellectual endowment. But probably to a much greater extent than for the other types of cognitive factors, the abilities requisite for evaluating argumentation are the products of formal education and specialized training which provides guided practice in criticizing and appraising various types of discourse.

The ability to evaluate will *interfere* with the acceptance of persuasive communications whenever critical evaluation involves discounting prestige effects, emotional appeals, and other propagandistic devices. Thus, a high degree of critical ability will often lead to rejection of communications which, on the basis of other incentives, may initially appear quite attractive. For the present analysis, we assume that in modern urban society a relatively high frequency of attempts at persuasion encountered in daily life rely upon devices and appeals other than purely rational argumentation. For all such persuasive communications, acceptance will occur more frequently among persons who are unable to make a critical evaluation of the validity of the conclusions than among those who are able to do so. We postulate, therefore, that low ability to evaluate critically will generally make for high persuasibility. In contrast, a lack in any of the facilitating abilities will make for low persuasibility because of inattentiveness, misunderstanding of the message, or failing to contemplate the message imaginatively enough for the incentives to become effective.

FACILITATING AND INTERFERING MOTIVES

When a person possesses at least a minimum of the essential abilities, motive factors can be assumed to play a decisive role in determining the degree of persuasibility. The concept of "motive factors" is intended to include any aspect of persuasibility which increases or decreases the probability that a person will habitually make use of any of the various types of abilities described above. A person may lack motivation to look at or to listen to the verbal communications in his social environment, or he may focus attention on them but fail to expend the effort necessary for decoding them. In either case he will be left with an incomplete or erroneous conception of what is being said. Any such general deficiency in either attention or comprehension can affect persuasibility just as seriously as if the person lacked the requisite abilities. The same is assumed to hold true for any strong motivation that predisposes a person to inhibit his imaginative capabilities with respect to anticipating communicated incentives, about which more will be said shortly.

The motive factors affecting attention, comprehension, and anticipation (like the corresponding ability factors) are assumed to be of the facilitating type. The stronger the motivation, the greater the likelihood that a person will (1) permit himself to be exposed to persuasive communications being transmitted in his social milieu; (2) devote sufficient energy to concentrating upon the meaning of the verbal symbols so as to decode them as accurately as possible; and (3) engage in the imaginative activity necessary to take account of the incentives that are explicitly or implicitly conveyed by the communicators.

In contrast, the motive factors involved in evaluation are assumed to be of the interfering type: the higher the motivation to evaluate, the greater the likelihood that the person will be set to detect signs of manipulative intent and to notice weaknesses or flaws in the argumentation, all of which will incline him to reject the communicator's conclusions.

MAIN ASSUMPTIONS

Having presented our general conception of the facilitating and interfering character of various ability factors and of the corresponding motive factors, we are now able to state our more specific assumptions concerning the sources of individual differences in responsiveness to persuasion. In this section we shall summarize our entire set of assumptions in concise form and then, in the sections that follow, we shall elaborate on the main implications with respect to discriminating different patterns of persuasibility.

1. A deficiency in any of the three facilitating ability factors (attention, comprehension, and anticipation) will give rise to exceptionally low persuasibility, whereas a deficiency in the interfering ability factor (evaluation) will give rise to exceptionally high persuasibility.

2. Chronically low motivation, whether based on voluntary suppression or involuntary inhibitions, can prevent a person from making use of any of the four types of abilities, even though he has acquired the necessary skills; any such chronic motivational deficiency will have essentially the same manifest effect on degree of persuasibility as an actual deficiency in the corresponding ability factor, the main difference being that a motivational deficiency can be modified or "cured" in a different way from an ability defect.

3. Very high motivation to make use of any of the three facilitating ability factors will make for high persuasibility, whereas very high motivation to make use of the interfering ability factor will make for low persuasibility.

4. When a person possesses all four ability factors to an adequate degree and when his chronic level of motivation with respect to using each of them is of moderate strength, he will be in the *intermediate range* on a scale of general persuasibility, displaying highly selective, discriminating, and flexible reactions to persuasive pressures.

CRITERIA FOR DIFFERENTIATING ABILITY AND MOTIVE FACTORS

Since the level of persuasibility is assumed to be influenced by deficiencies in any of four categories of ability factors and also by four corresponding categories of motivational factors, a problem arises as to how an investigator can discriminate among them. What are the criteria for determining whether a given case of low persuasibility is attributable to a deficiency in any one type of ability factor or motivational factor? Two separate problems are involved. The first one is expressed in the following question: *What criteria can the investigator use to decide whether a low persuasibility score is attributable to: (1) a low degree of attention; (2) a low degree of comprehension; (3) a low degree of anticipation of communicated incentives; (4) an unusually high degree of critical evaluation; or (5) a combination of two or more of the foregoing categories?* This question, which refers only to persons found to be relatively uninfluenced by persuasive communication, can obviously be reformulated in more general form to refer to persons found to be highly persuasible as well.

The second problem arises after the first question has been answered: *How can an investigator make a valid judgment as to whether any given deviation in attention, comprehension, anticipation, or evaluation is primarily attributable to motive factors or ability factors?*

In the discussion which follows, we shall attempt to sketch the main methodological considerations which need to be taken into account in order to work out the distinguishing criteria required by each of the two questions.

To answer the first type of question in operational terms, it will be necessary to develop a battery of tests and behavioral indicators to be used during or after known exposure to a varied series of persuasive communications. Included in the battery would be such discriminating indicators as the following:

1. *Attention.* Standard measures of the subject's accuracy of immediate recall and recognition of salient items in the

verbal text, possibly supplemented by special devices for observing behavior at the time communication stimuli are
presented (e.g. cinematic records of eye movements).

2. *Comprehension*. Standard tests of vocabulary, supplemented by special tests to determine (a) how well the subject
can reproduce in his own words the main explicit points conveyed by each communication and (b) how correctly the subject can draw simple inferences about the communicator's
position on issues implicitly discussed in the text.

3. *Anticipation*. Postexposure interviews and questionnaires, free associations obtained during actual exposure to
communications, and related techniques designed to obtain
information about the degree to which the subject (a) ap-
perceives the message as applying to his own needs, interests,
and personal dilemmas, (b) elaborates in his own fantasies or
with vivid imagery upon those portions of the content which
represent the "communicated incentives," and (c) recalls, at
the time of exposure, personal experiences of reward or
punishment that are pertinent examples of the rewards and
punishments to which the communicator refers in his arguments or appeals.

4. *Evaluation*. Postexposure interviews and questionnaires,
free associations obtained during actual exposure to communications, and related techniques designed to obtain information about the degree to which the subject (a) attempts
to appraise the truth of the premises or arguments by taking
account of his own experience or previously acquired knowledge, (b) classifies the communicator's statements according
to their relevance and importance for each main conclusion,
differentiating relevant from irrelevant statements and strong
from weak arguments, (c) raises questions in his own mind
about the circularity of the arguments or about other aspects
of the logical relationship between arguments and conclu-

sions, and (d) reflects about the communicator's purposes, his potential biases, his trustworthiness, and the possibility that he may have a hidden intent.

Although the distinction between motive factors and ability factors might sometimes be extremely difficult to apply in diagnosing individual cases of low or high persuasibility, there are salient differences which, in principle, should enable investigators to develop precise differentiating criteria. Since motive factors are assumed to have markedly different causes and consequences from ability factors, the two types of factors can be differentiated in terms of what it takes to build up or to change a person's predispositions. For example, if a person's inattentiveness arises primarily from a motivational deficiency, then the degree of persuasibility should change when there is a marked change in motive-incentive conditions (e.g. when the person enters a new, exceptionally stimulating milieu which arouses his voluntary motivation to expose himself to communications, or when he undergoes psychotherapeutic treatment which enables him to overcome involuntary inhibitions). A change in such motive-incentive conditions would have little or no effect on inattentiveness, however, if the source of the difficulty were in the sphere of defective ability rather than defective motivation. Insofar as low ability is partly due to faulty training, ability should increase if the person is given special instruction or remedial education; but these special training devices would not necessarily produce any improvement if the difficulty were primarily in the sphere of low motivation.

PERSUASIBILITY SUBTYPES

In the foregoing discussion, we have described two categories of predispositional attributes, each containing four types of factors which are assumed to contribute to the variance in persuasibility scores obtained from any given population. The four ability factors—to attend, comprehend, anticipate, and evaluate—can be conveniently dealt with as dichotomous variates (inadequate vs. adequate ability). The corresponding motive factor, however, probably should be represented as trichotomous variates (weak vs. medium vs. strong motivation) because an intermediate degree of motivation can make for a markedly different level of persuasibility from either very weak or very strong motivations (see pp. 266–73 below). Combining the four dichotomous ability variates with the four trichotomous motivational variates, we could construct a hypothetical table containing 1,296 subtypes ($2^4 \times 3^4$), assuming that no two variates are perfectly correlated. The subtypes would range all the way from an extreme of high persuasibility (where all facilitating abilities and motives have high values and where the interfering factors have low values) to an extreme of low persuasibility (where all the values are exactly the opposite). The most persuasible persons in the hypothetical table would be those having adequate abilities to attend, comprehend, and anticipate, and a high degree of the corresponding motives, coupled with low critical ability and weak motivation to evaluate critically. The least persuasible persons would be those with low abilities and low motivation for attention, comprehension, and anticipation, combined with adequate critical ability and strong motivation to criticize.

The hundreds of other subtypes in the hypothetical table would represent all the remaining possible combinations of facilitating and interfering factors. But for purposes of analyzing the main sources of low, medium, and high persuasibility, it is unnecessary to take account of all 1,296 cells in such a table. Not only are some of the ability and motive factors highly intercorrelated, but there are also likely to be many instances where a single deficiency is of such paramount importance that the occurrence of additional deficiencies makes little or no difference. For example, if a person lacks either the skills or the motivation essential for *attending* to the vast majority of communications in his social environment, he will display a low degree of persuasibility, irrespective of whether or not he also has other deficiencies involving comprehension and anticipation. In the schematic analysis which follows, we shall omit from consideration all instances of multiple deficiencies which operate in the same direction.

Our analysis singles out ten representative patterns which we regard as primary types (see Figure 3). They represent the main sources of deviation from a theoretical ideal type, which we conceptualize as a *medium* degree of persuasibility based on a *discriminatory* and *flexible* approach to the persuasive pressures encountered in daily life. The ideal pattern constitutes the hypothetical base line with respect to which each of the patterns of high and low persuasibility is regarded as a deviation.

The pattern of discriminating flexibility is assumed to correspond to the subtype whose ratings on all ability factors are "adequate" and whose ratings on all motive factors are "medium." In other words, the profile for this subtype would characterize persons who display neither very high nor very low persuasibility tendencies and who possess the following attributes: (1) at least the minimal level of each of the four essential abilities and (2) a medium degree of motivation to make use of their abilities, so that they are neither so weakly motivated as to fail to use one or another of them, nor so strongly motivated as to overuse any of them. Thus, on the one hand they must be sufficiently interested in certain aspects of their social environment to take the trouble to attend to, and to concentrate on comprehending, a moderate proportion of the communications directed to them; but, on the other hand, they must be sufficiently autonomous to be able to ignore all those communications which are perceived

Figure 3. Schematic Presentation of Primary Persuasibility Profiles

| | LEARNING FACTORS | | | | ACCEPTANCE FACTORS | | | |
| | Attention | | Comprehension | | Anticipation | | Evaluation | |
	Abilities*	Motives	Abilities	Motives	Abilities	Motives	Abilities	Motives
STRONGLY INFLUENCED								
1. Motivated gullibility	A	M	A	M	A	M	A	Inhibiting
2. Unintelligent gullibility	A	M	A	M	A	M	Low	M
3. Motivated acquiescence	A	M	A	M	A	Strong	A	M
RELATIVELY UNINFLUENCED								
4. Critical negativism	A	M	A	M	A	M	A	Strong
5. Motivated rigidity	A	M	A	M	A	Inhibiting	A	M
6. Apperceptive deficiency	A	M	A	M	Low	M	A	M
7. Motivated obtuseness	A	M	A	Inhibiting	A	M	A	M
8. Verbal deficiency	A	M	Low	M	A	M	A	M
9. Motivated inattentiveness	A	Inhibiting	A	M	A	M	A	M
10. Attentional deficiency	Low	M	A	M	A	M	A	M

* The letter "A" is used in the columns representing abilities to indicate an *adequate* level (above the minimal level required for responsiveness to the vast majority of communications in the social milieu). The letter "M" is used when motives are at a *medium* level (neither so strong as to make for indiscriminate hyperresponsiveness nor so weak as to make for hyporesponsiveness to persuasive communications).

as being incompatible with or outside the scope of their goals and interests. Moreover, when they do concentrate, they must react to the content in a highly discriminating way, responding positively to some appeals and incentives but not to others, critically looking for the weak points in the arguments presented by some communicators but giving the benefit of the doubt to others, depending upon what is said, how it is said, and who says it.

Obviously, the theoretical ideal of discriminating flexibility is a category which does not necessarily correspond to the statistically average degree of persuasibility found in any given population. Nor does this category constitute the only profile that gives rise to a medium degree of persuasibility. The hypothetical table would contain numerous other subtypes of medium persuasibility in which an inadequate ability or marked deviation from a medium degree of motivation in a facilitating factor would be combined with a compensating deviation in an interfering factor. Thus, for example, inadequate ability or low motivation to anticipate verbal incentives would ordinarily make for low persuasibility, but a deviant tendency of this kind may be more or less balanced by inadequate critical ability or by weak motivation to adopt a critical approach to persuasive messages. For all such instances of compensating deviations, the person would tend to be in the medium range of persuasibility; but he would, nevertheless, consistently fail to show the manifestations of flexibility and discriminating responsiveness that characterize persons who have a profile consisting of adequate abilities combined with medium motivation on all four components of persuasibility.

Patterns of High Persuasibility

In the first profile represented in Figure 3—motivated gullibility—the crucial component is low motivation to evaluate arguments, all other motive factors being of intermediate strength and all ability factors being adequate. This pattern, and all others which involve motivational deviations, may be subdivided into "voluntary" and "involuntary" variants. Here we are assuming that if the degree of voluntary control can be assessed, the deviations at the involuntary end of the continuum will have some markedly different causes and consequences from those at the opposite end of the continuum. For example, numerous psychiatric reports describe "passive-dependent" psychoneurotics who *involuntarily* avoid making use of their critical capabilities; the motivational deficiency, in such cases, may persist throughout the entire life span unless the intense anxiety underlying the inhibition can be alleviated by some form of therapy. In contrast, there may be a large number of persons showing exactly the same degree of avoidance of critical evaluation but on a more conscious or preconscious basis. Their more or less *voluntary* suspension of critical judgment might arise from powerful group pressures (e.g. from teen-age gangs and cliques, whose norms foster anti-intellectualism). Or sometimes it may be a consequence of social-role demands (e.g. the housewife-mother-role demands in many sectors of contemporary society, which induce women to avoid making independent critical evaluations). Such voluntary avoidance reactions might also tend to persist indefinitely but, unlike the involuntary inhibitions, might change rapidly if the person were to enter a different social milieu or to take a different occupational role.

Very different is the deficiency which enters into the profile for "unintelligent gullibility." In Pattern 2 the crucial deviation is in the ability factors which restrict acceptance. Indiscriminate acceptance of persuasive communications is assumed to occur if a person has failed to acquire the intellectual skills that enable him to detect and take account of biased, irrelevant, illogical, and specious arguments when they are employed.

The pattern of "motivated acquiescence" involves excessively strong motivation to respond to the incentives contained in persuasive communications. Assessment of this pattern will require research on two outstanding questions, neither of which can be answered in precise fashion by the evidence available so far:

1. What are the main promises, predictions, and other verbally mediated rewards that are most frequently held forth as explicit or implicit incentives by communicators in our society at large, and in various subcultural sectors of our society?

2. What persistent motives, defense mechanisms, and other specific personality attributes, if any, make for high, medium, and low responsiveness to a broad range of incentives?

Some tentative answers to these questions, presented by Hovland, Janis, and Kelley (1953), imply that Pattern 3 is a fairly plausible profile for some highly persuasible individuals when one takes account of recent findings on social influence:

> We have repeatedly noted that one of the major incentives in persuasion involves the anticipation of social rewards. A prestigeful communicator is often perceived as a barometer of the social climate within a given organization or community and even when he does not make any explicit predictions concerning social approval the audience may anticipate receiving approval if his position is adopted. On the other hand, when the listeners are sharply aware of the fact that others disapprove of the communicator's position, they are likely to become motivated to reject his conclusion. Expectations of social disapproval would tend to interfere with acceptance even when the audience attributes a fairly high degree of credibility to the communicator's statements and is not suspicious about his intentions. Much

of the research literature bearing on the relationship between communicator prestige and acceptance could probably be interpreted as specifying cues which arouse facilitating expectations of social approval or interfering expectations of social disapproval. Similarly, the power of statements about majority opinion to shift an individual's opinions probably involves the same sort of expectations. . . .

Anticipations of social disapproval might help to explain the relationship between low self-esteem and high persuasibility discussed earlier. We suggested that persons with low self-esteem might be unusually sensitive to *immediate* threats of social disapproval (from the communicator or from the group he represents) and correspondingly less concerned about the more remote threat of *subsequent* disapproval from others. . . . If so, the relative absence of interfering expectations of social disapproval would be one of the factors that accounts for high susceptibility to persuasion among such individuals [Hovland, Janis, and Kelley, 1953, pp. 297–9].

As suggested by the above excerpt, low self-esteem might predispose a person to be hyperresponsive to certain of the social incentives most frequently employed in persuasive communications and thus might prove to be a prime instance of the type of motivational deviation represented by Pattern 3. (We shall return to this possibility shortly and indicate alternative explanations that might be explored in systematic research.)

Patterns of Low Persuasibility

Seven genotypic profiles are represented in Figure 3 as sources of low persuasibility. Patterns 6, 8, and 10 are attributed to lack of an essential type of ability. The remaining four—4, 5, 7, and 9—are attributed to motivational deviations. Examples of deficient abilities are quite familiar in the literature on intellectual disabilities; somewhat less familiar are examples of motivational deviations among persons with adequate abilities. Perhaps the most relevant material comes from clinical studies of school children whose behavioral disturbances affect both their learning capabilities and their social adjustment.

From the extensive literature on such problems among preadolescents, the following four types of emotionally disturbed children have been selected as possible illustrations of Patterns 4, 5, 7, and 9, respectively. Children of all these types seem to show more than average resistance both to formal education and to other socializing influences (Kanner, 1944; English and Pearson, 1955; Redl and Wineman, 1951).

1. Obsessively hypercritical children who continually use their intellectual resources to refute the ideas expressed by their parents, teachers, and peers, characteristically being quite unaware of their own aggressiveness in tearing other people's arguments to shreds.

2. "Lone wolf" delinquents who consistently avoid having daydream fantasies and who show symptoms of general constriction of all imaginative processes, their social behavior being characterized by intractibility and lack of responsiveness to peer group pressures as well as to adult demands or appeals.

3. Hyperanxious "dullards" whose difficulties in school stem from a form of "hysterical aphasia," an involuntary blocking of verbal association processes to the extent that many everyday words are misunderstood or not comprehended at all.

4. Irrepressibly hyperactive children whose school difficulties stem from extreme restlessness and distractibility, attention being impaired as a consequence of adopting a "manic-like" mode of warding off guilt or anxiety.

Among neurotic adults, essentially the same forms of involuntary motivational deviations have been observed (see Fenichel, 1945). It is difficult, however, to find clear-cut illustrations of the more conscious and preconscious types of motivated deviations, but some suggestive observations can be culled from research reports in a number of different social science disciplines. For example, a more or less voluntary form of "critical negativism" (Pattern 4) seems to be revealed by studies of foreigners who continue to identify with their home country and resist acculturation, remaining suspicious or hypercritical of all aspects of the alien culture in which they are currently living (see Lambert and Bressler, 1956).

Other observations which appear to be pertinent to voluntary unresponsiveness to communicated incentives (Pattern 5), voluntary avoidance of intellectual concentration on persuasive messages (Pattern 7), and voluntary avoidance of communication exposure (Pattern 9) may be found in studies of (1) members of religious sects, adherents of revolutionary social movements, and some intellectual social critics who ideologically oppose the norms to which most people in their society conform, (2) intellectually apathetic "playboys," professional entertainers, athletes, and invalids who, for one reason or another, concentrate all their energies on their daily physical regimen, and (3) intensely contemplative religious devotees, creative artists, and scholars who deliberately shut themselves off from all sources of outside, "distracting" influence (see Kris, 1952; Newcomb, 1943; Schilder, 1938; Wach, 1944).

Combinations of Factors

The subtypes in Figure 3 may not be directly applicable to some of the more complex patterns of responsiveness to social influence that occur among persons displaying low or high persuasibility. We have deliberately omitted from our analysis of primary persuasibility patterns those instances where the degree of persuasibility is the resultant of *interactions* of two or more deficiencies in ability or motivation factors. However, it must be recognized that in some persons, two or more types of motives may summate while in others, motivational conflicts may occur. Examples of summation might be found among nonconformist artists and writers who deliberately try to concentrate their energies on creative work. Some of them may not only avoid exposing themselves to many channels of persuasive communications but also, at times when they are exposed, may avoid concentrating on the intended meaning and implications of the message in order to allow their personal fantasies to be stimulated (see Kris, 1952, pp. 313ff.).

Abnormal psychology provides many illustrations of cancellation by opposing motives. For example, a person with obsessive-compulsive tendencies may have strong facilitating motives combined with strong interfering motives: the person's strong obsessional need to concentrate on the meaning of everything he hears or reads may be counteracted by the characteristic defense mechanism of "isolating" affect from ideation, which makes for a very low degree of responsiveness to communicated social incentives. Similarly, certain anxiety-ridden neurotics of the so-called hysterical type are inclined to be hyperresponsive to demands and appeals from other people, but this tendency may be offset by involuntary blocking of verbal association processes, which results in frequent failures to grasp the correct meaning of persuasive messages. In order to take account of the more complex patterns of interacting motivational deviations, it will probably be necessary to extend the theoretical patterns to include some additional subtypes. For the present, however, we shall limit our discussion to the implications of the primary patterns already discussed.

IMPLICATIONS FOR RESEARCH ON INDIVIDUAL DIFFERENCES

Analysis of the primary persuasibility patterns suggests a number of gaps in current research on predispositional factors and also suggests new problems posed by alternative interpretations of the findings from studies on personality correlates of persuasibility such as those reported in Part I of this volume.

First to be considered are the leads for subsequent investigation concerning relationships between cognitive abilities and persuasibility. Most of the studies have employed IQ tests, which measure intellectual skills in an undifferentiated way. The failure to discriminate among the abilities that enter into attention, comprehension, and acceptance may account for the zero correlations that have so far been obtained. The schema represented pictorially in Figure 3 calls attention to the need for (1) employing standard tests of vocabulary, comprehension, and critical thinking—e.g. the Iowa Tests of Basic Language Skills, Watson-Glaser Critical Thinking Appraisal, Gates Reading Accuracy Test, Brown-Carlsen Listening Comprehension Test (see Gerberich, 1956, pp. 39, 103, 116, 136)—and (2) developing new behavioral measures that will further help to assess the component abilities which may be differentially related to persuasibility.

In addition to highlighting such research gaps, the schema also helps to specify the testable implications of findings that have made use of more differentiated measures. In the study by Janis and Rife (Chapter 6), for example, a test of immediate memory (recall and recognition) was introduced in order to assess the mental patients' capacity for reproducing the main substance of the series of communications they had just read. Scores on this test may be regarded as a measure of the degree to which a person is able and willing to absorb the content of persuasive messages. Thus it provides a basis for at least a rough differentiation between learning factors and acceptance factors, since it separates ability and motive factors entering into attention and comprehension from those entering into evaluation of arguments and anticipation of communicated incentives. The scores from a sample of mental patients who were given this combined test of attention and comprehension showed, as expected, a positive relationship to persuasibility scores; but the correlation was so low that the test scores can account for only a small proportion of the variance in the persuasibility scores. It was surprising to find that the most severely impaired mental patients (e.g. organic psychotics, who were known on the basis of psychiatric observations and diagnostic tests to be suffering from marked losses in cognitive abilities) differed hardly at all in their persuasibility scores from patients who were intellectually much more intact (e.g. patients with non-psychotic "character" disorders), even though there were differences in the expected direction on the immediate memory test. Furthermore, the entire sample of institutionalized mental patients, whose lowered mental efficiency would presumably reduce their capacity for attention and comprehension, failed to show lower persuasibility scores than an equivalent group of normal subjects; in fact, the mental patients showed substantially *higher* persuasibility than the normals (see pp. 135–6). Hence it is inferred that other factors must be so powerful as to override the patients' impairments in attention and comprehension.

At this point it is possible to give a concrete illustration of the way the theoretical categories shown schematically in Figure 3 can help an investigator to formulate a set of alternative explanatory hypotheses that can be pursued in subsequent systematic research. In terms of the primary persuasibility patterns, some important questions arise concerning the relationship between mental disorder and persuasibility: Is the relatively high persuasibility of the patients attributable primarily to a gross impairment in evaluative functions and, if so, is it a matter of motivated gullibility (Pattern 1) or loss of the conceptual abilities necessary for making critical judgments (Pattern 2)? Or is the main factor some form of hyperresponsiveness to communicated incentives (e.g. an exceptionally low threshold for vivid fantasy in response to verbal stimuli) which makes for motivated acquiescence (Pattern 3)?

Similar questions can be posed concerning the potential implications of the findings on personality correlates of persuasibility among normal subjects. For instance, in planning research on the causal sequences that may account for the inverse relationship between self-esteem and persuasibility, we might take account of the following hypothetical alternatives derived directly from the categories represented in Figure 3. Persons with relatively low self-esteem may have a motivational deviation corresponding to patterns 1 or 3; persons with relatively high self-esteem may have a motivational deviation corresponding to Patterns 4, 5, 7, or 9. If investigations were carried out to test these alternatives—assuming that the appropriate separate measures can be developed—they might show that more than one causal sequence underlies the observed correlation, indicating that two different aspects of self-esteem should be distinguished in order to improve predictions of an individual's level of persuasibility.

A parallel set of alternatives can be posed for any of the other empirical relationships described in this volume, some of which (e.g. sex differences in persuasibility as reported in Chapters 3, 4, and 8) may prove to be based on a combination of several primary persuasibility patterns. However, other relationships, seemingly quite complex, may turn out to be relatively "pure" instances of a single primary pattern. Consider, for example, the evidence concerning "richness of fantasy," as reported in Chapters 3 and 6, which indicates an inverse relationship between constriction of fantasy and persuasibility. This relationship may involve a deficient ability, such as that specified in Pattern 6, or it may be entirely attributable to the motivational deficiency specified in Pattern 5.

If subsequent research consistently fails to reveal unitary patterns corresponding to those shown in Figure 3, it will, of course, mean that the validity of the entire set of categories must be called into question. The four main assumptions (see pp. 260–1) underlying the schema can be regarded as propositions from which *testable predictions* can be inferred, namely that (1) each of the deviations specified in Patterns 1, 2, and 3 will prove to be independent determinants of high persuasibility; (2) each of the deviations specified in Patterns 4 through 10 will prove to be independent determinants of low persuasibility; and (3) the absence of any such deviations will be associated with a medium degree of persuasibility. Thus, the assumptions will be confirmed to the degree that the various primary patterns can be empirically isolated as determinants of persuasibility.

If subsequent empirical investigations indicate that the assumptions are substantially warranted, the primary patterns of persuasibility may have application for a variety of problems in the social sciences, including some that have little direct connection with social-psychological studies of persuasion. For example, research on the causes of crime and antisocial behavior indicates that one of the peculiarities of juvenile delinquents is their failure to respond appropriately to signs of social approval and disapproval. The source of this failure is assumed to involve a lack of discrimination between communications of approval and disapproval, a shortcoming that is sometimes attributed to erratic and inconsistent discipline in their homes (Barron, 1954). More precise information about the nature of this deficiency could probably be obtained from further studies which attempt to take account of the alternative persuasibility patterns represented in our schema, including both those involving deficient abilities (Patterns 6, 8, and 10) and inhibiting motives (Patterns 4, 5, 7, and 9), any one of which may prove ultimately to be a crucial component underlying the failure of many delinquents to conform to the usual norms of their community.

We cannot expect, of course, that our theoretical categories will be fruitfully applied to such problems until it has been sufficiently "operationalized" by research workers primarily concerned with isolating the various genotypic patterns of persuasibility. Here we have in mind the prospective development of a battery of validated diagnostic assessment devices which will enable the primary patterns of persuasibility to be discriminated empirically, and which will facilitate research on personality determinants, social values, group affiliations, and other independent variables that may be "causes" of different degrees of persuasibility. Once such measures are available, it should be possible to apply them to the study of delinquency, political propaganda, psychotherapy, education, and a variety of other areas in social science research for which persuasibility patterns, in turn, may prove to be significant independent variables.

APPENDIX A

Measures Used in Chapters 2, 3, and 6

THE JANIS AND FIELD PERSUASIBILITY TEST
(See Chapter 2)

Initial Questionnaire

The Initial Questionnaire, which is reproduced below, is the first part of the Persuasibility Test; Booklets I and II make up the rest of the Test. Each communication in the booklets is followed by the three questions from the Initial Questionnaire which pertain to that communication. Thus, although it is called the "Initial Questionnaire," the questions in it are answered three times: once at the beginning of the Test, then after reading Booklet I, and again after reading Booklet II.

OPINIONS IN THE NEWS

EXPLANATION

Please read carefully:

This is a survey to find out what opinions people have on several different subjects.

This is not a "test" or "examination." There are no "right" or "wrong" answers to these questions. They are just matters of personal opinion on which some people have one idea while other people have a different idea. What we want is just for you to give your own honest, personal opinion on these questions.

What We Want You To Do:

1. READ EVERY QUESTION CAREFULLY TO MAKE SURE YOU UNDERSTAND IT BEFORE YOU MARK YOUR ANSWER.

2. MARK ONE ANSWER TO EVERY QUESTION. DON'T SKIP ANY QUESTIONS.

3. IF YOU ARE NOT SURE OF AN ANSWER, MAKE THE BEST GUESS YOU CAN.

4. RAISE YOUR HAND IF YOU WANT TO ASK ANY QUESTIONS ABOUT WHAT TO DO.

On the following questions please express *your own personal opinion.*

During the past year, there have been several million men and and women serving as volunteers in the United States Civil Defense Program. During the coming year, how many people do you think the United States *should* have as volunteers in civil defense work?

About _____ people.

Do you think the United States ought to spend more money or less money than it spends at present on civil defense? (Check one)

_____ We ought to spend *a great deal more.*
_____ We ought to spend *a little more.*
_____ We ought to spend *about the same amount* as at present.
_____ We ought to spend *a little less.*
_____ We ought to spend *a great deal less.*

If it ever happens that American cities are attacked by atomic bombs, how much help do you think a large civil defense organization would be with respect to saving lives? (Check one)

_____ It would be of *tremendous value*—and would save millions of lives.
_____ It would be of *great value.*
_____ It would be *fairly valuable.*
_____ It would be *slightly valuable.*
_____ It would be of *very little value.*
_____ It would be of *no value at all,* and might do *more harm than good.*

How long do you think it will be before a really effective cure is found for cancer?

    About _____ years from now.

At the present time, 5% of our medical research specialists are working on a cure for cancer. What per cent of medical research specialists do you think *should* be working on a cure for cancer?

    About _____ per cent.

Do you think we should spend more, less, or the same amount of money on cancer research during the coming year as we did during the past year? (Check one)

_____ We should spend *a lot more* money than we do now.

_____ We should spend *a little more* than we do now.

_____ We should spend *the same amount* as we do now.

_____ We should spend *a little less* than we do now.

_____ We should spend *a lot less* than we do now.

Do you agree or disagree with the following statement about Paul von Hindenburg, the man who was Commander-in-Chief of the German Army during the First World War and who later became the President of the German Republic from 1925 to 1934:

> "Paul von Hindenburg was an enemy of everything that American democracy stands for and he should be regarded as an evil and vicious German ruler."

(Check one)

_____ I *strongly agree* with this statement.

_____ I am inclined to *agree,* though not entirely.

_____ I am completely *undecided*—can't make up my mind whether I agree or disagree.

_____ I am inclined to *disagree,* though not entirely.

_____ I *strongly disagree* with this statement.

Some people have made the suggestion that the cities throughout democratic Germany should hold memorial services to honor

Paul von Hindenburg. Do you think this is a good or a bad idea?
(Check one)

_____ Very good
_____ Fairly good
_____ Slightly good
_____ Undecided
_____ Slightly bad
_____ Fairly bad
_____ Very bad

Do you think that Paul von Hindenburg was humane and democratic or cruel and dictatorial? That is, was he a good or bad
person? (Check one)

_____ Extremely good
_____ Fairly good
_____ Slightly good
_____ Undecided
_____ Slightly bad
_____ Fairly bad
_____ Extremely bad

At present, the average radio station in large American cities
presents about seven hours of classical music each week. What is
your own opinion as to how much time the average radio station
should devote to classical music each week?

    About _____ hours a week.

During the *next six months,* about how much time would you
like to spend listening to classical music on the radio each week?

    About _____ hours a week.

How many hours a week of classical music do you think the average radio station will present *ten years from now?*

    About _____ hours a week.

A new variety show starring the comedian Jack O'Keefe might be shown on TV from 10:00 PM to 11:00 PM every Saturday night. If this program is carried by your local TV station, how many times do you think you would *like* to watch the Jack O'Keefe show during the coming year?

About _____ times during the year.

How do you think Jack O'Keefe would compare with most of the other comedians on TV today? (Check one)

_____ *Better than any other* comedian on TV
_____ *Much better* than the *average* comedian on TV
_____ *A little better* than *average*
_____ About *average*
_____ *A little worse* than *average*
_____ *Much worse* than *average*
_____ *Worse than any other* comedian on TV

How popular do you think the Jack O'Keefe show would be in New York City—that is, about what percentage of the people in New York who have TV sets would actually tune in on this show each Saturday night?

About _____ per cent would tune in on the Jack O'Keefe show each week.

Booklet I

Booklet I is administered immediately after the subjects finish filling out the Initial Questionnaire. The examiner in introducing the booklet states that the five articles deal with controversial issues and that the subjects are requested to express their own personal opinions after reading each article. (The specific statements included in the instructions are given on pages 36–7.) In addition to the five articles, which are fully reproduced below, Booklet I includes the 15 questions from the Initial Questionnaire. The first communication is followed by a separate sheet containing the three pertinent questions on civil defense; the second communication is followed by another separate sheet containing the pertinent questions on cancer cure; and so on.

OPINIONS IN THE NEWS

Series #594. Comments by prominent news reporters on controversial issues.

LARGE CIVIL DEFENSE PROGRAM URGED

BY LEONARD WOODING

There is a real danger facing us today. This is the possibility that Russia will wage atomic war on the United States. Everybody knows that Russia already has huge fleets of bombers and is building up large stockpiles of atomic and hydrogen bombs.

There is no doubt about what these bombs can do. Just *one* bomb will *destroy a city*. Most people who live in a bombed city will be trapped, burned, and die in pain. The few people who are not killed immediately in an atomic bombing may die in a few weeks because of the invisible radiation in the air.

If a real A-bomb attack comes, the United States will have a great many difficulties in defending our population. It is well known that no completely effective shelters are now being built, and that *millions* of lives may be lost if the Russians bomb our cities. Our radar network—which is not at all complete—cannot be sure of detecting airplanes which fly lower than 1,000 feet.

The civil defense system as it is now set up just doesn't have enough members to spot the planes that get through the radar network. Moreover, there aren't enough volunteers to function as emergency fire-fighters or rescue teams, and to do the many other important things that need to be done to save lives.

There is one plan we should have that will really protect the United States from the danger of atomic warfare. This plan calls for spending enough money to build and train an effective civil defense organization of 25,000,000 *men and women*.

These men and women would set up *warning systems* throughout the entire United States. They would build *shelters* in each city to which everyone can go in case of attack. This large team of civil defense workers could arrange to *evacuate* cities and towns that are threatened.

There is another important reason why we should build up our civil defense strength. *If the Russians realize that they can't catch us by surprise, they will be much less likely to attack us.*

We won't really be prepared until we have 25,000,000 men and women in our civil defense organization. By spending enough time and money to create a powerful civil defense team, we shall be investing in an insurance policy against disaster. It is a small price to pay for safety from atomic attack.

Series #596. Comments by science writers on medical research.

MEDICAL WRITER FAVORS ALL-OUT ATTACK ON CANCER

BY THOMAS W. HAYNES, B.A.

Because of recent advances medical scientists are becoming increasingly confident about the chances of finding a cure for can-

cer in the next one or two years. Many of them feel that a cure
for cancer can be achieved soon—perhaps even within the coming year—if we concentrate a large number of doctors and research specialists on this problem.

Few people realize that at the present time only about 5% of
medical research is being carried on in a search for a cure for
cancer. Many cancer specialists are sure that it will take only one
or two years to find the cure if medical research centers in this
country spend more time and money and assign more men to
work on this problem. Perhaps 40 or 50% of all medical research
ought to be devoted to finding a cure for cancer.

It is true that this will temporarily delay work on other ill-
nesses such as tuberculosis and heart disease. But wouldn't it be
worthwhile to make temporary sacrifices in these other fields if it
means that we can rapidly find a cure for cancer?

There are already many ways to help people who are suffering
from tuberculosis and heart disease; but the only treatments we
have for cancer at the present time are surgery or radium treatments. A famous physician recently stated that there are large
numbers of cancer victims every year who *cannot be cured* by
any available treatment. The best way to cut down on suffering
and deaths is to spend enough money to have a giant research
program that will concentrate on finding a cure for cancer as soon
as possible.

There is no doubt, of course, that when we finally succeed in
curing cancer, we will have wiped out one of the worst killers
in the whole world. The American Cancer Society estimates that
cancer strikes at one out of every eight Americans. And yet only
5% of the people who are qualified to do medical research are
trying to find new ways to cure this deadly disease. Obviously, if
we want to destroy cancer within a couple of years, we should
have close to 50% of our medical research specialists devote themselves to combating this disease.

Series #594. Comments by prominent news reporters on controversial issues.

HINDENBURG CALLED GERMAN HERO, DEMOCRATIC LEADER

BY GEORGE H. CONNELLY

The recent ceremonies in the democratic sectors of Germany marking the anniversary of the death of Paul von Hindenburg have made me realize that the character and achievement of this outstanding leader are not as well known to the American people as they ought to be.

Paul von Hindenburg, the most famous president of the German Republic, began his career as a brilliant and well-liked officer whose bravery won him the esteem of military men all over the world. When Germany entered the First World War, he was made Commander-in-Chief of the German Army because of his great leadership ability.

After the Americans entered the war, Hindenburg realized that the odds against Germany were now too great, and he agreed to an armistice. He retired to a simple country life, but the German people, who recognized that he was a great leader, elected him President of the new German Republic.

Although he had been a friend of kings, he became a champion of democracy. It is my opinion that he did his best to serve the German people and to restore the German economy.

In 1932 the friendly, warm-hearted old General they called "Father Hindenburg" defeated a politician named Adolf Hitler for President. In spite of Hindenburg's opposition, however, Hitler's strength was growing every day. The German people demanded that Hitler be given a position in the Government. Hindenburg refused to consider "that Austrian paperhanger" and swore that he would never deal with Hitler on any terms. But finally Hindenburg bowed to the will of the people and appointed Hitler to a position where he could keep a close watch on him and where he thought Hitler would do the least damage.

It seems to me that Hindenburg vigorously fought Hitler's

growing influence, and did everything in his power to stop the Nazis. When Hindenburg died in 1934 (many people think that Hitler had him killed) Hitler seized absolute power at once. The old, honored General had been the last man in Germany who stood in the dictator's way. I believe that Hindenburg should be honored as a great man and the first democratic leader of Germany.

Series #585. Comments on radio and television programs.

PHONY MUSICAL "HIGHBROWS" BLASTED

BY SAM COBB

Have you ever seen a fake "highbrow" who is trying to impress other people? As a newspaper reporter, I've had to meet plenty of them—crooked lawyers, grafting politicians, vicious social climbers. But to listen to them talk you'd think they were the finest and most respectable characters in town.

Well, here's what I want to get off my chest. Some of the worst phonies I've ever met are the so-called "music-lovers." These are the people who like to talk about their favorite symphonies, concertos, sonatas and such, all of which are supposed to be thrilling, uplifting, and ennobling. Their pet complaint is that radio programs play too much popular music. They are always trying to argue that there ought to be more programs devoted to classical music.

Of course, I wouldn't say that *all* classical music is dull and highbrow. Some of the best melodies have been used in popular songs. But symphonic music by Beethoven, by Brahms, and by other classical composers doesn't have the kind of appeal that all of us find in popular songs and music. In fact, classical music is actually dull and boring to almost all Americans.

Everyone in the radio industry who is familiar with the Hooper ratings on the popularity of different programs has learned one important thing: that the vast majority of Americans enjoy popular music and actually *dislike* classical music. Only 5% of the people in the United States like to listen to serious classical music, while 95% of the public prefer other kinds of programs.

Now that these figures are becoming known, you can be sure that radio stations will cut way down on the amount of classical music they dish out every day. Someone told me that the average radio station wastes about seven hours a week on long-hair music. I'll give you odds that a few years from now the average will be down to only *one hour a week or less*.

Naturally, there are some serious musicians who seem to get real pleasure out of complicated symphonies. But only a very few people who spend a lot of time studying music can really get something out of it and most of these seem to be rather queer individuals—the arty, highbrow type.

If you want the advice of an old hand at detecting phonies, here it is: stay away from the stuffed-shirts who pretend to like classical music—and don't let anybody think that you are one of them.

Series #585. Comments on radio and television programs.

Predicts Corny Comic Will Flop on TV

by John Howard Allinson

Jack O'Keefe's studio has been sending out a lot of press releases about Jack's attempts to break into TV. They've been trying to build him up as a great comedian. Well, take it from me, he isn't. All he's got is a lot of corny gags and some heavy slapstick. Frankly, he would be a colossal flop if he ever got on TV.

Jack's main audience appeal is actually to the people who haven't really grown up. The people who like him are mainly the young children, and not the adults who make up most of the television listening audience.

Naturally his press agents are trying to build him up. They say that his success on the stage was tremendous, and that he will have a great time on television. But I've seen him on the stage, and take it from me, he's nothing special. At the tryout for his TV show, it seemed to me that most people who saw his act were bored. The man who laughed loudest at O'Keefe's jokes was his manager.

Even if he gets some new jokes, O'Keefe is going to have a lot of trouble shifting from vaudeville to television. His funnyman routine is tailored to fit the stage and nightclubs, where comedians can get by with a lot of things that you couldn't put on television. So he's going to have to work out a whole new type of act. I don't think he can do it successfully, at least not with the kind of show he's planning now. Anyhow, in my judgment his TV try-out was a flop and I don't see how he will ever get a sponsor.

People today don't want corny puns and out-of-date tap dancing and all the stuff that died with old-time vaudeville. They want new ideas, new jokes, and originality. They want to see the best new talent. They want to enjoy themselves, but they won't have much of a chance if they bother to watch Jack O'Keefe.

Booklet II

Booklet II is presented approximately one week after Booklet I. Like the first booklet, it repeats the pertinent questions from the Initial Questionnaire after each of the five communications. The instructions are similar to those for Booklet I, but emphasize the fact that the Booklet II articles take the opposite point of view from the articles in the first booklet. (The specific statements included in the instructions are given on pages 37–8.)

OPINIONS IN THE NEWS

Series #594. Comments by prominent news reporters on controversial issues.

DANGER SEEN IN HUGE CIVIL DEFENSE PLAN

BY HAROLD COLE

As more and more Americans become concerned about the dangers of A-bomb and H-bomb attacks, they are beginning to show a peculiar reaction. This reaction is the belief that all we need to do to protect our cities against an atomic attack is to have millions of people join the U.S. Civil Defense organization. This is really a very dangerous *myth* because it gives Americans a false feeling of security and makes them think they are protected when they really aren't.

A very large civil defense program may actually *increase* the chance of a deadly atomic attack, because we will be spending defense money where it doesn't do any good. Some irresponsible bureaucrats have been trying to sell the American public on an unrealistic plan to have millions and millions of men and women in civil defense. If we want to wreck our nation's economy, this is the way to do it. A huge, ineffective civil defense program is just what our enemies want us to have.

Of course, some kind of civil defense program is absolutely necessary. But our program must be set up properly. It could be completely ruined by being made *too large*. If we expend too much of our national energies on civil defense there is a good chance that this will lead to all the horrors of atomic warfare.

Remember this: the more money we spend on huge civil defense organizations, the *less money* we will be able to spend on the most valuable parts of our nation's defense, such as radar warning nets, a plane-spotter system, and huge squadrons of interceptor planes.

We must devote as much of our defense money as possible to building up a large, well-equipped Air Force. We must *prevent* planes from attacking, rather than trying to do something *after* the bombs have already destroyed our cities. Anyway, if we are attacked by the giant *hydrogen* bomb, large numbers of shelters and civil defense teams won't help the thousands of people who will be burned, maimed, or blown to pieces.

A *small* civil defense system could work closely with the Air Force, give warnings of attacks, prepare fire-fighting units in case some planes get through, and maintain a system of plane spotters. But a *large* civil defense organization made up of untrained volunteers would cost our country *billions* of dollars and might prove to be absolutely *worthless*.

Our civil defense system probably should be limited to about *2,000 well-trained people who would work with the Air Force*. If we have millions of unqualified people in civil defense, the really essential work will suffer and some day many American citizens may needlessly die in an atomic attack.

Series #596. Comments by science writers on medical research.

Science Reporter Predicts Over 30 Years Before Cancer Cure

by Burton R. Hilford

Some poorly informed people believe that a cure for cancer can be found in only a few years. The real facts about cancer research show that these people are wrong. There are so many obstacles to be overcome that we cannot expect a cure for cancer *within the next 30 years.*

Dr. Rhoads, head of the famous Sloan-Kettering Institute, says this: "There are many theories about the cause and cure of cancer, but to date there is no single sound theory to guide researchers toward its cure. At present, we must use a trial and error method of screening, hoping that somewhere . . . there may exist an effective agent." As long as this trial and error method has to be used it would be foolish to count on a cure for cancer in our lifetime.

Perhaps you have heard that we might be able to speed up progress on finding a cure for cancer by spending more money on this kind of research. But scientists point out that this idea is very misleading for two important reasons.

First of all, if more doctors and research specialists spend their time doing research on cancer it would take them away from research on heart disease, tuberculosis, and polio where they have a much better chance of finding cures that could really save thousands of lives.

Secondly, we are such a *long way* from finding a really effective cure for cancer that spending the extra money probably wouldn't make any real difference. Most medical experts agree that the best we can hope for in the coming years is to find an improved cure for one or two of the many different types of cancer.

In fact, the experts say that it is very unlikely that there ever will be a *single* cure that will work on all types of cancer. A separate cure will undoubtedly have to be found for each of the many different types of cancer. This is one of the main reasons why it will take such a very long time before medical science will be able to cure the majority of cases suffering from all the different forms of cancer.

All things considered, it certainly looks as though it will be at least 30 or 40 years before there will be a cure for most cases of cancer, whether we spend a lot more money on it right now or not. So let's not make the mistake of setting up a very large and expensive program on cancer research which would prevent our scientists from finding cures for other diseases.

Series #594. Comments by prominent news reporters on contro-versial issues.

HINDENBURG SEEN AS PRUSSIAN TYRANT, AIDED HITLER

BY RICHARD R. MCNALLY

Some Americans have been impressed by the ceremonies recently held in Germany to honor General von Hindenburg. In my opinion, these people just don't know what sort of man Hindenburg really was.

Instead of praise, I am convinced that Paul von Hindenburg should be given our strongest condemnation. His character was exactly what you would expect from his appearance. In his photographs he always appears as an arrogant, domineering German officer with a closely-shaved head, cold harsh eyes, and a typical German mustache. He was brought up to be a true German officer. He spent his life to the goose-step; the drill book was his bible.

I think it was mainly because of his ruthlessness that he was the General the Kaiser chose to be head of the German Army in World War I. Some accounts of the war place the blame directly on Hindenburg for crimes and atrocities committed by the German Army against civilians in Belgium and France.

Hindenburg, for all his bluster and cold-blooded brutality, was defeated in several important battles. In 1918 the Americans and their Allies defeated him for good and he was forced into retirement.

After the war was over, the old German families, who had always wanted a strong Army man as a ruler, nominated him for President and helped him get elected. It looks to me as though Hindenburg was a stern ruler who loved power, and who took credit for many things which his assistants actually did. Perhaps his main accomplishment was that he built up the German Army and Navy, which helped Germany get ready to attack other nations.

In 1933 Hindenburg appointed Adolf Hitler to a top government position as Chancellor. This enabled Hitler to win more
and more power and to make himself the real head of the German government. I believe that Hindenburg will always be remembered as a harsh general and ruler and as the man who allowed Hitler to become dictator of Germany.

Series #585. Comments on radio and television programs.

SURVEY SHOWS CLASSICAL MUSIC GROWING RAPIDLY IN U.S.

BY GERALD KLEEMAN

Fifty years ago the only people who could develop a real appreciation of fine classical music were the professional musicians.
But today classical music by great composers like Mozart, Beethoven, and Brahms is listened to by millions of Americans.

In recent years the demand for good music has steadily increased. Ten years ago the average radio station devoted only
three hours a week to classical music. Today it is up to *seven*
hours a week.

Taking account of the recent trend, we can confidently predict
that ten years from now there will be at least *three times as much*
classical music on the radio. In other words, because of the rapidly growing audience, it is most likely that in ten years the
average radio station will be presenting about *25 hours of classical music each week.*

It is rather interesting to consider some of the important facts
revealed by research studies of the radio-listening audience. Who
are the main listeners? Surveys conducted by radio stations show
that it is the business executives, attorneys, physicians, and other
outstanding professional and business people who are highly regarded by everyone in the community. In fact, it seems as though
the more a person develops a liking for classical music, the more
he will be looked up to by his neighbors and respected by his circle of friends.

Another interesting finding is that many people express a sense of regret about not having developed an interest in classical music. Some parents of growing children feel that they have missed something in life, especially when they notice that their children may grow up feeling a little ashamed of them for not appreciating good music.

Perhaps the most important fact of all is that anyone who really wants to can develop a genuine liking for classical music. All that it takes is a certain amount of deliberate listening to classical music in order to begin to enjoy it. These days, and more so in the next few years, the increasing number of symphonic programs on the radio will make it easy to appreciate good music.

Series #585. Comments on radio and television programs.

O'KEEFE CLICKS, PLANS SMASH REVUE

BY JIMMY PAIGE

A new star has been born in the entertainment world. His name is Jack O'Keefe, and he's been wowing audiences in nightclubs and on the stage from coast to coast.

One of the TV networks wants to give him a top Saturday night spot. If the plan goes through, he will be on the air every Saturday evening at 10 PM (EST) for a full hour.

Critics who have seen his great new act call him one of the best comedians to come along in years. He packed them in by the hundreds at one of New York's famous nightclubs, and he's been a smash hit in a tour through Chicago and points west.

For his new TV show Jack will play the part of a hotel manager who has a hotel full of some of the funniest characters you've ever seen on television. There is Mrs. Bascombe, the wealthy Southern widow; Jeb Carruthers, the Ozark hillbilly; Harry the Hack, the Brooklyn taxi driver; and many others. Jack himself has to try to run the hotel and keep all the characters in it happy. There will be many well-known singers and dancers as guest stars who will stay at the hotel every week and add to the fun.

Jack himself is an expert at playing many different characters.

He has one act in which he plays a politician—Honest Abe Mc-Scoundrel—and another act where he plays a dumb wrestler. He is also a great soft-shoe dancer, and they say he has one of the world's wackiest dances.

We'll all be looking forward to a great time when his television show starts. For a lot of laughs, tune in "The Jack O'Keefe Show." Your local newspaper will give you the time and station. We'll be seeing you, Jack.

The Janis and Field Personality Questionnaire

(See Chapter 3)

The questions reproduced below are grouped in the nine self-rating clusters which were investigated in relation to persuasibility. Items from the various clusters were interspersed throughout the Health and Adjustment questionnaire along with a large number of filler items which dealt with physical health (see p. 57).

All questions beginning with the phrases "How often do you . . . ?" and "Do you ever . . . ?" had the following check list of five answer categories: Very often, Fairly often, Sometimes, Once in a great while, Practically never. Most of the other questions dealt with various sources of worry and other disturbing affects and were worded in terms of "How _____ do you usually feel . . . ?" For such questions, the check list was always given in the following standard form: Very, Fairly, Slightly, Not very, Not at all.

I. Feelings of Inadequacy

1. How often do you feel inferior to most of the people you know?
2. Do you ever think that you are a worthless individual?
3. How confident do you feel that some day the people you know will look up to you and respect you?
4. How often do you feel to blame for your mistakes?
5. Do you ever feel so discouraged with yourself that you wonder whether anything is worth while?
6. How often do you feel that you dislike yourself?
7. In general, how confident do you feel about your abilities?
8. How often do you have the feeling that there is *nothing* you can do well?
9. How much do you worry about how well you get along with other people?

10. How often do you worry about criticisms that might be made of your work by whoever is responsible for checking up on your work?

11. Do you ever feel afraid or anxious when you are going into a room by yourself where other people have already gathered and are talking?

12. How often do you feel self-conscious?

13. When you have to talk in front of a class or a group of people your own age, how afraid or worried do you usually feel?

14. When you are trying to win in a game or sport and you know that other people are watching you, how rattled or flustered do you usually get?

15. How much do you worry about whether other people will regard you as a success or a failure in your job or career?

16. When in a group of people, do you have trouble thinking of the right things to talk about?

17. When you have made an embarrassing mistake or have done something that makes you look foolish, how long do you usually keep on worrying about it?

18. Do you find it hard to make talk when you meet new people?

19. How often do you worry about whether other people like to be with you?

20. How often are you troubled with shyness?

21. When you are trying to convince other people who disagree with your ideas, how worried do you usually feel about the impression you are making?

22. When you think about the possibility that some of your friends or acquaintances might *not* have a good opinion of you, how concerned or worried do you feel about it?

23. How often do you feel worried or bothered about what other people think of you?

II. Social Inhibitions

1. Do you prefer to work *with others* rather than alone?

2. How important is it to you to have some really *close friends* of your own age?

3. When you need to make an important decision do you usu-

ally work things out entirely for yourself rather than get someone else's advice?

4. How often do you feel that you would prefer to become so absorbed in your own work or hobbies that you would not care about having any friends?

5. How often do you wish that you would *not* have any responsibility to do things for other people?

6. When you are invited to go some place where there will be a large number of people, do you try to avoid going?

7. Do you enjoy talking with people?

8. How often do you have the feeling that you would be better off if you were to live in a place where there are no people around who know you?

9. Do you prefer to spend your evenings *alone*?

10. How often do you prefer to be by yourself rather than with other people?

11. How often do you feel that you would prefer to be left alone by all your relatives and friends so that you would have no obligations toward others?

III. Test Anxiety

1. *Before* taking an examination in school, how worried do you usually feel?

2. *While* taking an examination in school, how worried do you usually feel?

3. *Before* taking an examination in school, do you usually perspire?

4. *While* taking an examination in school, do you usually perspire?

5. *Before* taking an examination in school, does your heart usually beat faster?

6. *While* taking an examination in school, does your heart usually beat faster?

7. *Before* taking an examination in school, how uneasy do you usually feel?

8. *While* taking an examination in school, do your emotional feelings interfere with or lower your performance?

IV. Richness of Fantasy

1. When you are thinking about some pleasant event that might happen in the future, is it hard or easy for you to imagine what it will really be like?

2. When you read an interesting story or novel do you ever imagine how *you* would feel if the events in the story were happening to you?

3. When you imagine things that might happen to you in the future, do you picture them in your mind almost as if they are real?

4. When you read a sad story, do you ever feel really sorry for the people in the story?

5. When someone tells you about something unpleasant or dangerous that might really happen to you, how worried or upset do you usually feel?

6. At times when you are hoping that some pleasant experience will occur, do you ever imagine it so vividly in your own mind that you can practically see and feel what the experience would be like?

7. When you read stories or novels, do you see in your mind's eye the things you are reading about?

8. When someone tells you about something very unfortunate that has happened to a person you know, how sad do you usually feel?

9. When you see a good mystery show in the movies or on TV, do you get really excited by what is going on?

10. Do you have vivid or lifelike daydreams?

11. How often do you have realistic daydreams in which you imagine yourself doing various things that you would like or hope to do?

V. Hyperaggressiveness

1. Some people feel so disgusted that they get angry about a lot of little things that ordinarily wouldn't bother them at all. How often do you feel that way?

2. During the past three days, how many times have you argued or quarrelled with someone?

3. During the past three days, how many times have you made criticisms of other people?

4. How often do you feel cross and grouchy?

5. How often do you get so angry that you feel like smashing things?

6. Do you ever go out of your way to make things unpleasant for somebody you don't like?

7. How often do you lose your temper?

8. During the past three days, how often have you felt angry at someone?

9. Do you find that you often have to tell people to mind their own business?

10. Do you ever feel mean and full of hatred toward other people?

VI. Argumentativeness

1. How often do you feel that you want to do the opposite of what other people want you to do?

2. How angry do you feel when someone tries to make you do something you don't want to do?

3. Do you feel annoyed when people try to tell you how to do something?

4. Do you feel annoyed at times when people try to convince you to change your personal opinions?

5. Is it easy or hard for people to win arguments from you?

6. In an argument, do you find it difficult or easy to give in when you begin to realize that the other person may be partly right?

VII. Suspiciousness

1. When you are in the presence of strangers, do you ever wonder whether they might cheat you or try to get something out of you?

2. How often do you feel that most people cannot be trusted?

3. How often do you feel suspicious of other people?

4. Do you ever wonder what hidden reason another person may have for doing something nice for you?

VIII. Obsessive and Compulsive Symptoms

1. Do you ever have the experience of being unable to get rid of some unimportant thought or idea which keeps coming into your mind over and over again?
2. After you have made a decision about something, do you continue to have doubts and keep thinking that maybe you ought to change your mind?
3. How often do you make up rules for yourself so that you will be sure to do the right thing and to avoid making mistakes?
4. Do you ever spend some time counting or observing things which are not very important, such as the cracks in the sidewalk?
5. How often do you set up and follow a schedule for yourself so that you know exactly what you will be doing during each hour of your spare time?

IX. Symptoms of Neurotic Anxiety

1. Do your hands ever tremble enough to bother you?
2. Are you ever bothered by having nightmares (dreams that frighten or upset you very much)?
3. During the past three days, how often have you had the feeling that something dreadful is about to happen to you?
4. Have you ever been bothered by your heart beating hard at times when you were *not* exercising or working hard?
5. Are you ever bothered by your hands sweating so that they feel damp and clammy?
6. At the present time how often do you bite your fingernails?
7. Have you ever been troubled by "cold sweats" at times when you were *not* exercising or working hard?
8. Do you often have trouble in getting to sleep?
9. During the past three days, how often have you felt worried or upset?
10. Are you ever bothered by nervousness?

APPENDIX B

Persuasibility Measures Used in Abelson and Lesser Studies

(See Chapters 7, 8, and 9)

PERSUASIBILITY BOOKLET

Pictured Objects

1. Hard-top car * vs. convertible (1920 style)
2. Flapper * vs. Gibson girl
3. Elm tree vs. evergreen *
4. Hottentot vs. Australian bushman *
5. Pagoda * vs. Taj Mahal
6. Platypus vs. armadillo *
7. Oriole vs. mallard *
8. African daisy * vs. tulip
9. Viking vs. Cossack *
10. Pattern * vs. design (wallpapers)
11. Brussels sprouts * vs. broccoli
12. Centaur vs. satyr *
13. Sampan * vs. galley ship
14.†Marie Antoinette vs. Cleopatra *
15. Top hat vs. derby hat *
16. Luna moth vs. swallowtail butterfly *
17. Urn * vs. flagon
18. Man with forked chin beard * vs. man with Franz Josef beard
19. Silver shark vs. flatfish *

INCOMPLETE STORIES

The test given here is the Mother Persuasibility measure. When the subject is a boy, substitute "Johnny" for "Susie." Another

---

* Denotes the picture the communicator "prefers."

† The data in Tables 17, 22, and 23 pertain to the booklet containing the first 14 pairs. The data in Table 25 pertain to the 19-item booklet.

name should be used if the subject is named or has a sibling named Susie (Johnny). To use the stories as a Father Persuasibility measure, substitue "father" for "mother" and make the following changes, respectively, in stories 1 and 5: "wash the car" instead of "hang out the wash" and "fixes something" instead of "irons some clothes."

Warm-up Stories (Not Scored)

i. Susie and her mother went to see some people Susie had never seen before. Susie and her mother went to see some surrealists. Susie's mother said, "Susie, be nice to the surrealists." Maybe Susie was very nice to the surrealists or maybe she did not like them at all and was mean to them. Or maybe she did something else.

ii. Susie is playing outside. She runs in the house to get something to take outside. Susie's mother says, "Don't slam the door, Susie. Close it quietly." Maybe Susie banged the door as hard as she could or maybe Susie was very careful and closed it quietly. Or maybe even Susie just closed it the way she always does. I wonder what Susie did.

Scored Stories

1. Susie's mother has something she doesn't want Susie to see. Susie's mother says, "Susie, don't look at it." Susie's mother goes outside to hang out the wash. While her mother is out, does Susie try to look at it?

2. Susie's mother has two boxes of cookies. Susie starts to take a cookie from the *big* box. Susie's mother says, "I think the *little* box has better cookies, Susie." Which cookie does Susie think she'd like better—the cookies from the big box or the ones her mother thought were better—the cookies from the little box?

3. Susie and her mother are going for a walk. It's a beautiful sunshiny day. Susie's mother says, "Walk on the sidewalk. Don't walk on the grass." Does Susie walk on the sidewalk as her mother says or on the grass?

4. Susie's mother says boys' bikes cost less money than girls' bikes. Which does Susie think cost less money—boys' bikes as Susie's mother says or girls' bikes?

5. Susie and her mother are at home. Susie is going to look at a book while her mother irons some clothes. Susie's mother says, "Sit down in *this* chair. Don't sit in the *other* one." Which chair does Susie sit in—the one her mother said to sit in or the one her mother said not to sit in?

6. Susie's mother says that in Norway, a country far away, sometimes you can't see the moon for many months even if you look hard for it. Does Susie think that she can't see the moon in Norway?

7. No one lived in the house next door to Susie for a long time. Then a family moved in with a little girl just Susie's age. Susie's mother said to Susie, "That little girl is not nice. Don't play with her." Does Susie play with her?

8. Susie has drawn two pictures. Susie's mother says that the one on the left is prettier than the one on the right. Which one does Susie think is prettier—the one on the left that her mother thinks is prettier or the one on the right?

9. One day Susie's mother said to Susie, "Susie, stay away from simians." Does Susie go near simians?

10. Susie and her mother are talking about a city far away. Susie's mother says that most of the people in that faraway city are mean. Does Susie think they're mean?

11. Susie and her mother are on a picnic. Susie is cooking her own hamburger. Susie's mother says, "Susie, don't touch it." Does Susie try to touch it?

12. Susie broke one of her toys. Susie started to fix it. Susie's mother said to fix it with glue—glue will fix it better than string. Which does Susie use to fix it—glue as her mother says or string.

13. One day when it is raining outside Susie's mother turns on a radio program for Susie to listen to. She says, "Susie, this is a good program." Does Susie think she'll like the program?

14. Susie's mother tells Susie about some kinds of music. One kind is called a mazurka. Susie's mother says mazurkas sound beautiful. Does Susie think they do?

15. Susie's mother tells her about a flower called a maypop. Susie's mother thinks maypops are very ugly flowers. Does Susie think maypops are ugly?

16. One day Susie's mother comes over to Susie. Susie's mother says, "Susie, you must wash the canine." Does Susie wash it? [If the child asks what a canine is, say— 'Spose Susie didn't know. What would she do? If the child says she would ask her mother, then say— Then Susie's mother tells Susie what a canine is. Then does Susie wash it? etc.]

17. Susie's mother says most firemen have pet cats. Does Susie think they do?

18. Susie's mother was telling Susie what to do. Susie's mother told her to act like a conformist. Did Susie act like one?

RECORDED OPINIONS

Adult Persuasibility Script I

1.* Do you think everyone should vote?
   Mother: I think it's everybody's duty to vote.
   Father: But if a person doesn't want to vote, he shouldn't have to. It's a free country after all.

2. They say that pretty soon doctors will know so much that nearly everybody will live to be a hundred years old. Do you think this is so?

* Dummy items.

> F : Yes, medical science is advancing very rapidly. In the very near future almost everyone will live to be a hundred.
>
> M: I agree completely.

3.* There are stories that some monkeys can learn to talk. Do you think this is possible?

> F : Monkeys probably can learn to talk. They're about the smartest animals there are.
>
> M: I doubt that. Only human beings are smart enough to learn to talk.

4. Do you think that there are some people who can really read other people's minds?

> F : That's a lot of nonsense. No one can read minds.
>
> M: That's what I say. There's no such thing as mind reading.

5. Do you think that traveling by airplane is as safe as traveling by car?

> M: No. Traveling by car seems safer to me.
>
> F : I agree. Plane travel isn't safe—too many accidents.

6.* Is it true in business that "honesty is the best policy"?

> M: Definitely not. You can't be honest and make money too.
>
> F : That's silly. Honesty *is* always the best policy.

7. Do you think husbands should tell their wives *everything*?

> M: Yes, definitely, otherwise how can a wife trust her husband?
>
> F : I agree. It seems to me that a husband should tell his wife everything.

8. Is our country heading for bad times?

> F : Yes, I'm afraid so. Things have been too good.
>
> M: Right, I think we're going to have a depression.

9. Do you think men look all right in pink shirts?

> M: Pink is for women. Men look silly in pink.
>
> F : That's what I say. Men shouldn't wear pink shirts.

* Dummy items.

10. Should everyone take vitamin pills every day?
    F : Yes, everyone should take vitamin pills.
    M: Sure, vitamins are good for everyone.

   Peer Persuasibility Script I

1.* Which would you rather have, a goldfish or a turtle?
    A. Turtles bite. I don't like turtles.
    B. Turtles are more interesting than fish. I like turtles better.
    C. I'd rather have a goldfish.
    D. What's the difference? They both swim in water.
    E. I don't like turtles or fish. I'd rather have a space gun.

2. If you told somebody something over and over again while he was asleep, would he remember it when he woke up?
    A. I don't think he'd remember it. That's stupid.
    B. Bet he would. Bet he'd remember it when he woke up if you said it enough times.
    C. If you said it over and over again, I think he'd remember it.
    D. I think so too. I think people can learn while they're asleep.
    E. Me too. If you said it enough times I think he'd remember it when he awoke.

3. Do you think there will ever be a woman president of the United States?
    A. Yeah, I think there'll be a woman president some day.
    B. I don't think so. I believe men will always be president.
    C. That's what I say. There'll never be a woman president.
    D. I don't think a woman will ever be president of the United States.
    E. I agree. There won't ever be a woman president.

4. When a person who doesn't have much hair has a haircut he pays just as much as another person with plenty of hair. Is that fair?

* Dummy items.

A. I think it's fair that everybody should pay the same price for a haircut.

B. It doesn't seem right to me that a person who doesn't have much hair should pay as much.

C. Everybody should pay the same for a haircut.

D. That's what I say.

E. I agree. People with a little hair should pay the same as people with plenty of hair.

5. Are policemen nicer than firemen?

A. No, firemen are nicer men than policemen.

B. I think so too. Firemen are nicer.

C. I like policemen better. Policemen are nicer than firemen.

D. I don't think so. I think firemen are nicer.

E. Me too. I think firemen are nicer than policemen.

6.* Do you think that some day there won't be any more movies?

A. Yes, pretty soon nobody'll go to the movies.

B. There will always be movies. I always go.

C. A lot of people go to the movies nowadays.

D. I think pretty soon there won't be any movies.

E. Not me. There'll always be *some* movies anyhow.

7. Do you think there are animals living on other planets, like Mars?

A. No, that's silly.

B. I don't think there are animals on any other planet.

C. I doubt that there are any animals living on Mars.

D. It doesn't seem likely that there are animals on any other planets.

E. I think there are. I betcha there are animals living on other planets.

8. Do you think it's more healthy to swim in the ocean or in lakes?

A. I think ocean swimming is healthier.

B. Seems that way to me. Swimming at the ocean is more healthy than swimming in lakes.

* Dummy items.

C. Of course swimming in the ocean is healthier than swimming in lakes.

D. I don't think so. I always thought that swimming in lakes was healthier than swimming in the ocean.

E. Not me. I think ocean swimming is healthier than lake swimming.

9. Which is more important about a job, how much money you earn or how interesting it is?

A. I think money is more important.

B. No. I think how interesting it is is definitely more important. It'd be terrible to work at a job you weren't interested in.

C. How interesting the job is is definitely more important.

D. Interest is the more important thing.

E. I agree. Interest is more important in a job.

10. Do you think men who wear vests are old-fashioned?

A. Yes, definitely. I don't like men who wear vests.

B. I don't think men who wear vests are old-fashioned.

C. Men who wear vests *are* old-fashioned.

D. I think so too. Nowadays men shouldn't wear vests.

E. Sure. Vests are old-fashioned, all right.

Adult Persuasibility Script II

1.* Which do you think is most important, developing your mind or keeping in good physical shape?

M: I think that keeping healthy is the most important thing.

F : Seems to me that learning things is more important.

2. Would you rather watch people swim or watch people ice-skate?

M: Watching people swim is more enjoyable.

F : I agree. I'd rather watch people swim.

3. Which do you like better, Thanksgiving or the Fourth of July?

* Dummy items.

M: I think the Fourth of July is very exciting.

F : I've always enjoyed the Fourth of July myself.

4. Would you rather watch a basketball game or a football game?

   M: I think that basketball is exciting to watch.

   F : Yes; I'd rather watch basketball than football.

5.* Do you think that in the near future nearly everyone will live to be a hundred years old?

   F : Definitely. Science is advancing very rapidly.

   M: Well, doctors know a great deal. I think some day perhaps, but not in the near future.

6. Do you agree that traveling by airplane is as safe as traveling by car?

   F : No. Traveling by car seems safer to me.

   M: I agree. Plane travel isn't safe. Too many accidents.

7. Would you rather see a rodeo with cowboys and horses or a real auto race?

   F : Seems to me that watching an auto race would be more enjoyable.

   M: Yes. I'd prefer watching an auto race too.

8. Do you think that men look all right in pink shirts?

   M: Pink is for women. Men look silly in pink.

   F : That's what I say. Men shouldn't wear pink shirts.

9. Do you agree that husbands shouldn't keep secrets from their wives, that they should tell their wives everything?

   M: Yes. Otherwise how can a wife trust her husband?

   F : I agree. A husband should tell his wife everything.

10. Would you rather go for a long trip on a large ship or take a ride in an airplane?

    F : I'd rather take a long boat trip.

    M: Me too. I should think that a long ocean voyage would be wonderful.

* Dummy items.

11.* Do you think that everyone should vote?

    M: I think that it's everybody's duty to vote.

    F : But if a person doesn't want to vote, he shouldn't have to. It's a free country after all.

12. Do you think that there are some people who can really read other peoples minds?

    F : That's a lot of nonsense. No one can read minds.

    M: That's what I say. There is no such thing as mind reading.

13. Should everyone take vitamin pills every day?

    F : Yes. Everyone should take vitamin pills.

    M: Sure. Vitamin pills are good for everyone.

14. There are stories that some monkeys can learn to talk. Do you think this is possible?

    F : Monkeys are supposed to be the smartest animals. They could probably learn to talk.

    M: With enough practice, I think monkeys could learn speech.

Peer Persuasibility Script II

1.* Do you think that there are creatures like people living on Mars?

    A. Sure. Maybe not exactly people but like people.

    B. I doubt that there's life on Mars.

    C. Gee, I'm really not sure.

2. If you told somebody something over and over again while he was asleep, would he remember it when he woke up?

    A. If you said it over and over again, I think he'd remember it.

    B. That's what I say; I think people can learn while they're asleep.

    C. Me too; if you said it enough times, he'd remember it.

3. Which would you rather take care of, a flower garden or a vegetable garden?

  * Dummy items.

316   PERSONALITY AND PERSUASIBILITY

    A. I should think taking care of a flower garden would be more interesting.

    B. Yeah, watching vegetables grow sounds dull.

    C. Mmm, I think taking care of a flower garden would be better too.

4. Which part of the weekend do you usually enjoy more, Saturday or Sunday?

    A. It's pretty close, but I think I generally have a better time on Saturday.

    B. (drawn-out mmm of reflection, then quick) Yeah, me too.

    C. I enjoy Saturdays more too.

5.* Which do you think are nicer, policemen or firemen?

    A. I think they're both about the same. Depends on the person.

    B. I've always liked firemen better; sometimes they letcha ride on their trucks.

    C. But policemen are always ready to help you out. I think policemen are nicer.

6. Would you rather watch a sunrise or a sunset?

    A. I've always heard sunrises are more beautiful.

    B. Yes, I'd rather watch a sunrise.

    C. Me too. I think sunrises are nicer than sunsets.

7. Do you think there will ever be a woman president of the United States?

    A. No, I think men will always be president.

    B. That's what I say, there'll never be a woman president.

    C. I don't think a woman will ever be president of the United States either.

8. Do you think the trees look nicer in the spring when they are just beginning to turn green or in the fall when they are just beginning to turn all different colors?

    A. Seems to me trees look nicer in the spring.

    B. I agree. It's really beautiful when all the trees are turning green.

* Dummy items.

C. Yeah, trees in the spring look nicer than trees in the fall.

9. Would you rather work in a grocery store or a department store?
    A. I think I'd prefer a department store.
    B. Working in a department store would be more fun than in a grocery store.
    C. I'd like working in a department store better too.

10.* Which is more important about a job, how much money you earn or how interesting it is?
    A. I think how interesting it is is definitely more important. It'd be terrible to work at a job you weren't interested in.
    B. But you need money to live. How much money you earn earn is definitely more important.
    C. They're both important I guess. I don't know which is more important though.

11. Would you rather go fishing or hunting?
    A. I guess I'd rather go hunting.
    B. Sure, hunting's more exciting.
    C. Yeah, I think hunting's more fun than fishing.

12. Do you think it's fair that when a person who's nearly bald has a haircut he pays just as much as another person with plenty of hair?
    A. Sure, it doesn't make any difference if you have a lot of hair or just a little.
    B. That's what I say. Everybody should pay the same for a haircut.
    C. Yeah, I think it's fair that everybody should pay the same price for a haircut.

13. Do you think it's more healthy to swim in the ocean or in lakes?
    A. I've always thought the ocean was a healthier place to swim.
    B. Me too. I think the ocean's healthier.

* Dummy items.

C. That's what I say. It's better to swim in the ocean than in lakes.

14. Do you think men who wear vests are old-fashioned?
   A. Yes, definitely. I don't like men who wear vests.
   B. Men who wear vests are old-fashioned.
   C. I think so too. Nowadays men shouldn't wear vests. They're old-fashioned, all right.

PARENT QUESTIONNAIRE

Items 1, 2, and 5 are scored 4, 3, 2, 1 for the respective answers. Items 3, 4, 6, and 7 are scored 1, 2, 3, 4 for the respective answers. Item 8 is scored as follows: 0 if "leader" is circled, but not "follower"; 2 if "follower" is circled, but not "leader"; and 1 if neither or both are circled.

1. Does your child copy you in your gestures and your way of speaking?

   often   occasionally   very seldom   never

2. When your child doesn't have anything to do and you suggest things for him (her) to do, does he (she) take up your suggestion?

   almost always   usually   sometimes   seldom

3. Does your child dislike the friends of you and your husband?

   often   occasionally   very seldom   never

4. Does your child insist on having his (her) own way whenever you and he (she) disagree?

   often   occasionally   very seldom   never

5. How easy is it for you to talk your child out of an opinion?

   very easy   easy   hard   very hard

6. When you tell your child how to fix something or do something, does he complain that he doesn't like your way of doing it?

   often   occasionally   very seldom   never

7. When you express an opinion on some matter that your child knows nothing about, does your child get sassy and contradict you?

    often   occasionally   very seldom   never

8. Try and put yourself in another person's place in describing your child. Circle all the words below that you think describe your child.

affectionate	bright	clean	conceited
cheerful	lazy	grouchy	selfish
stubborn	friendly	untruthful	helpful
spoiled	popular	a leader	a follower

OPINION QUESTIONNAIRE

1. Which team do you like better, the Dodgers or the Yankees?

    Dodgers   Yankees

2. Which color do you like more, green or brown?

    green   brown

3. Would you rather take a walk in the rain or in the snow?

    rain   snow

4. Would you rather live in California or in Vermont?

    California   Vermont

5. Would you rather live in Mexico or in Canada?

    Mexico   Canada

6. Which time of day do you like better, morning or night?

    morning   night

7. Would you rather see a funny movie with a lot of music or a murder mystery?

    funny musical   murder mystery

8. Would you rather stay home or go to a friend's house on a rainy day?

    stay home   friend's house

9. Would you rather eat vanilla or chocolate ice cream?

    vanilla   chocolate

10. Would you rather take a short trip on a bus or a train?

    bus   train

11. Would you rather go for a long trip on a large ship or take a ride in an airplane?

    ship   airplane

12. Would you rather see a movie with Danny Kaye or one with Marilyn Monroe?

    Danny Kaye   Marilyn Monroe

13. Would you rather read a book that tells all about the life of a bumblebee or one that tells about the early pioneers of our country?

    bumblebee   early pioneers

14. Would you rather watch people swim or watch people ice-skate?

    swim   ice-skate

15. Would you rather watch a basketball game or a football game?

    basketball   football

16. Would you rather see a rodeo with cowboys and horses or a real auto race?

    rodeo   auto race

17. Would you rather buy clothing for yourself or buy a gift for someone else?

    clothing   gift

18. Would you rather take care of a flower garden or a vegetable garden?

    flower garden   vegetable garden

19. Do you think a joke is funnier if it is about adults or if it is about children?

> adults   children

20. Do you think dogs or cats make better pets?

> dogs   cats

21. Do you think most women look better in high-heel shoes or flat-heel shoes?

> high-heels   flat-heels

22. Would you rather play checkers or a card game?

> checkers   card game

23. Would you rather swim in the ocean or in a lake?

> ocean   lake

24. Would you rather build a snowman or shovel snow off the sidewalk?

> snowman   sidewalk

25. Do you think the trees look nicer in the spring when they are just beginning to turn green or in the fall when they are just beginning to turn all different colors?

> spring   fall

26. Do you think walls look better painted a light color or a dark color?

> light color   dark color

27. Which do you like better, Thanksgiving or Fourth of July?

> Thanksgiving   Fourth of July

28. Would you rather drink milk or some kind of soda?

> milk   soda

29. Which kind of car do you like better, a Ford or a Cadillac?

> Ford   Cadillac

30. Would you rather go fishing or go hunting?

fishing   hunting

31. Would you rather eat grapes or a banana?

grapes   banana

32. Would you rather work in a grocery store or a department store?

grocery store   department store

33. Which part of the weekend do you usually enjoy more, Saturday or Sunday?

Saturday   Sunday

34. Would you rather watch a sunrise or a sunset?

sunrise   sunset

35. Would you lend your new car to a friend?

yes   no

36. Would you rather take a trip to a place where you have already been or to a new place?

already been   new place

37. Do you think it's better to be good-looking or smart?

good-looking   smart

38. Do you prefer fiction or nonfiction books?

fiction   nonfiction

39. Do you think a thief should be sent to jail or given a second chance?

sent to jail   given second chance

40. Would you rather buy a book of humor or a book about music?

humor   music

41. Would you rather hire someone to do odd jobs around the house or do them yourself?

hire someone   do yourself

42. Would you rather eat out in a restaurant or eat at home?

    restaurant   at home

43. Would you rather play baseball or watch a baseball game?

    play   watch

44. Would you rather play basketball or build a snowman?

    basketball   snowman

45. Would you rather ride on an airplane or watch a football game?

    airplane   football game

46. Would you rather take a trip on a ferry or read a book?

    ferry   book

47. Would you rather dig vegetables or pick flowers?

    vegetables   flowers

48. Mr. & Mrs. Blank are planning to go on a sight-seeing trip. They can go with another family and share expenses or they can go alone, which is more expensive. If they go with the other family it will mean going some places they don't want to go but that the other family wants to see. If they go alone they can spend their time only seeing the places they really want to see. Does Mrs. Blank think they should go alone or with the other family?

    go alone   with other family

49. Mrs. Blank breaks the windshield of her car because of carelessness. She knows that if she tells the insurance agent that she doesn't know how the windshield got broken, the insurance company will pay for the damage; and if she tells the truth about how the windshield got broken she will have to pay for a new one herself. Does Mrs. Blank think that she should tell the truth about how the windshield got broken and pay for a new one?

    yes   no

50. Mrs. Blank goes shopping for a new cage for her canary. She finds a cage that she likes, and then she sees another one that is even nicer-looking but that costs twice as much money. Which one does Mrs. Blank buy?

    nice cage   costs twice as much

REFERENCES

Italic numbers at the end of each reference refer to pages in the present volume.

ABELSON, R. P. and MORRISETT, L. N., Jr., 1959. After the over-all F-test, what? To appear in *Brit. J. Stat. Psychol. 185.*

ADORNO, T. W., FRENKEL-BRUNSWICK, ELSE, LEVINSON, D. J. and SANFORD, R. N., 1950. *The authoritarian personality.* New York, Harper. *6, 70, 83, 86, 219, 235*

ALLPORT, G. W., 1954. The historical background of modern social psychology. In *Handbook of social psychology,* Vol. 1, ed. G. Lindzey. Cambridge, Mass., Addison-Wesley, pp. 3–56. *53*

ANDERSON, J. P., 1940. A study of the relationships between certain aspects of parental behavior and attitudes and the behavior of junior high school pupils. *Teach. Coll. Contr. Educ.,* No. 809. *211*

ARNETT, C. E., DAVIDSON, HELEN H., and LEWIS, H. N., 1931. Prestige as a factor in attitude changes. *Sociol. and Soc. Res., 16,* 49–55. *208*

ASCH, S. E., 1948. The doctrine of suggestion, prestige and imitation in social psychology. *Psych. Rev., 55,* 250–76. *56*

ASCH, S. E., 1952. *Social psychology.* New York, Prentice-Hall. *12, 143, 245*

AUSUBEL, D. P., 1955. Relationships between shame and guilt in the socializing process. *Psychol. Rev., 62,* 378–90. *180*

AUSUBEL, D. P., BALTHAZAR, E. E., ROSENTHAL, IRENE, BLACKMAN, L. S., SCHPOONT, S. H., and WELKOWITZ, JOAN, 1954. Perceived parent attitudes as determinants of children's ego structure. *Child Develpm., 25,* 173–83. *180*

BALDWIN, A. L., 1948. Socialization and the parent-child relationship. *Child Develpm., 19,* 127–36. *176, 194*

BALDWIN, A. L., 1949. The effect of home environment on nursery school behavior. *Child Develpm., 20,* 49–61. *176, 208*

BARRON, M. L., 1954. *The juvenile in delinquent society.* New York, Knopf. *279*

BASS, B. M., 1956. Development and evaluation of a scale for measuring social acquiescence. *J. Abnorm. Soc. Psychol., 53,* 296–9. *146, 148f.*

BELL, ELAINE G., 1955. Inner-directed and other-directed attitudes. Unpublished doctoral dissertation, Yale University. *70, 79*

BELL, H. M., 1934. *The adjustment inventory* (student form). Stanford, Stanford University Press. *210*

BELOFF, H., 1958. Two forms of social conformity: acquiescence and conventionality. *J. Abnorm. Soc. Psychol., 56,* 99–104. *147, 205*

BERELSON, B. R., LAZARSFELD, P. F., and McPHEE, W. N., 1954. *Voting: a study of opinion formation in a presidential campaign.* Chicago, University of Chicago Press. *142*

BERENDA, RUTH W., 1950. *The influence of the group on the judgments of children.* New York, King's Crown Press. *142f.*

BERKOWITZ, L. and LUNDY, R. M., 1957. Personality characteristics related to susceptibility to influence by peers or authority figures. *J. Pers., 25,* 306–16. *11, 56*

BETTELHEIM, B., 1943. Individual and mass behavior in extreme situations. *J. Abnorm. Soc. Psychol., 38,* 417–52. *208*

BETTELHEIM, B. and JANOWITZ, M., 1950. *Dynamics of prejudice.* New York, Harper. *6*

BIRD, C., MONACHESI, E. D., and BURDICK, H., 1952. Studies of group tensions: III. The effect of parental discouragement of play activities upon the attitudes of white children toward Negroes. *Child Develpm., 23,* 295–306. *142*

BISHOP, BARBARA M., 1951. Mother-child interaction and the social behavior of children. *Psychol. Monogr., 65,* No. 11 (Whole No. 328). *177, 180, 194*

BLUM, G. S., 1949. A study of the psychoanalytic theory of psychosexual development. *Genet. Psychol. Monogr., 39,* 3–99. *115*

BLUM, G. S., 1954. Procedure for the assessment of conflict and defense. Unpublished manuscript, University of Michigan. *116f.*

BROGDEN, H. E. and THOMAS, W. F., 1943. The primary traits in personality items purporting to measure sociability. *J. Psychol., 16,* 85–97. *19*

BURTT, H. E. and FALKENBERG, D. R., 1941. The influence of majority and expert opinion on religious attitudes. *J. Soc. Psychol., 14,* 269–78. *208*

CATTELL, R. B., 1957. *Personality and motivation structure and measurement.* Yonkers, World Book Co. *174, 189*

COFFIN, T. E., 1941. Some conditions of suggestion and suggestibility: a study of certain attitudinal and situational factors influencing the process of suggestion. *Psychol. Monogr., 53,* No. 4 (Whole No. 241). *219*

COHEN, A. R., 1953. The effects of individual self-esteem and situational structure on threat-oriented reactions to power. Unpublished doctoral dissertation, University of Michigan. *105f.*

COHEN, A. R., 1954. Some explorations of self-esteem. Unpublished manuscript, University of Michigan. *115, 117*

COHEN, A. R., 1956. Experimental effects of ego-defense preference on interpersonal relations. *J. Abnorm. Soc. Psychol., 52,* 19–27. *109f.*

COHEN, A. R., 1959. Situational structure, self-esteem and threat-oriented reactions to power. Chapter 3 in *Studies in social power,* ed. D. Cartwright. Ann Arbor, University of Michigan Institute for Social Research. *102, 107*

CRISWELL, JOAN H., 1937. Racial cleavage in Negro-white groups. *Sociometry, 1,* 81–9. *186*

CRISWELL, JOAN H., 1939. A sociometric study of race cleavage in the classroom. *Arch. Psychol.,* No. 235. *186*

CRONBACH, L. J., and MEEHL, P. E., 1955. Construct validity in psychological tests. *Psychol. Bull.*, 52, 281–302. *159*

CRUTCHFIELD, R. S., 1955. Conformity and character. *Amer. Psychol.*, 10, 191–8. *56, 143, 147f., 149, 154, 159, 189, 197, 245*

DIGGORY, J. C., 1953. Sex differences in the organization of attitudes. *J. Pers.*, 22, 89–100. *59*

DITTES, J. E., and KELLEY, H. H., 1956. Effects of different conditions of acceptance upon conformity to group norms. *J. Abnorm. Soc. Psychol.*, 53, 100–7. *198*

DOLLARD, J. and MILLER, N. E., 1950. *Personality and psychotherapy*. New York, McGraw-Hill. *22*

DUNCKER, K., 1938. Experimental modification of children's food preferences through social suggestion. *J. Abnorm. Soc. Psychol.*, 33, 489–507. *142*

ENGLISH, O. S. and PEARSON, G. H. S., 1955. *Emotional problems of living*. New York, W. W. Norton. *272*

EYSENCK, H. J. and FURNEAUX, W. D., 1945. Primary and secondary suggestibility: an experimental and statistical study. *J. Exp. Psychol.*, 35, 485–503. *143*

FENICHEL, O., 1945. *The psychoanalytic theory of neurosis*. New York, Norton. *122, 273*

FERGUSON, L. W., 1944. An analysis of the generality of suggestibility to group opinion. *Character and Pers.*, 12, 237–43. *19, 29, 146, 149*

FESTINGER, L., 1954. A theory of social comparison processes. *Human Relat.*, 7, 117–40. *168*

FESTINGER, L., 1957. *A theory of cognitive dissonance*. Evanston, Row, Peterson. *170*

FISKE, D. W., 1949. Consistency of the factorial structures of personality ratings from different sources. *J. Abnorm. Soc. Psychol.*, 44, 329–44. *19*

FLESCH, R., 1946. *The art of plain talk*. New York, Harpers. *11*

FLUGEL, J. C., 1945. *Man, morals and society*. New York, International Universities Press. *23*

FREUD, ANNA, 1946. *The ego and the mechanisms of defence*, transl. Cecil Baines. New York, International Universities Press. *208*

FURNEAUX, W. D., 1946. The prediction of susceptibility to hypnosis. *J. Pers.*, 14, 281–94. *143*

GERBERICH, J. R., 1956. *Specimen objective test items*. New York, Longmans, Green. *275*

GOLDSTEIN, S., 1952. A projective study of psychoanalytic mechanisms. Unpublished doctoral dissertation, University of Michigan. *115*

GRAHAM, ELAINE. See Bell, Elaine G.

GRIMES, F. V., 1948. An experimental analysis of the nature of suggestibility and of its relation to other psychological factors. *Studies in Psychol. Psychiatry, Catholic Univ. Amer.*, 7, No. 4. *219*

HARTLEY, E. L., 1946. *Problems in prejudice*. New York, King's Crown Press. *7*

HARTSHORNE, H., MAY, M. A., and SHUTTLEWORTH, F. K., 1930. *Studies in the nature of character. III. Studies in the organization of character*. New York, Macmillan. *142*

HARVEY, O. J. and RUTHERFORD, JEANNE, 1958. *Relationship of status in the informal group to influence and influencibility at differing age levels*, Tech. Rept. No. 3. Nashville, Tennessee, Vanderbilt University. *251*

HATTWICK, B. W., 1936. Interrelations between the preschool child's behavior and certain factors in the home. *Child Develpm., 7*, 200–26. *180*

HAYWARD, R. S., 1935. The child's report of psychological factors in the family. *Arch. Psychol.*, No. 189. *211*

HELFANT, K., 1952. Parents' attitudes vs. adolescent hostility in the determination of adolescents' sociopolitical attitudes. *Psychol. Monogr., 66*, No. 13 (Whole No. 345). *142*

HELSON, H., BLAKE, R. R., MOUTON, JANE S., and OLMSTEAD, J. A., 1956. Attitudes as adjustments to stimulus, background and residual factors. *J. Abnorm. Soc. Psychol., 52*, 314–22. *147, 149, 151*

HERTZMAN, M. and PEARCE, JANE, 1947. The personal meaning of the human figure in the Rorschach. *Psychiat., 10*, 413–22. *90*

HIRSCHBERG, G. and GILLILAND, A. R., 1942. Parent-child relationships in attitude. *J. Abnorm. Soc. Psychol., 37*, 125–30. *142*

HOCHBAUM, G. M., 1954. The relation between group members' self-confidence and their reactions to group pressures to uniformity. *Amer. Sociol. Rev., 19*, 678–87. *56*

HOFFMAN, M. L., 1953. Some psychodynamic factors in compulsive conformity. *J. Abnorm. Soc. Psychol., 48*, 383–93. *23f., 143, 208, 219*

HOLLENBERG, ELEANOR and SPERRY, MARGARET, 1951. Some antecedents of aggression and effects of frustration in doll play. *Personality, 1*, 32–43. *194*

HOVLAND, C. I., HARVEY, O. J., and SHERIF, M., 1957. Assimilation and contrast effects in reactions to communication and attitude change. *J. Abnorm. Soc. Psychol., 55*, 244–52. *12*

HOVLAND, C. I., JANIS, I. L., and KELLEY, H. H., 1953. *Communication and persuasion*. New Haven, Yale University Press. *1, 4f., 8f., 20f., 29, 39, 56, 62, 189, 195, 198ff., 209, 236f., 256, 270f.*

HOVLAND, C. I., LUMSDAINE, A. A., and SHEFFIELD, F. D., 1949. *Experiments on mass communication*. Princeton, Princeton University Press. *5, 59f., 256*

HOVLAND, C. I. and MANDELL, W., 1952. An experimental comparison of conclusion-drawing by the communicator and by the audience. *J. Abnorm. Soc. Psychol., 47*, 581–8. *10*

HOVLAND, C. I., MANDELL, W., CAMPBELL, ENID H., BROCK, T., LUCHINS, A. S., COHEN, A. R., McGUIRE, W. J., JANIS, I. L., FEIERABEND, ROSALIND L., and ANDERSON, N. H., 1957. *The order of presentation in persuasion*. New Haven, Yale University Press. *v, 10*

HOVLAND, C. I. and PRITZKER, H. A., 1957. Extent of opinion change as a function of amount of change advocated. *J. Abnorm. Soc. Psychol., 54*, 257–61. *146, 149, 208*

HOVLAND, C. I. and WEISS, W., 1951–52. The influence of source credibility on communication effectiveness. *Publ. Opin. Quart., 15*, 635–50. *11, 71, 73*

HULL, C. L., 1952. *A behavior system.* New Haven, Yale University Press. *22*

JAHODA, MARIE, 1956. Psychological issues in civil liberties. *Amer. Psychol., 11*, 234–40. *143*

JANIS, I. L., 1954. Personality correlates of susceptibility to persuasion. *J. Pers., 22*, 504–18. *29f., 55, 62, 148f., 188f., 195, 235*

JANIS, I. L., 1955. Anxiety indices related to susceptibility to persuasion. *J. Abnorm. Soc. Psychol., 51*, 663–7. *29f., 55f., 62, 65, 148f., 189, 235*

JANIS, I. L. and FESHBACH, S., 1954. Personality differences associated with responsiveness to fear-arousing communications. *J. Pers., 23*, 154–66. *10, 29*

KANNER, L., 1944. Behavior disorders in childhood. In *Personality and the behavior disorders,* Vol. 2, ed. J. McV. Hunt. New York, Ronald, pp. 761–93. *272*

KATZ, D., SARNOFF, I., and McCLINTOCK, C., 1956. Ego-defense and attitude change. *Human Relat., 9*, 27–45. *10*

KATZ, D., McCLINTOCK, C., and SARNOFF, I., 1957. The measurement of ego defense as related to attitude change. *J. Pers., 25*, 465–74. *10*

KELLEY, H. H. and THIBAULT, J. W., 1954. Experimental studies of group problem solving and process. In *Handbook of social psychology,* Vol. 2, ed. G. Lindzey. Cambridge, Mass., Addison-Wesley, pp. 735–85. *11*

KELLEY, H. H. and VOLKART, E. H., 1952. The resistance to change of group-anchored attitudes. *Amer. Sociol. Rev., 17*, 453–65. *9, 11*

KELMAN, H. C., 1950. Effects of success and failure on "suggestibility" in the autokinetic situation. *J. Abnorm. Soc. Psychol., 45*, 267–85. *75*

KELMAN, H. C., 1959. *Social influence and personal belief: a theoretical and experimental approach to the study of behavior change.* Unpublished manuscript. *3, 143f.*

KING, B. T., 1955. The relationship between persuasibility and parental domination. Unpublished doctoral dissertation, Yale University. *149, 209*

KLAPPER, J. T., 1949. *The effects of mass media.* New York Bur. Appl. Soc. Research, Columbia University (mimeo.). *12*

KLOPFER, B., AINSWORTH, MARY D., KLOPFER, W. G., and HOLT, R. R., 1954. Vol. 1 of *Developments in the Rorschach Technique.* Yonkers, World Book Co. *90ff.*

KRIS, E., 1952. *Psychoanalytic explorations in art.* New York, International Universities Press. *273f.*

KUDER, G. F. and RICHARDSON, M. W., 1937. The theory of the estimation of test reliability. *Psychometrika, 2*, 151–60. *212*

KUHLMANN, F. and ANDERSON, R. G., 1952. Kuhlmann-Anderson Test Handbook. Princeton, Personnel Press. *163*

KULP, D. H., II, 1934. Prestige, as measured by single-experience changes and their permanency. *J. Educ. Res.*, *27*, 663–72. *208*

LAMBERT, R. D. and BRESSLER, M., 1956. *Indian Students on an American campus.* Minneapolis, University of Minnesota Press. *273*

LAYMAN, EMMA M., 1940. An item analysis of the adjustment questionnaire. *J. Psychol.*, *10*, 87–106. *19*

LAZARSFELD, P. F., BERELSON, B., and GAUDET, HAZEL, 1944. *The people's choice.* New York, Duell, Sloan and Pearce. *12*

LESSER, G. S., 1952. Maternal attitudes and practices and the aggressive behavior of children. Unpublished doctoral dissertation, Yale University. *180, 194f.*

LESSER, G. S., 1957. The relationship between overt and fantasy aggression as a function of maternal response to aggression. *J. Abnorm. Soc. Psychol.*, *55*, 218–21. *195, 197*

LINDZEY, G. and BORGATTA, E. F., 1954. Sociometric measurement. In *Handbook of social psychology*, Vol. 1, ed. G. Lindzey. Cambridge, Mass., Addison-Wesley, pp. 405–48. *189*

LINTON, HARRIET B., 1952. Relations between mode of perception and the tendency to conform. Unpublished doctoral dissertation, Yale University. *70*

LINTON, HARRIET B., 1954a. Rorschach correlates of response to suggestion. *J. Abnorm. Soc. Psychol.*, *49*, 75–83. *74, 90, 99*

LINTON, HARRIET B., 1954b. Autokinetic judgments as a measure of influence. *J. Abnorm. Soc. Psychol.*, *49*, 464–6. *76*

LINTON, HARRIET B., 1955. Dependence on external influence: correlates in perception, attitudes, and judgment. *J. Abnorm. Soc. Psychol.*, *51*, 502–7. *70, 99*

MACCOBY, ELEANOR E., MATTHEWS, R. E., and MORTON, A. S., 1954. Youth and political change. *Publ. Opin. Quart.*, *18*, 23–39. *142, 177*

MACFARLANE, JEAN W., ALLEN, LUCILE, and HONZIK, MARJORIE P., 1954. *A developmental study of the behavior problems of normal children between twenty-one months and fourteen years.* Berkeley, University of California Press. *205*

MACHOVER, KAREN A., 1949. *Personality projection in the drawing of the human figure.* Springfield, Illinois, C. C. Thomas. *71*

McKINNON, KATHERN MAE, 1942. *Consistency and change in behavior manifestations.* New York, Bureau of Publications, Teachers College, Columbia University. *189*

MARINHO, H., 1942. Social influence in the formation of enduring preferences. *J. Abnorm. Soc. Psychol.*, *37*, 448–68. *142*

MARPLE, C. H., 1933. The comparative susceptibility of three age levels to the suggestion of group versus explicit opinion. *J. Soc. Psychol.*, *4*, 176–86. *208*

MASLOW, A. H., 1939. Dominance, personality, and social behavior in women. *J. Soc. Psychol.*, *10*, 3–39. *56*

MEYERS, C. E., 1944. The effect of conflicting authority on the child. *Univ. of Iowa Stud. Child Welf.*, *20*, 33–98. *176, 180, 194*

MUELLER, D. D., 1945. Paternal domination: its influence on child guidance results. *Smith Coll. Stud. Soc. Work, 15*, 184–215. *208*

MURPHY, G., MURPHY, LOIS B., and NEWCOMB, T. N., 1937. *Experimental social psychology*, rev. ed. New York and London, Harper. *237*

MURRAY, H. A., 1943. *Thematic Apperception Test manual*. Cambridge, Harvard University Press. *197*

MYERS, T. R., 1935. Intra-family relationships and pupil adjustment. *Teach. Coll. Contr. Educ.*, No. 651. *211*

NEWCOMB, T. M., 1943. *Personality and social change*. New York, Dryden. *9, 273*

NEWCOMB, T. M., 1950. *Social psychology*. New York, Dryden. *198*

NEWCOMB, T. M., 1953. An approach to the study of communicative acts. *Psychol. Rev., 60*, 393–404. *168*

NEWCOMB, T. M., 1956. The prediction of interpersonal attraction. *Amer. Psychol., 11*, 575–86. *202*

NEWELL, H. W., 1936. A further study of maternal rejection. *Amer. J. Orthopsychiat., 6*, 576–89. *180*

PARSONS, T., 1953. Age and sex in the social structure of the United States. In *Personality in nature, society and culture*, eds. C. Kluckhohn, H. A. Murray, and D. M. Schneider. 2d ed., New York, Knopf, pp. 363–75. *59*

PAYNE, D. E. and MUSSEN, P. H., 1956. Parent-child relations and father identification among adolescent boys. *J. Abnorm. Soc. Psychol., 52*, 358–62. *180*

PINTNER, R., CUNNINGHAM, B. U., and DUROST, W. N., 1946. *Pintner-Cunningham Primary Test*. Yonkers, World Book Co. *163*

QUENOUILLE, M. H., 1952. *Associated measurements*. London, Butterworths Scientific Publications. *165*

RADKE, MARIAN J., 1946. The relation of parental authority to children's behavior and attitudes. *Univ. Minn. Inst. Child Welf. Monogr. Series*, No. 22. Minneapolis, University of Minnesota Press. *176, 194*

RAZRAN, G. H. S., 1940. Conditioned response changes in rating and appraising sociopolitical slogans. *Psychol. Bull., 37*, 481 (abstract). *13*

REDL, F. and WINEMAN, D., 1951. *Children who hate*. Glencoe, Illinois, Free Press. *272*

RICHARDS, T. W. and SIMONS, M. P., 1941. The Fels Child Behavior Scales. *Genet. Psychol. Monogr., 24*, 259–309. *19*

RICKMAN, J., 1950. Psychodynamic notes. In *Tensions that cause wars*, ed. H. Cantril. Urbana, University of Illinois Press, pp. 167–208. *253*

RIESMAN, D., 1950. *The lonely crowd*. New Haven, Yale University Press. *79f.*

ROBERTS, MARY P., 1934. A study of children's play in the home environment. In *Univ. Iowa Child Welfare Studies. Vol. VIII: Researches in parent edu-*

cation, II, ed. G. D. Stoddard. Iowa City, University of Iowa Press, pp. 33–98. *176*

SAMELSON, F., 1957. Conforming behavior under two conditions of conflict in the cognitive field. *J. Abnorm. Soc. Psychol., 55*, 181–7. *9*

SARASON, S. B. and MANDLER, G., 1952. Some correlates of test anxiety. *J. Abnorm. Soc. Psychol., 47*, 810–17. *61*

SARNOFF, I., 1951. Identification with the aggressor: some personality correlates of anti-Semitism among Jews. *J. Pers., 20*, 199–218. *7*

SARNOFF, I. and KATZ, D., 1954. The motivational bases of attitude change. *J. Abnorm. Soc. Psychol., 49*, 115–24. *143*

SCHILDER, P., 1938. *Psychotherapy*. New York, W. W. Norton. *273*

SHAPIRO, D., 1952. Psychological factors in friendship choice and rejection. Unpublished doctoral dissertation, University of Michigan. *105*

SHERIF, M., 1935. A study of some social factors in perception. *Arch. Psychol.*, No. 187. *75*

SHERIF, M., 1936. *The psychology of social norms*. New York, Harper. *75*

SMITH, M. B., BRUNER, J. S., and WHITE, R. W., 1956. *Opinions and personality*. New York, Wiley. *7*

STOTLAND, E., THORLEY, S., THOMAS, E., COHEN, A. R., and ZANDER, A., 1957. The effects of group expectations and self-esteem upon self-evaluation. *J. Abnorm. Soc. Psychol., 54*, 55–63. *111*

SYMONDS, P. M., 1939. *The psychology of parent-child relationships*. New York, Appleton-Century. *176, 194*

TERMAN, L. M., JOHNSON, WINIFRED D., KUZNETS, G., and McNEMAR, OLGA W., 1946. Psychological sex differences. In *Manual of child psychology*, ed. L. Carmichael. New York, Wiley, pp. 954–1000. *56*

THIBAUT, J. W. and STRICKLAND, L. H., 1956. Psychological set and social conformity. *J. Pers., 25*, 115–29. *143*

THOMAS, E. and BURDICK, H., 1954. Self-esteem and defense preference as related to social behavior. Unpublished manuscript, University of Michigan. *108, 110*

TOLMAN, E. C., 1951. A psychological model. In *Toward a general theory of action*, ed. T. Parsons and E. A. Shils. Cambridge, Harvard University Press, pp. 279–361. *22*

TRAGER, H. G. and RADKE-YARROW, MARIAN, 1947. Early childhood airs its views. *Educ. Leadership, 5*, 16–24. *142*

WACH, J., 1944. *Sociology of religion*. Chicago, University of Chicago Press. *273*

WEINBERG, S. M., 1952. *Society and personality disorders*. New York, Prentice-Hall. *23*

WEINER, M., CARPENTER, JANETH T., and CARPENTER B., 1956. External validation of a measure of conformity behavior. *J. Abnorm. Soc. Psychol., 52*, 421–2. *143*

WEISS, W. and FINE, B. J., 1955. Opinion change as a function of some intrapersonal attributes of the communicatees. *J. Abnorm. Soc. Psychol., 51,* 246–53. *7*

WEISS, W. and FINE, B. J., 1956. The effect of induced aggressiveness on opinion change. *J. Abnorm. Soc. Psychol., 52,* 109–14. *7*

WHITE, R. W., 1956. *The abnormal personality.* 2d ed., New York, Ronald Press. *122*

WITKIN, H. A., 1950. Individual differences in ease of perception of embedded figures. *J. Pers., 19,* 1–15. *70, 77*

WITKIN, H. A., LEWIS, H. B., HERTZMAN, M., MACHOVER, KAREN, MEISSNER, P. B., and WAPNER, S., 1954. *Personality through perception.* New York, Harper. *66f., 70, 74, 77, 87ff., 90f., 99*

WITTENBORN, J.R., 1956. A study of adoptive children. *Psychol. Monogr., 70* (1,2,3), (Whole Nos. 408–10), 1–115. *194*